T. C. Ivens was born in Northampton in 1922 and was educated at Northampton Grammar School and the Seale-Hayne Agricultural College. Between 1944 and 1947 he was in command of HM minesweepers. *Still Water Fly-Fishing* was his first book and was originally published in 1952, when it had immediate success and soon became a classic on the subject. From 1953–6 he was on the staff of *Fishing Gazette*, and contributed three pieces on trout fishing to the three-volume work, *The Art of Angling*. He contributes regularly to *Angling* and is a keen sea angler and photographer.

Richard & Keil

Happy Easter
Greeting.

Jido

March '76.

Pan Anglers' Library

STILL WATER FLY-FISHING

A modern guide to angling in reservoirs
and lakes

T. C. IVENS

REVISED EDITION

PAN BOOKS LTD : LONDON

First published 1952
Revised and enlarged edition published 1970 by
André Deutsch Ltd
This updated edition published 1973 by Pan Books Ltd,
33 Tothill Street, London SW1

ISBN 0 330 23810 8

Made and printed in Great Britain by
Cox & Wyman Ltd, London, Reading and Fakenham

Contents

List of diagrams

Acknowledgements

I wish to acknowledge my debt to the many people without whose help this book would have been less complete.

To the late Editor of *The Fishing Gazette*, Robert L. Marston, whose friendly criticism helped to make such a success of the articles from which the first edition of this book developed; to Patricia Marston, late of *The Fishing Gazette*, for permission to publish extracts from my more recent writings and to quote from published correspondence; to Brian Harris, Editor of *Angling* and Bill Adamson and E. Horsfall, joint Editors of *Anglers' Annual*, for permission to quote from several of my contributions; to Drs O. L. Meehean, W. Hagen and A. V. Tunison of the US Fish and Wildlife Service and to Mr E. D. le Cren of the Freshwater Biological Association, all of whom exchanged long informative letters with me; to Mr D. F. Leney, of Surrey Trout Farms, and Alex Behrendt of Two Lakes for information on Fishery Management and Mr K. B. S. Brown, of Blagdon and Chew, whose information on hatchery work in England was most helpful, and who, with Mark Holford, of Durleigh and Sutton Bingham, provided information on the use of Compensation Water to rear growing trout without artificial feeding; to Dr T. T. Macan, of the Freshwater Biological Association, who assisted with the chapter on stocking; to Messrs A. Smith and A. R. Kelly of the Pemberton-Warren Trout Acclimatization Society, who gave me most helpful information on their pioneer project in Western Australia; to Mr R. B. Finney, whose genius with a camera and enthusiasm in a new sphere of activity resulted in some very interesting photographs; to the late Edgar May, the famous amateur caster, who gave me some very helpful information for the chapter on casting; to Barrie Welham who cooperated to produce the chapter on stalking big trout; to Dick Shrive of Northampton who taught us all to fish deep for Rainbows and helped to produce Chapter 15; to Richard Walker, whose friendship I enjoy and whose opinions are always to be respected however heretical they may at first seem; to the late Captain 'Len' Parker, master craftsman of the Hampshire Avon, who was always willing to pass on to others the information he gained in a lifetime of angling; to John Rowe, past Secretary of the Mid-Northants Trout Fishers' Association, who continued the co-ordination of the Association's fishery work and made the results of his researches available to me; to Leslie Stewart, Fishery Officer to the Lancashire River Authority for information on trout migration in a lake now under investigation.

Lastly, and perhaps most importantly, my thanks are due to all those men whose company by the waterside has made my fishing so enjoyable.

T. C. IVENS

Preface

It is twenty-one years since *Still Water Fly-Fishing* was first published. During that time Chew Valley, Sutton Bingham, Weir Wood, Grafham, Hanningfield and many other reservoirs have been opened, and it is now certain that virtually all reservoirs will be opened for fishing within the next three years.

The number of still water enthusiasts has grown apace and today probably there are more fly fishers in the Midlands than anywhere else in Britain and they enjoy a quality of sport unequalled elsewhere in our island.

River trout fishing is everywhere at a premium and will become increasingly so, for water abstraction and conservation are completing the ruin begun long ago by pollution. Almost everywhere, too, stocks in rivers have to be maintained by turning in sizeable fish, fed on offal or pellets in a hatchery almost up to the date of capture.

By contrast, our fertile reservoirs support a large population of growers, and the fish we catch are wild fed at least from the 4-in or 8-in stage of growth, though several hard-fished waters have recently stocked 10-in to 12-in fish which are takeable by opening day and which reach 2 lb or more by September. On several waters we now catch fish wild fed on plankton from birth, for a new rearing system has been introduced and is already providing yearlings of unsurpassable quality at minimal cost. You will read about it in Chapter 21.

For the last few seasons we have fished a Midland water, Grafham, which, by reason of its great depth, stratifies. The enormous fishing pressure and lack of marginal weed beds there has challenged much that was written about bank fishing in the past and demanded solutions that were nigh impossible until the recent development of supple lines which would float effectively on rough or scum-covered water, and other lines which would sink rapidly to great depth. These new lines have had and will continue to have a marked influence on rod design, and my first two chapters have been re-written and enlarged to embrace the most recent experience.

Boat fishing has come back into its own through the availability of reliable outboard motors and because we have now developed specialized techniques far superior to the old 'cast and lift' style of fishing employed on northern and Scottish waters from a drifting boat.

Again, observation of surface-feeding fish, particularly those that feed on calm lanes, has resulted in many more fish being taken in the mid-day and afternoon period. Both these topics are thoroughly discussed in Chapters 12 and 17.

But above all the development of deep-fishing techniques from boats has led to the capture of enormous numbers of rainbow trout which at certain seasons of the year appear not to feed at the surface. Indeed, we may be near to a solution of the enigma of the vanishing rainbow trout.

At Northampton some years ago we set up an advisory association to help manage the Mid-Northamptonshire Water Board Reservoirs. The story of the association and the work that it did is described in Chapter 18. Advisory associations remain in most areas a very useful means of securing recognition by and help from a public authority which, because of its first duty to safeguard public health, cannot relinquish its overall supervision of the fishery in favour of an outside body.

But Grafham is run with a new spirit. The Great Ouse Water Authority anticipated the Ministry of Land and Natural Resources' circular addressed in September 1966 to all water undertakings, and created what is virtually an inland holiday centre for sailors and anglers alike. Every weekend of spring and summer some 1,000–1,500 anglers and sailors enjoy their sport in complete harmony with elbow room for all.

I regret that I am less enthusiastic about the activities of bird watchers who, in 1967, succeeded, despite their small numbers, in sterilizing, so far as anglers are concerned, much of the southwest (upwind) shore where many of us fished very successfully in 1966.

There are some who feel that insistence upon fly-only seriously reduces their chance of sport, and I know of waters where bank fishing with the fly is almost hopeless. But once you depart from fly, where do you stop ?

Others regard it as sporting to catch trout on a legered lobworm or live minnow; still more anglers may prefer to groundbait with maggots and fish a single maggot on a 14 or 16 hook.

That fly-fishing is an aid to conservation is nothing more than another way of saying that many anglers are indifferent performers with a fly. On our shallow reservoirs skilled fly fishers have little difficulty over most of the season in regularly killing their limit of large trout. Examine the returns of a club and you will find some members regularly have limit bags, 50 per cent of the total catch falling to 5 per cent of the rods. Despite jealous comment to the contrary, those bags will have been made by fair but essentially skilled fly-fishing.

In this book I have revealed as much as I know about the behaviour of trout in lakes and the methods of fly-fishing likely to be successful and I sincerely hope that what has been written will encourage the beginner to persist with the fly rod and master it. The rhythm and beauty of fly casting are sources of delight and satisfaction in themselves, and over a season the bag of a skilled fly fisher will prove at least equal to that of the threadliner. Barrie Welham, in Chapter 13, takes the supremacy of the fly even further when he demonstrates its effectiveness for those very big brown trout which many of us have long thought should be angled for with a 'wobbler' sprat!

Nevertheless, it is probably as little true to say that the methods outlined in this book are applicable to all still waters holding trout wherever they may be, as it would be to suggest that Skues' description of nymphing on a chalk stream could be applied also in every respect to the Teign, the Ure, or for that matter the Klamath. Because so many anglers have said in effect 'all still waters are the same', I have tried in Chapter 19 to explain just why this is not so.

Although my methods were devised upon the trout reservoirs of the Midland Plain, they apply in greater part to eutrophic* lakes everywhere, and letters from readers in almost every country of the Commonwealth testify abundantly to that fact. If the trout are large, averaging 2 lb or over, then the flies should be used in the sizes advocated. Where the fish average perhaps 1 lb then the flies might well be two sizes smaller. Where lakes are of the oligotrophic† type, and bottom feed is restricted, fish will be

* See Chapter 20.
† A word explained on page 257.

relatively easier to take on fly, and the dry fly may well from time to time give better results than the wet fly. Leader strength too may require amendment. Clearly, 0·10-inch points would be folly when fishing for those heavy New Zealand trout.

In 1952, I wrote: 'Just as Skues writing of nymphing in rivers has contributed something of importance to my technique, so I hope those who fish rivers may find ideas of mine which could be adapted to river work.'

It is already clear that lake techniques are extremely useful for night sea-trout fishing, and also for brown trout and sea-trout (and salmon too) in slowly moving pools. I think we shall find many more applications as time goes on.

By far the biggest problem in revising this book has been how best to deal with Grafham reservoir. What has already appeared in print is as true of most Midland waters as it was when it was written twenty-one years ago, and is just as valuable as it was then. But Grafham's special problems have demanded untypical solutions to which I have devoted special chapters so as to avoid writing in almost every paragraph 'except at Grafham, where . . . etc.'

Assume, then, except under Grafham headings, that I am writing about Eyebrook or Chew Valley or Durleigh or Blagdon and similar waters up to about 35 feet in depth.

T. C. Ivens
St Albans
April 1973

Part One

CHAPTER 1

On the choice of a rod

Although it is true that the man with but one rod loses no sleep or fishing time deciding which rod he will take with him, Hobson's Choice where rods are concerned is not an enviable situation. Although far from being well off, I have always acted on the premise that one should not attempt to make a single rod serve widely differing purposes. Rather should one acquire several rods, each suited to a different type of fly work.

I have met many men with a selection of rods at their disposal, but all too often 50 per cent of each collection consists of rods of similar type. Until 1951 few anglers would have possessed a rod suitable for reservoir trouting, and only since about 1960 have tackle makers as a whole acknowledged the need for specialized equipment by producing new rods, or, in some cases, judging from their continuing inadequacy, by renaming old models!

Our Midlands reservoirs provide the finest fly fishing in Britain: certainly no river now produces wild fish which average so great a weight or which are in such grand condition, and yet from the tackle point of view these reservoirs might until recently have been non-existent. Possibly this was because until 1952 there was no book dealing in detail with 'Blagdon-type' waters. Earlier writers refer to Blagdon, but with the exception of G. D. Luard they appear to have used boats. Mr Luard, I feel, half hit upon the basic truth of reservoir fishing, namely, that the well-equipped and skilled bank fisherman will often take more fish than the man fishing from a drifting boat.

Ashore or afloat, reservoir angling requires special skills which can be achieved only with specialized tackle. Contrary to the general impression, long casting is frequently as necessary from a boat as from the bank, and particularly is this so in calm weather. Except on rare occasions the 'traditional' loch outfit is unsuitable.

The river fisherman with no experience of reservoirs may well wonder why specialized tackle is so necessary. I believe he will find the reasons as he reads on, for I have been at pains to give as accurate a picture of reservoir fishing as is possible on paper.

Many of the best reservoirs occupy shallow valleys, and water of only 6 ft depth is often to be found as much as 100 yards from the shore. Such marginal shallows with their extensive weed beds are usually the best holding water on the reservoir. The angler must be able to cover as much of this 'belt' as possible. His problem, unlike that of the river angler, is not the avoiding of overhanging trees, nearby shrubs and so on, but the casting of as long a line as possible as often as he is able. He will not be bothered by the flora (or fauna) of the hinterland, for he will usually wade 10 yards or more out from the margin, which is usually clear of vegetation. (Water authorities usually take care to keep trees and rushes well above high-water mark to prevent decaying vegetation from fouling the bottom.) Thus the problem of casting a narrow loop does not present itself. Even fishing from the dams does not necessitate a narrow loop; you merely throw high at the back.

I have often seen powerfully built, fit men on the water using 9 ft 6 in rods weighing about 6½ oz. At the end of a day of long casting – that is, casting an average distance of 23 yards to 28 yards, they are all but collapsed with fatigue. It is so unnecessary – the collapse, not the long casting. In nearly every case you find that the man is the proud owner of a first-class split-cane rod by

16

a first-class maker, but that his rod is tip-actioned and designed for throwing a short line with a narrow loop on a river.

Such outfits are the devil on a reservoir. I once had one. The rod was delightful until I had 18 yards of line in the air. At that point its upper part became overloaded and liable to break off.

By definition a tip-actioned rod is one whose bending is focused nearer to the top than to the butt. The upper part of the rod assumes a marked curve because it is not powerful enough to resist bending and thereby force the lower part of the rod to work. Long casting demands that the whole rod contribute to the effort; but many rods are so constructed that the top can be overloaded while the butt is idle. Since only part of the rod is working fully, only that part can release much energy. On the other hand, a rod which works through its full length imparts a much greater impulse to the line and obviously is better suited to long casting with normal fly lines. Again, once any part of a rod has reached its optimum, no increased effort on the part of the angler will effect noticeable increase in distance. So, in 1946, said Joannès Robin, author of *La Canne à Mouche à Truite, Objet d'Art*.

Today we have three approaches to reservoir long casting, each requiring a different sort of outfit.

Method One requires a butt-actioned split-cane rod from 9 ft 4 in to 10 ft, matched very probably with one of the American, supple, free-shooting, plastic-dressed, double-taper lines.

Method Two requires a rod of 9 ft to 9 ft 6 in matched to a standard torpedo head or forward-tapered line which, if it is to stay afloat, must be one of the plastic-dressed floaters.

Both outfits are essentially 'traditional' and are used without a qualm of conscience by radicals of the new school and purists of the old.

Method Three is something else again. A very powerful two-piece fibre-glass rod 9 ft 6 in to 10 ft long, differing from most fibre-glass rods in that the top joint is almost as stiff as a spinning rod. The rod is matched to a ten-yard shooting head of AFTM 10 level line spliced to 35 lb BS monofil shooting line or fine level plastic-dressed line.

In the case of method one, the rod must be capable of handling 22 yards of line in the air and be capable furthermore of initiating a forward impulse to the line great enough to allow up to 6 yards more line to be shot. In other words we want a rod capable of casting 28 yards of line and a longish nylon leader at the end of it. Such a rod must have an easy all-through action for, in high summer, when long casting is perhaps most necessary, it is sometimes essential to use small flies or nymphs to fine nylon. By 'fine', so far as big fish waters are concerned, I mean ·009 in, and an absolute minimum of ·008 in. Fishing finer means frequent breakage in fish which become conditioned to become non-risers. This demonstrates neither skill nor sportsmanship.

Often, too, a fish has to be held hard, or slid over the top of a weed bed, therefore resilience is required of a rod. Rigidity and resilience (ability to flex without fracture) militate against one another, as was stated by Robin in *La Pêche Indépendante*, and indirectly by Dick Walker in his thesis on *Split Bamboo Constructions*.

A rigid rod would break sooner or later under the rough treatment mentioned, and even if it remained unfractured itself, would cause many breakages when 'holding' fish.

For method one long casting I have designed three outfits all of similar action but of differing strengths to suit the differing powers of the anglers who use them. Outfits of the method one type are my first choice and when reservoir fishing I now use them in two strengths, 'Lake' and 'Ravensthorpe'. Both rods are matched by AFTM DT-6 lines and their easy power enables me to cast all day long without fatigue.

The 'Ivens Original', the most powerful of the series, which is matched by an AFTM DT-7 line, gets an occasional airing at Grafham and is the first choice of Mike Brady, a companion who enjoys an advantage of both muscle and years. But it has now become my standard greased-line salmon rod.

When casting with a butt-actioned rod one habitually follows through after punching; one does not attempt to 'stop' the action. This is possibly because the whole rod is moving and possesses high momentum of its own: it is physically impossible to 'stop' it at eleven o'clock as one can a light, tip-actioned rod. This 'follow through' or 'drift' is said to result in the wide loop associated with butt-actioned rods, but as you will read in Chapter 5, this probably is not the true cause. However, it is that 'follow through' that makes casting with butt-actioned rods far less tiring than casting and stopping a tip-actioned rod.

For method two long casting I use a 'Ravensthorpe' matched to an AFTM 7 weight-forward line. This line is the equivalent, as we shall explain in Chapter 2, to the AFTM DT-6 line, which also is used for long casting with the 'Ravensthorpe'.

This outfit helps me to achieve maximum casting distance from a sitting position in a boat. It compensates for the lack of toe-to-hand muscular power which one develops only when standing with both feet comfortably planted on solid ground. Standard weight-forward lines with 20 yards of fine dressed shooting line do not cast as far as the shooting heads described under outfit three, but have the great advantage that they can be figure-of-eight recovered in the hand which monofil most certainly cannot. During 1970 a glass-fibre rod has been hard tested with AFTM 7 and 8 weight-forward lines and has proved excellent. Prototypes of such butt-action fibreglass rods are now in use and should soon be in production.

Method three has progressed from the Ivens Superflyte, an 8 ft 8 in steepish-tapered fast-actioned split-cane rod introduced in 1967 for long casting heavy shooting heads spliced to monofil shooting line, to the 9 ft 10 in Ivens Ferrulite rod introduced by Davenport and Fordham in 1970.

Glass fibre, as tournament results show, has long been superior to split cane for sheer distance work, and our shooting heads with monofil backing are as near as damn it tournament tackle. So it seemed sensible to use glass fibre to replace the 1967 'Superflyte'. The problem with glass has always for me been its inability to handle double tapered lines well because butt-action was virtually unobtainable. The top joint was always too light in weight to help the relatively large diameter butt to work, and it was usually too soft at the tip to accept a line load that was adequate to flex the butt. Soft tips have the further disadvantage that driving in hooks at a distance is a chancy business.

Which brings us to the real point of method three: the need for a rod to drive in lure hooks as large as 4's or 6's at distances up to 40 yards, and above all to throw a size ten fast sinking shooting head and lift it for recasting. The basic 'stick' might be described as halfway between a fly rod and a spinning rod.

The method three outfit is probably most useful when wading, giving its best results when one can adopt a stance similar to that of a tournament caster reaching out for distance. By using a line raft to prevent the monofil shooting line sinking deep one casts consistently 36–40 yards – 45 yards is no problem when you really need it, though I have absolutely no confidence in my ability to drive home a hook at that distance . . . particularly with so much stretchy monofil between me and the fish.

The outfit is also useful when boat fishing with a sinking shooting head as described in Chapter 2 and again in Chapters 15 and 17. It is indispensable for the Dick Shrive method of deep fishing.

The rods I have described are made by Davenport & Fordham of 3, Thames Street, Poole, Dorset, and are obtainable through your usual dealer.

An outfit to be ideal must be kind to the fisherman. He must be reasonably fresh to make the most of the evening rise, though, truth to tell, however exciting the rise may be it never seems to produce the fish it appears to promise. Nor must it be an outfit that goes well only when casting down or across wind, for some of the finest reservoir-fishing is to be had casting into the teeth of a strong wind on a lee shore.

The easy-action method one rods throw a line 20 yards into a wind, and, quite as helpful if you are casting with trees behind you, they will also roll-cast splendidly . . . something quite impossible with weight-forward tapers or shooting heads unless the head is at the top ring.

As we have said, reservoir fishing demands continuous long casting and great concentration. The less you have to rest, the longer your fly is in the water, and all other things being equal, the length of time you are fishing will determine the size of your bag, over a period. Your ability to stand up to a day of 'The Contemplative Man's Recreation' on a reservoir, will largely depend on the efficiency of the rod (and line) you are using for the job in hand.

Whether we like it or not it is probable that within ten years, virtually all rods will be made of glass, or more sophisticated materials such as carbon fibre, because good quality Tonkin cane is becoming very difficult indeed to obtain.

Split-cane rods remain excellent but many makers still fit ferrules which are so designed that there is a ·02 in (approx) step down in the diameter of the stick immediately above the ferrule, and it is therefore not surprising that breaking-off above the male ferrule is so common a failure. Again, although the node of the culm is recognized as a weak spot, we continue to group the nodal points of the strips in threes instead of spiralling them, thereby avoiding more than one node at a given point along the stick.

Although varnish finishes cause flash, a sure fish scarer, anglers insist on high gloss, and Davenport & Fordham tell me that they have difficulty in selling the very durable matt finishes, which I demand for my own rods.

I was astonished last year to find that a number of my 'Superflyte' rods had been sent out with intermediate tyings every half-inch or so through the rod length. There was once a time when such tyings served, occasionally, to prevent strips of cane from separating after an animal-glue had broken down, perhaps due to the penetration of water. But modern resin glues are boil-proof and tyings add nothing but cost to the rod. In response to my objection Tony Fordham confirmed that many anglers still insisted upon decorative tyings and it was his job to satisfy the purchasers' requirements. I suppose it is equivalent to the unnecessary and very much more expensive chasing that one finds on sporting guns.

Nor have I ever understood why anglers prefer to buy rods whose silk whippings have retained their brilliant colour only because the varnish had been prevented from soaking into the silk by reason of a prior coat of dope. The first time the rod is used every whipping cracks.

When a modern resin varnish is applied to clean silk, nylon or Terylene whippings it penetrates through the whippings to the surface of the cane. Rod, whipping and varnish then flex together and remain in perfect condition for years.

But the most easily cured fault in our modern fly rods remains the use of agate butt and end rings. It is quite impossible to avoid the occasional cracked ring when travelling and, into the bargain, agate substitute rings, particularly the transparent ones, groove badly.

All these lined rings could well be replaced by the rust-proof and virtually unbreakable steel-alloy or hard-chrome rings used by most USA manufacturers and by Pezon & Michel and also on the English 'Apollo' rods.

Until the last two or three seasons I have been content with hard-chromed, intermediate bridge rings of various types, but whereas with oil-dressed silk lines it was the line which wore out, it is now the relatively hard plastic dressing of the modern fly line which wears out the intermediate rings. The rate of wear has been greatly aggravated by the speed-fishing techniques now widely used when fishing big lures for rainbow trout.

My own rods now sport 'Chromex' butt and tip rings, and the old-fashioned hard-steel snake intermediate rings which are less prone to grooving than any other. The trouble is that so many anglers insist on buying things that look expensive rather than things which the designer knows are effective.

This list of shortcomings of the English rod must make some readers feel like asking why on earth I use them. The plain fact is that deficient in some respects as they are, they are still the most beautiful tools for their price produced anywhere in the world. While a first-class split-cane rod in England can be bought for as little as £15 its counterpart in America would cost very much more.

The American angler is tackle-conscious – perhaps too much so – and his tackle industry is quick to put new technology to practical use. The result has been some very weird pieces of equipment of truly amazing variety, and doubtful utility, but the casting records have travelled westward nonetheless. There are encouraging signs today that the British tackle maker is much more receptive to new ideas than he was five years ago, and the angling press has increased the space devoted to reports of tests of new equipment. Probably the controlling factor is the angler and in the field of fly fishing there has been an astonishing development of new techniques in recent years with which the industry has coped better and quicker than would have been the case thirty years ago.

Certainly traditionalism within the industry is taking a beating. Some of the oldest firms have vanished from the scene whilst others have been taken over or have amalgamated with rivals. Commercial rough and tumble is bringing its usual beneficial results.

The 'Casting Tournament' has long been regarded in England as a sporting event in which 'freak tackle' is made to do things which would scare any fish clean out of the water. Nevertheless, it must be admitted that the rules are equal for all, and the 4 oz rod with the greatest power–weight ratio is likely, when used with a suitable line, to put up the best performance. There is little doubt that tournament casting has done much to improve all tackle.

In recent years, however, there has been a marked swing away from purely tournament gear towards competition casting with normal fishing tackle.

'Skish' as the new competitive casting is named, is organized in the USA on national lines, clubs competing in divisions much as do our football clubs. The formation of these clubs has considerably widened the choice of casters for international tournament work, since the man who promises to shape well gets necessary practice and coaching.

Here, few men would consider going to a professional for tuition in casting. Most are content to spend an hour or two with a friend and then muddle along by the waterside as best they can. I speak from experience, for I too muddled along in the same way. Chance brought me into contact with a really good amateur caster, the late Phil Lupton of Harrogate. We visited his casting pool, and within half an hour he had ironed out a faulty stance and diagnosed several other faults. A month later I was casting 5 yards further than I had ever cast before, and with exactly the same tackle.

When some twenty years ago my series of articles in *Fishing Gazette* first appeared, several readers expressed polite disbelief as to the distances (28–30 yards) I then claimed to cast. It was noticeable that none of them was a reservoir specialist. There is little doubt that today the best potential tournament distance-casters are to be found amongst the reservoir anglers and to be in the picture at all you need to punch out 35–40 yards. Certainly the average river fisherman can rely upon good tuition and good example of style from many of the men he will meet on a reservoir. Given such contacts and the necessary specialized equipment, there is little doubt that the novice reservoir angler will add 10 yards to his cast in a season in the 'reservoir school of casting'.

CHAPTER 2

A plain man's guide to fly lines

Good fly casting results when a competent caster uses a well-made fly rod matched to a line of the correct weight. Note that I use the word 'weight' and not the word 'size'.

To most anglers today the emphasis on weight is so blindingly obvious that it is difficult to appreciate that it is only in the last seven or eight years that we have come to classify our lines by a size number related to the weight of the 30 ft of line nearest to the fly: the AFTM rating, as it is now known.

Those of us who learned our fishing before the Second World War are sometimes still confused by the competing tackle manufacturers' descriptions of their products, not only because they described lines of similar casting potential by different codes before the war, but because they still appear to do so today, AFTM ratings notwithstanding.

Let us go back for a moment to the beginning of the century . . . which, I hasten to add, I don't remember!

The oil-dressed silk line was then a fairly recent development. The silk varied slightly in quality and in weight and one maker braided his lines more tightly than another. Lines of apparently similar thickness, therefore, had different weights, even before the dressing was applied.

The dressing, basically of raw linseed oil, was at first applied by hand, each coat being honed to provide a key for its successor. By constant repetition of similar processes each manufacturer was able, within limits, to turn out lines of a given size which would behave sufficiently similarly as made no matter.

Probably the two most popular oil-dressed silk lines were Hardy's 'Corona Superba' and Malloch's 'Kingfisher', which in the USA was known as 'King Eider'. In 1937 Hardy's listed the two heavier Corona Superba trout fly lines as 'Medium ICI' and 'Heavy IBI', the former having points ·023 in in thickness with centre ·040 in and the latter ·024 in in thickness and ·048 at the centre. Very unusually in those days the weights were given: the ICI line was listed as 15 drams while the IBI was said to weigh approximately 1 oz 3 drams. The corresponding Malloch lines were given numbers 3 and 4 and to the best of my recollection the ICI Corona Superba was equivalent to a size $3\frac{1}{2}$ Kingfisher. Messrs Farlow's oil-dressed silk fly lines, which were of similarly good quality, approximated to the Kingfisher lines so far as casting performance was concerned.

Despite the discrepancies of nomenclature between competing manufacturers, most anglers knew what they were about until, shortly after the Second World War, makers began to braid fly lines from nylon and Terylene in addition to silk. Nylon was the lightest of the three materials and Terylene the heaviest, about 30 per cent heavier than nylon.

It soon appeared that linseed oil was not a suitable material for dressing a nylon line by reason of the lack of key between the nylon and the oil and also because a nylon line stretched markedly and the oil sheared from its surface.

Although I managed to hand-dress a Terylene salmon line with linseed oil, the two materials were not apparently compatible so far as factory dressing was concerned and very shortly American and British manufacturers, notably Milward's here, marketed nylon and Terylene lines dressed with synthetic resins which keyed so well to the braided fibres that it was virtually impossible to strip the dressing from the line. We thus had the first dressed lines which would stand up to abrasion and which did not deteriorate if left wet on the reel after a day's fishing, though they certainly needed to be stretched when next you came to use them.

At this point, then, we had fly lines, perhaps of similar diameter, at point and belly, made of three materials of different weight, each of them dressed with an oil or resin of different weight. If one line suited a fly rod, it was almost certain that the other two lines, despite similar thickness, were unsuitable for that same rod.

The position in 1960–62 was impossibly confused. Farlow's 1960 catalogue listed 'Air Cel' floating lines and 'Wet Cel' sinking lines by a letter code linked to the table then standard for American manufacturers and shown in the table below. The only thing that you could say with certainty when this coding system was applied to floating and sinking lines was that if an

HDH Air Cel was right for your rod an HDH Wet Cel most certainly was not right for it. On the next page of the same catalogue, Farlow's listed Kingfisher silk lines under the original number code. There was no method by which one could be sure of ordering a line of the correct size for one's rod.

In 1961, Hardy's catalogue listed Corona double-taper trout fly lines by number and weight and by the same American letter code denoting thickness shown in the table opposite, but it was still impossible to tell how the sizes related to the Kingfisher lines in the Farlow catalogue of the previous year. The whole problem was further aggravated by the fact that one maker's lines were frequently factored by other manufacturers under different trade names. Again some manufacturers attempted to relate size of line to length of rod without in any way attempting to define the weight and strength of the rods. To cap it all, several manufacturers marketed economy lines 22 yards long, while at least one offered size 1 lines as 30 yards, size 2 as 31, size 3 as 32, and size 4 as 34 yards.

For fifty years now tournament casters throughout the world have experimented with torpedo heads of various lengths and tapers, and consequently of varying weights, until they found the line which gave them their best distance with a given rod. They then weighed it! They knew that same rod would always perform well with heads of different length and different taper provided their weights were the same. When they chopped up lengths of line to manufacture their compound tapers it was no haphazard process because their raw materials (level dressed lines) were known to weigh so many grains per foot length.

In Britain there was very little contact between tournament casters and anglers, although most tournament casters are excellent anglers. In America, contact between anglers and casters has been very much better, primarily because casting is virtually a national sport.

The tackle used in skish casting is standard fishing tackle. Not surprisingly therefore, the relative weights of the various standard fly lines sold in the USA became well known to a very wide circle of anglers, and it was but a short step then to the devising of a number classification which was related to the weight or casting properties of the line as opposed to an arbitrary description given to it by its manufacturer.

Table 1 Summarized Confusion

Maker, Catalogue, Date, Name of line	Line Description	Meaning
Hardy, 1937, 'Corona Superba'	IEI	Points ·021 in, Centre ·030 in
Hardy, 1937, 'Corona Superba'	IBI	Points ·024 in, Centre ·048 in
Hardy, 1937, 'Tournament'	IBI	Points ·030 in, Centre ·044 in
Hardy, 1961, 'Corolene'	HEH, HDH, HCH, FCF, DAD	Each letter referred to a diameter from the by then generally accepted American size code: AAA ·070 in AA ·065 in A ·060 in B ·005 in C ·050 in D ·045 in E ·040 in F ·035 in G ·030 in H ·025 in I ·020 in
Farlow, 1960, Air Cel DT (Floater)	HEH, HDH, HCH, GBG, GAG	Each letter represented a diameter from the above American table but Wet Cels had a specific gravity 20 per cent higher than Air Cel. GAG Air Cel was approximately the same weight as GBG Wet Cel.
Farlow, 1960, Wet Cel DT (Sinker)	HEH, HDH, HCH, GBG	
Farlow, 1960, Kingfisher DT	Size Nos 2, 3, 4 and 5	No diameters or weights given but Kingfisher lines had long had sizes related to belly diameters thus: No. 2–·040 in, No. 3–·045 in, No. 4–·050 in

Milward, 1960	Brand of line	Flycraft		Flymaster		Twincraft	
		DT	FT	DT	FT	DT	FT
re 'Coltcraft' 9 ft rod	Size recommended	HDH	ICH	HCH	ICH	HDH	IBHCI

There was a similarly variable range of line sizes for each of 29 rods.

The American Fishing Tackle Manufacturers' Association's (AFTMA) code

The AFTM number code ranges from 1 to 12 in ascending order of line weights. Today you can be quite sure that if an AFTM size 6 line by Scientific Anglers suits your rod then AFTM 6 by Gudebrod or Malloch will also suit your rod. Although some manufacturers have retained their old descriptions, all use the AFTM rating at least as an alternative. I am indebted to Messrs Farlows for permission to reproduce below the comparison table published in their 1967 catalogue to which I have added a further table covering Gudebrod lines.

You will notice, still, that most manufacturers continue to provide after the AFTM number a letter-coded description of the taper again related to the thicknesses of lines from the American Code given in Table 1 above. Note how clearly Table 2 brings out the performance difference between lines of similar thickness, the HCH Air Cel and Gudebrod floaters having AFTM rating 6, while HCH Wet Cel and Gudebrod sinkers are rated AFTM 8. Note that it also shows that the same rod will handle a DT-6-F line as efficiently as WF-6-F . . . !

And this is where we come to what is probably the greatest confusion of all. Paradoxically, long casting, which means for the purposes of this book, a rod that is matched by a DT-6 line, sinker or floater, requires one or two sizes larger in a weight-forward line. Here is how this comes about.

When you false cast and aerialize a gradually increasing length of line, there comes a time when the rod is said to be working nicely. This is the moment when the weight of line outside your rod tip is matched to the power of the rod. You can get this feeling with a short length of heavy line, or a long length of fine line (provided you can move it through the air fast enough) and if, as Eric Horsfall Turner and the late Captain Tommy Edwards tell us in their excellent book *The Angler's Cast*, we were to cut off that length of line which lay outside the tip ring and splice to it a length of nylon monofilament, we should then have an excellent casting head and minimal shooting-line drag when we needed long-distance casts.

Outside the field of reservoir and lake fishing, the emphasis is on casting accuracy rather than distance. Accuracy is achieved only when the rod is working properly with its correct weight of

Table 2 The AFTMA Code

How the code works

The new nomenclature incorporates the AFTMA size number, plus additional information defining the characteristics of the line.

Example: DT 6 F

The first letter(s) indicate the profile, eg L = level; DT = double-taper; WF = weight forward.

The number in the middle indicates the number size in the AFTM scale (weight).

The final letter indicates the character of the line, eg F = floating; S = sinking.

The table below shows that a double-taper No 6 floating Air Cel is interchangeable for casting purposes with a DT – 6 – F Gudebrod line, or the No 2 Kingfisher balanced line (a weight-forward taper), or the Wet Cel level 'E'.

AFTM size no	Air Cel Supreme			Wet Cel			Kingfisher (silk)			Level	Flymaster (nylon)		Flycraft (terylene)			Gudebrod G5 (floater)			Gudebrod (sink-R)		
	Double taper	Weight forward	Level	DT	WF	Level	Double taper	Balanced taper	Level	Level	DT	WF	DT	WF	Level	DT	WF	Level	DT	WF	Level
1															I						
2															H						
3			F												G						
4	HEH		E				1			1		HEH		HEH	F						
5	HDH	HDG	D					1							E			E			E
6	HCH	HCF	C	HHH		E	2	2		2	HHH		HHH		D	HDH	HCF	D			D
7	GBG	GBF	B	HDH	HDG	D	3	3		3	HDH		HDH		C	HCH	GBF	C	HDH		C
8	GAG	GAF	A	HCH	HCF	C	4	4/30		4	HCH	ICH	HCH	ICH	B		GAF	B	HCH	HCF	
9	GAAG	GAAF		GBG	GBF	B	5	4/40		5	EBg	EBG	FCF	EBG	A	GAG	GAA/F			GBF	B
10	G3AG	G3AF		GAG	GAF	A	6	5		6		GAAF		GAAF	AA					GAF	
11	G4AG			GAAG			7			7			DAD								
12	G3AKG			G3AKG																	

line outside the rod tip. And for river fishing the casting distance usually ranges from 12 to 18 yards.

Thus in establishing AFTM ratings for lines of all types – weight-forward, shooting head, double-taper, or level – the rating has been based on the weight of the 30 ft of line nearest the fly (10 ft of leader plus 30 ft of line plus 9 ft of rod length equals about 15 yards distance ... an average river cast).

In reservoir fishing, however, it is customary when using a double-taper line to aerialize anything from 18 to 22 yards before shooting a further 6 or 8 from the hand. If, therefore, we are to avoid overloading a rod, any double-taper that we use when long casting must be one or two sizes lighter than that used when river fishing over a shorter distance.

But with a weight-forward line, whether short or long casting, the weighty belly of the line will be outside the top ring and needs to be the same weight as the 18 or so yards of double-taper line which I aerialize when long casting. That is to say, I need a WF-7 line. The rod will, in fact, accept WF-8 lines, though I prefer the lighter line which increases the rod's length of life by keeping it underloaded.

Let me illustrate this. When I am dry-fly fishing with a comparatively short line on the upper Test, I use the 'Ravensthorpe' with an AFTM 7 double-taper line. That same size 7 line overloads the 'Ravensthorpe' rod when I am false casting a much longer line on the lower Test or on a reservoir and I then customarily use a size 6 double-taper line.

So here is the rule. When reservoir fishing use a weight-forward line at least one size heavier than the double-taper which is correct when you are long casting. If your rod butt is marked with the AFTM rating of the matching line thus, #6 or #7 or #8, choose for reservoir fishing a DT line one size lighter. On the river, for short casting, the line size is the same for any type of line.

The treatment of dressed fly lines

Plastic-dressed fly lines require little or no special treatment. They take no harm put away wet after a day's fishing and there is no need to strip them from the reel even during the close season ... always provided that they are stored in a dark and cool place. Like all lines, however, they pick up scum and this will reduce their free-shooting qualities, when it does no harm and a great deal of good to wipe them down with a moist soft rag sprinkled with a few drops of green liquid soap.

As I have already said, these plastic dressings are extremely tough and are virtually inseparable from their braided cores. Nonetheless, after two or three seasons the dressings will be found to have cracked and the floaters become prone to sinking over at least part of their length. There is nothing then that you can do with them for although they won't float properly, nor will they sink fast and reliably. Worse still, that hard and cracked dressing has a marked abrasive effect on your rod rings and in half a dozen outings you can badly groove or even cut through intermediate rings other than the snake type.

Despite their durability, plastic-dressed fly lines still do not give as many seasons' effective use as the old Kingfisher oil-dressed silk lines. Occasionally when using the 'Lake' or 'Ravensthorpe' rods I have returned to a No 3 DT Kingfisher and have been astonished at the improvement it effects in casting upwind, because, for a given weight, it is somewhat finer than a plastic-dressed floating line. But after an hour or two of fishing broken water in a high wind its flotation wanes and I am glad to return to a modern line that does what I want it to do.

Over the last eight years I have used floating and sinking lines by Gudebrod and by Scientific Anglers (who manufacture the Air Cel and Wet Cel range). I have found no difference in the life of either brand and whilst I have the feeling that Air Cel lines shoot rather more freely, any slight advantage is perhaps offset by the greater suppleness of the Gudebrod line which better lends itself to figure-of-eight line recovery.

But the advantage of plastic-dressed fly lines is not limited to their free-shooting and 'knock-about' durability: I changed over to them because they made possible and enjoyable techniques that hitherto were so tedious to apply that one avoided them. They have made oil-dressed silk fly lines obsolete so far as the reservoirs are concerned.

Floating lines

My techniques in the 1940s and 1950s were dominated by the need to keep the line afloat. Once it sank you were faced with the task of drying it out before it could be redressed to carry on fishing.

We experimented with longer and longer nylon leaders of ever more complex taper so as to be able to fish a fly deep while the line remained at the surface. True, the effect of that long leader was also to separate the wake of the line from the fly and presumably from any trout that was following the fly.

I was well aware that by wiping the line down with detergent, one could sink it to considerable depth when fishing from the dam and so catch fish at great depth at certain seasons of the year when other methods were quite hopeless. But knowing how hard it was to get a silk line to float properly once it had been sunk, one avoided sinking it. Again a sunken silk line soaked up so much water that casting it placed a dangerously unfair strain on the rod.

The Jersey Herd was developed from the need to create a fly so heavy that it would remain below the surface when line was recovered fast, an occasion when lightweight flies skated across the surface leaving a wake that scared trout away.

Somehow it has all become so simple now. A floating line today really does float, all day long, week in week out, all except for the last few feet of the taper which is designed to sink and so ensure that the nylon leader and the fly fish below the surface leaving no wake. But that short sinking tip, unlike any part of a silk fly line that sinks, never sinks more than a few inches below the surface and certainly does not drag down that part of the line which is intended to remain fishing in the surface. Note I say 'in' rather than 'on', for a plastic-dressed line does not rely upon surface tension to remain afloat. It is actually lighter than water.

Another version of the floating line has a 10 ft sinking tip which enables a bank fisherman readily to fish a fly at the bottom with a leader no more than 12 ft long and still have the sensitivity and rapid tighten to a taking trout which is never achieved with a deep-sunk line.

Sinking lines

A line that is designed to sink, and sink fast, should be, and is, braided and dressed from heavy materials. This weight gives it a very real advantage casting in a wind and such lines have the same free-shooting surface as the floaters.

The important point is to accept the fact that with these fast-sinking lines you can fish your fly at the bottom in 30 ft of water or in the thermocline of a stratifying water almost as readily as you can fish the surface water with a floater. As a rough guide I find that using a WF-7-S line and with 25 yards of line and leader between me and the fly, it takes about 60 seconds for the fly to get down about 20 ft. The heavy shooting heads mentioned below get down faster of course.

Bear in mind that the line sinks very much more rapidly than the relatively fine and light nylon leader and that the line will touch the bottom before the fly.

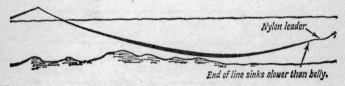

Nylon leader.

End of line sinks slower than belly.

Diagram 2.1a   Double-taper sinker

Whole line sinks fast.

Diagram 2.1b   Level sinker

Diagram 2.1a shows roughly the relative positions of line, leader and fly when a double-taper fast-sinking line is allowed to sink before line recovery is begun. Which brings us to our first point. There can be no more mistaken choice than a double-taper sinker. A level sinker (at one third the price) is very much more suitable since it has much more weight and sinking speed near to the fly as is demonstrated in diagram 2.1b.

Both the above illustrations, however, make it clear that there is always a considerable belly of line which reduces the sensitivity of the method. A take is usually felt as a slow drag, at times almost indistinguishable from weed.

It is in sunk-line fishing that weight-forward lines really come into their own. The weight is all in the short head which will be thicker and heavier than the belly of a DT or level line. Bear in mind, too, the AFTM rating of your weight-forward line will be at least one size bigger than the double-taper line which matches your rod when long casting. The relative weights per foot length of the bellies of AFTM 6-DT and AFTM 7- and 8-WF are as 4 is to 5 and 6¼.

Applying Stokes' Law, an AFTM 8 weight-forward head will sink half as fast again as an AFTM 6 level line. Conversely the shooting line, be it monofil or a very fine size 'H' Air Cel level shooting line, will sink much more slowly and the line will tend to lie as shown in diagram 2.3a.

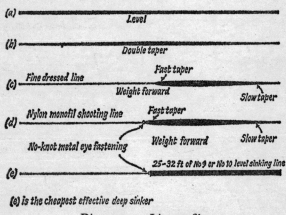

(e) is the cheapest effective deep sinker

Diagram 2.2   Line profiles

But why use a weight-forward line when we are really looking for maximum weight at the far end of the line? For the past two seasons I have experimented with relatively short lengths of AFTM 8, 9 and 10 Wet Cel level line spliced to monofil or Air Cel 'H' shooting lines. They are very cheap indeed and they perform excellently. Probably the lie of the line in the water is much as shown in diagram 2.3b, and this is as near as we shall get in sunk-line fishing to a straight line from rod tip to fly.

Size 10 level Wet Cel line is ·060 in in diameter and foot for foot it is two and a quarter times as heavy as the belly of a DT-6-S Wet Cel with corresponding much faster rate of sinking.

34

near short level shooting head, let us face it, seldom alights with
Adelicacy of a properly tapered momentum-reducing end to
the line. But whilst splashy casting is fatal when fish are feeding
your the surface, and an abomination to a competent angler at
any time, there is no question that splash matters little when
fish are lying very deep.

Whatever the design of your sunken line there is no need at
all to use a leader longer than 10–12 ft. Lines below the surface
seem scarcely to deter feeding fish where wake from a surface
fished line can put a fish off immediately. A relatively short
leader means freedom from the wind hazard which so bedevils
casting with 20 ft and 25 ft leaders.

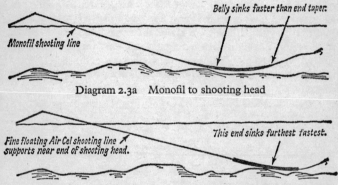

Diagram 2.3a   Monofil to shooting head

Diagram 2.3b   This combination comes closest to a direct line from
rod tip to deep-sunk fly.

Although I use monofil shooting lines with shooting heads of
all types, I find that Air Cel 'H' level floating line is far less
prone to snarl than monofil, and infinitely less likely to get
caught up when boat fishing. Probably 25 lb breaking strain
monofil is the smallest size that one should use for practical
fishing as opposed to pure distance casting. I now use nothing
less than 35 lb BS and find the extra weight and stiffness reduce
snarls and help the shooting head to turn over. I support Dick
Shrive's view that snarls and kinking are inevitable in a wind
and the used length of shooting line should be cut away and
re-spliced every two outings.

35

A new type of floating head

The very effective comparatively crude shooting heads we have described are just not good enough for surface fishing for, as we have said, line splash will put down rising trout.

According to my reasoning, if one can cast effectively with a level shooting head, and fish with finesse with a double-taper line it ought to be possible to devise a heavy shooting head of considerably more simple taper than a forward-tapered line and which therefore ought to be available at considerably lower cost than a forward-tapered line or a weight-forward shooting head.

I felt that all I needed was, in fact, a length of heavy level line with a taper at either end to give it good alighting qualities and to make it reversible for increased life. Such a line, I reasoned, ought to be marketable at about two-thirds the price of a standard double-taper line, and so it has proved. 'Superflyte' lines, as they are known, are about the same weight and length as comparable weight-forward tapers, and cast very well indeed, spliced either to monofil or fine dressed shooting lines. They are marketed by Davenport & Fordham. Their profile is shown in diagram 2.4.

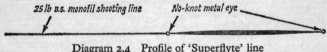

25 lb B.S. monofil shooting line   No-knot metal eye

Diagram 2.4   Profile of 'Superflyte' line

Building your own lines

There was very little point so far as surface fishing was concerned in splicing together lengths of level line in order to make your own fishing lines. But for very deep fishing there is a great deal to be said for buying lengths of dressed sinking level line and Air Cel shooting line in order to fish deeper, quicker and with more sensitivity. The object, after all, is to get your fly down to where the fish can see it as quickly as possible without the need to add lead to the cast!

May I at this point heartily recommend to you a thorough study of all that Eric Horsfall Turner and the late Captain Tommy Edwards have had to say in Chapter 13 of *The Angler's Cast* about building lines. If only plastic-dressed lines could be teased out in preparation for splicing as easily as the old oil-dressed silk lines!

The best method I have found is to remove about one inch of the dressing from the two ends to be spliced by dipping them for a minute or two in cellulose thinners. The dressing then strips off the braided core as a soft plastic tube.

After drying for half an hour the two ends are covered with impact adhesive (Evostik) and when touch-dry are lapped to give a union. The join is then overwhipped, whip-finished and sealed with a coat of Evostik. The resulting whipping, being the same thickness as the line on either side, passes readily through the rings.

Connecting line to leader

Several American manufacturers provide 'No knot' eyelets which by means of barbs on the pointed shank secure a permanent hold when pushed up the centre of the end of the fly line. The leader is then secured to the eyelet by the tucked half-blood knot (diagram 4.6). I often use these eyelets at *both* ends of my line, the other being secured to the monofil shooting or backing line. Retying a knot is much quicker than remaking a splice.

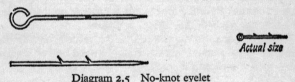

Actual size

Diagram 2.5   No-knot eyelet

'No knot' eyelets have three disadvantages.

The eyelets are not easy to insert and I find it best to place them in a fly vice and push the line onto the point, sometimes with the aid of pliers, using paper to mask the serrated jaws.

After a few days' use it will be found that the eyelet has caused the line dressing to crack just above the eye. The eyelet must then (by means of a razor blade) be cut out and reinserted.

Lastly there are occasions when the sinking tip of the line must be made to float with line grease so that the flies can be fished at the surface or only an inch or so below it. And you may occasionally wish to fish the dry fly! On such occasions that small eyelet has the effect of hastening the sinking of the tip.

An excellent alternative to eyelets for connecting the leader nylon is the knot shown in diagram 4.9. It is, of course, the knot the coarse fisher has for years used to tie on his spade-end hooks.

Which line will be best?

I will say now what will be repeated over and again throughout this book. Your fishing technique must be related to how the fish are feeding or are believed to be feeding.

If you can see fish feeding at the surface within 30 yards' range, by far the best outfit is a double-taper floater with a rod such as the 'Ravensthorpe' or the 'Lake'. The outfit is sensitive, throws a long line lightly and, above all, to lift off the 25-yard line and leader from the water and cover a rising fish with a simple lift and throw movement takes perhaps three seconds. This is something difficult to do with a weight-forward line which must be stripped in until the heavy belly is just outside your top ring if you are to avoid straining or breaking your rod.

Nymphing is often evident from flat patches appearing amidst the ripple or, when the big fish are about, one often sees great upwellings of water commencing feet below the surface. Probably you will wish to fish small nymphs very slowly and will fish the better for the delicacy of contact afforded by the 'Lake' or the 'Ravensthorpe' with a floating double-taper line spliced to 2 yards of AFTM 5 level sinker.

When fish are showing more than 30 yards away the casting problem is paramount and a weight-forward line or a shooting head then comes into its own.

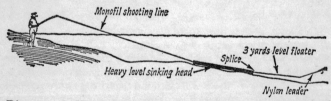

Diagram 2.6 Heavy sinking head rubs the bottom, but the fly rides clear of bottom snags.*

When fish are not showing and refuse to come up for a fly fished near the surface you would do well to use any of the

* In all diagrams, line profiles have been exaggerated to emphasize their differences.

following: a level sinker or, better, a sinking weight forward or, better still, a sinking shooting head and get your fly right down to the bottom or down to the thermocline if you are fishing from a boat.

Dick Shrive of Northampton has developed a most interesting 'composite' line for bank fishing. Basically it is a shooting head which sinks to the mud, the fly and leader being held off the bottom and clear of most snags by a length of floating line spliced to the weighty sinking portion. Diagram 2.6 shows the probable behaviour of such a line.

Casting with a sinking line

Nothing in casting will more surely destroy a rod's action than attempting to lift off a line which is submerged. Indeed, if you attempted it for an hour I could almost guarantee that within that time you would break the rod. The secret of picking off safely is to recover line until you have about 8 yards outside the tip ring, then raise the rod slowly and roll-cast forward. The line rolls easily before you on to the surface of the water when it may be immediately picked off and false cast to the rear in the ordinary way.

CHAPTER 3

The reel and other tackle

Reels and backing lines

As a river fisherman you probably feel safe with 30 yards of double-taper line and 20 yards of backing. As a reservoir fisherman, I used to feel safe with 30 yards of double-taper line and 60 yards of backing. As a result of one or two near tragedies, I now *hope* I am safe with a 30-yard double-taper line and 100 yards of backing.

On a river the banks set a limit to the distance a trout can run. That is true of a reservoir, too, but in this case the other bank may be 800 yards away, and you cannot follow a fish out to the middle!

My first large reservoir trout, a fish of 5 lb 3 oz, took me down to my last 10 yards of line when I was using a total of 90 yards. A week later exactly, after I had gone over to the 130-yard line, a fish took out well over 100 yards of line in each of the two long runs he made before the hook tore free. (I shall have something to say on small hooks in Chapter 6.)

You see, reservoir trout are cruisers by habit: they do not dive for a hole under the bank or for the shelter of a rock as does the river fish. Having no home, so to speak, they often head out into the lake and keep going. A fish hooked in shallows usually makes a very long fast run for deeper waters and, as we have said, these reservoirs have wide, shallow margins and the fish has some way to go.

When fishing in the deep water off the dams the fight is one of depth rather than distance, but now and then up comes the exception that tests the rule. On 18 May 1952 while I was fishing a 'Jersey Herd' from the dam, a fish hit me and immediately made a fast surface-run over the horizon. I had visions of a 10-pounder which were not shattered until I saw the fish fifteen minutes later – foul-hooked in the tail. When I netted him some ten minutes later the hook dropped free. He pulled the balance down to 3 lb 10 oz.

I moved away from Northampton in 1953. After working in Surrey for three years I moved to the north of England and lived in and near Skipton in the West Riding. My business journeys all over the north of England and southern Scotland, gave me splendid opportunity to fish for sea-trout and salmon but access to reservoirs holding large fish was limited and confined usually to vacations.

There were times when I re-read my comments on the need for a long backing line and wondered what had happened to those splendid fish that made plenty of backing so essential in the 1948–52 period. For, truth to tell, between 1952 and 1966 I can recall only five reservoir trout that took over 30 yards of line and four of these were rainbow trout at Chew Valley.

For some years I lived in Hemel Hempstead, distant one hour and five minutes from Grafham Fishing Lodge. Owing to a business trip to Libya, I missed the opening weeks of the 1966 season and by the end of the month when I had my first full day there the early days of slaughter were coming to an end. Nevertheless, from 2 PM during a sweltering afternoon I took six rainbow trout, three of which took line like the big brownies in Hollowell's hey-day. The biggest, 5 lb 9 oz, came when dusk was almost darkness and showed merely as a dimple near where I knew the fly must be. Her answer to the tighten was a savage, tearing, reel-screaming run such as you occasionally get when a grilse or a small summer salmon turns down-stream in a shallow sunlit pool and heads for the sea.

When at last she jumped she was beyond the point of the bay and out in the main body of water, 90 or more yards away. Five times she jumped against the energy-sapping drag of the long sunken line. Then, her steam all but spent, line came rapidly back onto the reel and a few moments later she was in the net . . . where the hook fell out.

Probably this is as good a moment as any to remind ourselves that very fast-growing brown or rainbow trout in new reservoirs are every bit as soft mouthed as newly run sea trout. There is a lot of flesh and fat covering a relatively light frame of bone.

Most anglers who fish Grafham regularly, well know what these big rainbows can do. The days of long backing lines are with us again.

There was a time when most of us used braided flax or Cuttyhunk as backing and only a large reel such as a 3¾ in Hardy St George would carry the amount of line one needed. Today the usual backing line is a 100-yard length of twisted or braided nylon or Terylene from 15 to 18 lb breaking strain and this, and the accompanying 30 yards of fly line, are easily carried on a 3½ in contracted-drum fly reel. Increasingly, since using shooting heads I have used 100 or 150 yards of 35 lb nylon monofil as shooting line and backing.

Over the last ten years or so, I have fished with reels by Morrit, Hardy, Noris Shakespeare, Young, and Pezon & Michel ranging in price from £1·50 to around £10. All have behaved satisfactorily. Today, I ask only that a fly reel shall be of simple design, easily taken apart to wash out sand (though this is more necessary on a river bank than a reservoir) and that the reel saddle should fit the standard screw reel fitting on an English fly rod.

In recognition of the tendency of nylon monofil wound onto a spool under tension to contract and perhaps burst or seriously distort the reel drum I always wind on a few yards of soft string as a cushion before I wind on the monofil backing line.

From time to time we read that the left-hand-wind fly reel is much to be preferred to the usual right-hand-wind reel. Writers emphasize the dangers of changing the rod to the left hand in those tricky moments immediately following the 'take'.

This criticism of right-hand-wind reels does not apply to lake fishing for no matter which hand you wind with, one hand must hold the rod while the other will handle recovered line. It is nonsense to think of changing the rod hand, or winding recovered spare line back onto the reel before one is on terms with the fish and by that time there is no danger in passing the rod to the left hand.

Line in the hand, or on the water, or in the bottom of the boat, as the case may be, is always a hazard and particularly so when, as frequently happens, the fish runs towards you. This is the one occasion when I concede real value to the automatic fly reel which, when you press the trigger, will whip in line at fantastic speed. Barrie Welham uses an automatic reel to catch those very large trout down at Two Lakes but these fish have little opportunity to make the distance runs common in reservoirs.

I feel a great need for a conventional contracted-drum fly reel of about 4 in diameter to which has been added a clockwork mechanism which would gather in all stray line as soon as I hit a fish, the reel action thereafter being by normal manual operation: no gears, no springs, no necromancy to come between me and the fish. Meantime the geared recovery 'Fish-Hawk' by Noris Shakespeare effects a reasonable compromise.

Waders

If wading is permitted, then, for bank fishing, it must be regarded as essential. If, like me, you are blessed with big feet, then you have an advantage in that your ordinary full thigh waders are long in the leg and enable you to wade well out without resorting to trousers waders, which are, in any case, forbidden in the rules of an increasing number of reservoir fisheries. If you fish only reservoirs, then waders with metal-studded soles are unnecessary, but if, like me, you enjoy opportunities to fish rocky-bedded trout and sea-trout streams from time to time, studded soles you must have if you would wade in safety.

When fishing from the stones of dams, which become dreadfully slippery after a shower, you would be well advised to slip off your waders and put on a pair of rope-soled shoes. These will at least permit you to swim for it if you slip. I once spent a nerve-racking hour-and-a-half fishing at Ravensthorpe with an elderly companion from a steep dam with a hedge at the top. I packed up fishing and spent my time getting his fly out of the hedge, rather than have to fetch him out of the water when he attempted to scramble up and down the stones. Needless to say, he saw no risk and wrongly thought I was activated by altruistic motive only.

The most comfortable waders available are those distributed by Millard Bros and of Canadian origin. I have two pairs: one is in use and the other is back at home hanging up with bags of Silica Gel crystals in the feet to absorb perspiration from the previous day's fishing.

With such waders you will find that by ordering your usual shoe size you will have room for a thick pair of socks and perhaps a felt sock beneath your foot. I have found that with some other makes it is advisable to order one size larger than your shoes which will permit you to wear thick socks or sea-boot stockings inside your boots to increase your wading comfort in the cold water of early spring. Never wear tight waders. They restrict your circulation and your feet and lower limbs become unbearably cold.

Carrying your fish

There is probably no fish container which will keep fish in better condition than a wicker creel, though it is doubtful if many of the post-war generation of fly fishers have ever seen one let alone possessed one. But creels are of little use if your fish average 2 to $2\frac{1}{2}$ lb as ours do.

When bank fishing, I carry a big, strong, canvas haversack with separate compartments for tackle and fish and place my fish in large polythene food bags which are cheap enough to discard after use. An excellent alternative (and the usual container at Grafham) is a 1 cwt polythene fertilizer sack which can be washed out and used over and over again. It has the advantage of being strong enough to hold 25 or 30 lb of trout slung over your shoulder as you stagger back a mile or so to the car. The polythene laundry bags with handles available from launderettes are also excellent. In hot weather, however, polythene bags can ruin fish in a matter of hours.

The net

The ordinary throw-up net used in river fishing is useless for big reservoir trout. I use a net of my own design consisting of a triangular 20-in steel frame screwed into a handle 2 ft 7 in long. It is secured by a cord loop over my head. When a fish is hooked and all is well the dog leash clip is unhitched with the left hand and the net front is rested on the bottom with the handle against my tummy for instant use. The net is very deep and needs to be, for quite often we deal with fish over 4 lb in weight, and fish of maybe 8–12 lb are there to be caught. The net in no way interferes when you are fishing. And how wonderful it is to make a clean job of netting a heavy fish at the first attempt. It remains true that I have never lost a fish at the net when using this implement, and it has secured salmon up to $11\frac{3}{4}$ lb.

I now mesh my own nets using 40 lb breaking strain twisted Terylene which has been immersed on its spool in boiled linseed oil and varnish and allowed to dry. This overcomes the springing-apart tendency of a sheet-bend mesh knot tied in untreated Terylene.

Long-handled nets have enjoyed increased popularity in the last few years, probably because bank fishing pressure has increased to such an extent that many anglers move about very little. Indeed at times if you move from your 'pitch' you might well have to walk half to three-quarters of a mile before you could find a space to wade out again.

With individual anglers staying put, so to speak, for the whole day, there has been a return to landing nets with 4- and 5-foot handles, which are spiked into the mud ready to hand when a fish is to be landed. Long-handled nets of this kind are ideal for boat fishing in which context the short-handled net is quite unsuitable. Needless to say the long-handled net has the same large frame and deep net already recommended.

Fishery rules notwithstanding, long-handled nets are often left out in the water whilst their owners rest on the bank. When it comes to 'territory' we are still very primitive animals, I fear.

Reservoir tackle for river fishing

Events have shown that the tackle we have described is by no means confined to reservoir fishing. Except on really big rivers the 'Original' is now my first choice as a floating-line salmon rod. It throws all the line one needs, and picks it off cleanly. I find too, that it kills fish quicker than a 12-footer, the best performance being an 18 lb fish completely played out and killed in ten minutes.

The 'Lake' is a delightful sea-trout rod, powerful, without being hard on the soft mouths of newly run fish, and it handles heavy fish (including nocturnal salmon!) as well as those easily lost acrobatic half-pounders that swarm through so many rivers in late July and August. My favourite night-fishing rod is, however, the 'Ravensthorpe'. It throws a long line so effortlessly and, being lighter in the hand, one tightens more surely to those angel wings that brush the fly in the quiet dark of a slow-running pool.

Both the 'Ravensthorpe' and the now-withdrawn 'Tarn' (a lighter 'Ravensthorpe') happily permit the use of AFTM 5 line (either double-taper or level) giving a delicacy of contact with the fly quite impossible with heavy-line outfits.

Being butt-actioned, all the rods of the series will switch-cast very nicely, making them particularly useful when fishing down a pool with wooded or high banks. Nor does their marked butt-action prevent a narrow loop being thrown when it is necessary. One's casting action influences the width of the loop much more than is generally realized.

I have felt it better to deal with weatherproof clothing in the chapter on boat fishing and under the heading of 'Clothing, equipment and companions' (page 180).

CHAPTER 4

Nylon and the reservoir fisherman

Nylon, of course, has little strength when first extruded like spaghetti through a hole in a steel plate. The chain-molecule of nylon is very long, 1,000 atoms or more, and the substance achieves its high tensile strength when these long molecules are forced to lie parallel to one another when the relatively soft, worm-like, extruded form of nylon is drawn out by stretching, while running over a system of rollers revolving at different speeds. Before this stretching, the molecules lie higgledy-piggledy; after stretching, their ends have been drawn in, and the monofilament exerts its greatest resistance to those stresses which operate parallel to its axis. Drawn metallic tubing gains its tensile strength from a similar molecular rearrangement. If analogy is possible, we may liken our nylon molecules to wool fibres. Worsted yarns have their fibres parallel to the axis and fine yarns are comparatively strong. Woollen yarns on the other hand show no such neat arrangement of the fibres, and diameter for diameter are weaker than worsted yarns.

When, however, these drawn substances are subjected to vibration, and forces are exerted at right angles to the axis of the drawn substance, the orientation of the molecules is broken down, and they again slowly assume their old unordered arrangement, and the tensile strength is markedly reduced. A breakage can then occur without any great load being applied. In the case of metals, we came in youth to recognize the malaise in the form of fractures to the copper petrol-feed of our first motor-cycles. In the 1950s fatigue was responsible for a series of air disasters to high-flying jet airliners. Today's schoolboy takes it for granted.

Nylon suffers the same malaise, which sets in after prolonged or repeated flexure under load. I first encountered it when on holiday in 1950 whilst using a Mitchell reel and German nylon to spin for sea trout. The line initially broke at an evenly applied load of 6¾lb, but after only two hours' use the dry breaking load had been reduced to 4¼ lb. I did not experience anything like so great a loss of strength when using a length of nylon as a fly cast and by a process of elimination I concluded that it was the bending over the pick-up arm which had engendered this weakness which extended over the whole length of used line. To the naked eye, weak and strong portions of the line appeared exactly similar.

Again in 1957 on Border Esk a friend's line broke after he had played a huge salmon for over an hour. Breaking strain had fallen from a tested 10 lb to 4¼ lb.

High-quality nylon monofilament is now so cheap that fatigue breakages should never occur if we destroy after reasonable use or excessive loading what may appear a perfectly good leader or line. After landing a heavy trout I always replace the whole of the level length of nylon immediately above the fly.

Waste nylon should be taken home and burnt. Never leave it on the bank for birds become entangled in it. In one case the stuff had cut through a coot's leg to the bone; in another I found a blackbird held fast by a loop tightened round its tongue.

Stored nylon loses strength

In recent years, as a result of testing unused spooled nylon left over from previous seasons, I have established beyond all doubt that nylon deteriorates with age. In an extreme example a spool of 18 lb BS monofil bought in 1960 had dropped to 10 lb BS by 1964.

This is what one would expect of an 'organic' molecule and at the beginning of each new season I buy new 25-yard or 50-yard spools of monofil from ·014 in down so as to be quite sure that the finer sections of a made-up leader are at maximum strength.

Nylon casts well when you understand it

So often, I hear the complaint that nylon will not cast into a wind, that it lands in a 'bird's nest', or that it lags behind the line when long casting. Usually if I know the angler well enough to ask him questions or make suggestions, I find that he uses a nylon cast consisting either of a 3-yard continuous length of mono-filament or a tapered nylon cast bought from his tackle dealer.

Over the years I have kicked the tackle maker as hard as most other specialist anglers, but the last ten years or so have seen many changes of attitude and most manufacturers of repute are glad to market gear designed and sponsored by recognized authorities. But rubbish is still sold from time to time and usually it happens because the maker himself is not a first-class angler, lacks a designer and never finds out the errors of design in his products. Let me digress to illustrate this point.

An angler has two fly rods. In his novice, river-fishing days his long cast will be no more than 18 yards and at that distance both rods can appear quite satisfactory. While his capability as a caster remains '18 yards with the wind' he is most unlikely to discover that, while one set of tackle is suitable for casting up to 22 yards, the other is quite capable of giving him 30 yards or more. In fact, I would go further: it *could* happen that because the long-casting outfit never has its power developed, the angler could believe that the less desirable rod, which was being forced to work with only a short line aerialized, was in fact the better outfit. It is, I agree, more likely that at 18 yards the better rod would be showing its worth, but please see my point: it would only be showing its worth to a man who really appreciated how a 30-yard rod should behave. Again, the difference in design of two outfits, one of which has a 22-yard capacity and the other a 30-yard capacity is unbelievable: Ted Trueblood writing in *Field and Stream* about sixteen years ago, claimed that he had achieved a 20-yard cast using a broomstick as a rod.

It is the addition of distance beyond 22 yards in which tackle design becomes important, and the perfection of tackle for long casting is essentially a job for a man who can get and has to get distance in his fishing.

Double-taper nylon leaders

Reservoir trout fishing in the Midlands demands very long casting, and, when bank fishing, more often than not one has to cast across or upwind. Money spent on a most perfectly balanced rod and line of 30 yards or more potential, is money wasted unless the design of the leader for use with the outfit is of similarly high order.

The failure of a nylon leader to straighten is often due to bad casting, but the most competent caster can have difficulty when long casting with an inadequately designed nylon leader.

Generally it will be found when casting that fine level monfil leaders have insufficient momentum to straighten beyond the line when the line is coming to rest. Let us examine the significance of diagram 4.1.

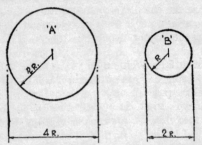

Diagram 4.1   Cross-sections of two lengths of nylon

The area of cross-section 'A' is $\pi 4R^2$ and the diameter to be pushed through the air is 4R. Circle 'B' has a cross-sectional area of πR^2 and a diameter of 2R. From this we see that for equal lengths of monofil, the one with diameter 4R will be four times as heavy as that with diameter 2R. In other words, when we double the diameter, we multiply the momentum at a given speed by four, the ratio of wind resistance to weight decreases, and the leader will travel farther before coming to rest.

The first angling writer to take advantage of this mathematical solution was Al McClane, Angling Editor of *Field and Stream* who, in 1949, published a series of tapers for 'speed' casting.

I chose two of McClane's tapers and found them in all conditions, including high adverse winds, completely efficient. In simplest terms, McClane gained leader momentum and overcame wind resistance by using much thicker lengths of nylon in his casts, and at the same time he redistributed the weight and, in fact, evolved the double-taper leader.

Although my recent employment of sunken lines, or sinking tips to floaters has offered easier solutions of many problems, I give in the table below those of McClane's tapers which are most useful in reservoir fishing, followed by three tapers of my own (C, D and E) which meet the need for a really long leader when fishing in conditions of bright sunlight. These very long leaders were developed to test Hewitt's theory, that it was better in bright conditions to lengthen the leader than to reduce the size of the point. Certainly appreciable lengthening of the leader appears to give as good results as a finer point, without any of the risks.

(I deliberately use the word 'leader', which the Americans use to describe the nylon at the end of the line, so as to avoid the reader's confusing this piece of equipment with the actual throwing or casting of the fly.)

(A) 40 in of ·018 in; 36 in of ·017 in; 7 in of ·016 in; 7 in of ·014 in; 7 in of ·013 in; 7 in of ·012 in; 28 in of ·010 in; length 11 ft. General purposes.

(B) 26 in of ·020 in; 24 in of ·018 in; 22 in of ·016 in; 18 in of ·014 in; length 7 ft 6 in. Heavy flies in strong cross or adverse winds.

(C) 12 in of ·016 in; 12 in of ·018 in; 16 in of ·020 in; 12 in of ·018 in; 12 in of ·016 in; 12 in of ·014 in; 12 in of ·012 in; 12 in of ·011 in; 15 in of ·010 in; length 9 ft 7 in. This is a variation of a taper which McClane took down to ·008 in, too light for work where fish are heavy. This is a grand taper for use under normally windy conditions and will allow for good casting upwind. This leader will serve the novice-caster much better than the longer 'D' and 'E' tapers below.

(D) 18 in of ·016 in; 18 in of ·018 in; 30 in of ·020 in; 14 in of ·018 in; 14 in of ·016 in; 10 in of ·015 in; 10 in of ·014 in; 10 in of ·013 in; 10 in of ·012 in; 12 in of ·011 in; 22 in of ·010 in; length 14 ft. This leader is not easy to handle, but I have found that any awkwardness there may be is compensated for by the fact that fewer fish are put down in bright weather. The leader is also useful for fishing a nymph deep down.

(E) 12 in of ·016 in; 12 in of ·018 in; 20 in of ·020 in; 12 in of ·018 in; 12 in of ·016 in; 12 in of ·015 in; 12 in of ·014 in; 12 in of ·013 in; 12 in of ·012 in; 20 in of ·010 in; length 11 ft 4 in. A very useful leader in light wind, and under sunny conditions.

There are endless variations of these tapers possible, and the reader must experiment until he finds a balance which suits his own rod and line. Using monofil up to ·025 in in diameter I have successfully experimented with leaders up to 25 ft in length.

Knotless tapered leaders

In 1955, I thoroughly tested knotless tapered leaders in which the weight decreased uniformly from loop to point, and my report on them was published in the *Fishing Gazette* under my editorial pen-name, 'Gannet'. In crossing and following winds I found a 12½ ft leader tapering from a ·017 in loop down to ·0105 in behaved well, and, when reduced to 9 ft length, was also reasonably good upwind. An effective 18½ ft leader was improvised by adding 18 in of ·018 in monofil, 36 in of ·020 in, and a looped 18 in length of ·018 in to the thick end of the 12½ ft taper.

This material was also available in continuous lengths and could be cut so as to provide double-taper profiles.

The development of new types of fly lines and the 'cocktail' combinations of spliced sinking and floating line described in Chapter 2 have made it much less necessary to use the very long leaders of the 1950s and early 1960s. Only when deep fishing from the shore do I now bother with them, and as mentioned in Chapter 2, Dick Shrive, probably the foremost exponent today of deep-fishing techniques, has now found them unnecessary from the bank. His solution closely resembles the 'balanced crust' method of keeping parboiled potato out of the herbage at the lake bed when carp fishing. It goes without saying that Shrive was a top-class coarse fisher long before he began fly-fishing for trout. He is yet another graduate of the Northampton School!

Today, whenever a leader length of 9 to 15 ft will suffice for my purpose I seem most frequently to employ a 'Platil' knotless taper to 35/100 (·014 in) or to 30/100 (·012 in) next to the line with lengths of level monofil added to step me down to my customary point size 24/100 or 26/100 (·009 in or ·010 in).

Dyeing nylon monofilament a certain shade of purple has been stated to render it less visible to fish. It may be so, but I prefer my leader material to be non-reflecting and, generally, of a neutral grey colour. Neutral greys will emit whatever colour of light is shone upon them; in other words, grey nylon will tend to become the greens and browns of weed and mud. It is hard to conceive of any nylon being invisible in water unless it has a non-reflecting surface, has the same refractive index as water, and is as transparent as water itself. The only form of dyeing which appears to me at all logical is that used for 'camouflaged' finishes. These rely upon colour changes to break up the line of the monofil and thereby reduce its visibility. I have caught many fish on camouflaged nylon, but it is impossible to say whether I have caught more than I would have done on a neutral grey material.

Increasingly since 1965 there have been a number of monofils with highly polished surfaces offered. I do not like them, but the trouble can be reduced by the time-honoured silver-nitrate treatments! (Page 46 – *This Fishing* – Captain L. A. Parker.)

But it is seldom that the fish will be concerned with the reflected colour of the leader material. More often than not in fly-fishing, the leader will be seen in silhouette, when, no matter what its colour, it will appear as a dark line against a lighted 'window'. Again, Hewitt's photographs show that objects lying in the surface cause depressions in the surface 'skin' through which light passes, to appear on the bottom as light-spots. What dye can overcome this defect?

Nylon knots

Nylon is intolerant of inadequate knotting, giving perhaps only 20 per cent of its breaking strength with a wind-knot (overhand

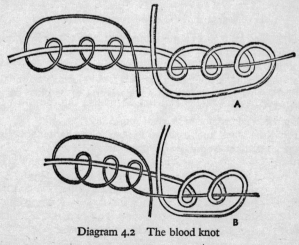

Diagram 4.2   The blood knot

knot) in its length whereas fibrous yarns and braided lines still retain reasonable fighting strength when so misused.

The knots that follow are all simple and reliable. They are for their purpose the strongest nylon knots developed.

The 'blood' knot 4·2A is an excellent knot for joining two strands, but I find in larger sizes that it pays to take two turns with the heavier strand and three with the lighter as in B. By this means the knot is drawn up evenly, and is stronger than the unevenly tightened knot which results from using three turns on both sides. The point is, that the lighter strand is more easily bent and tends to tighten before the heavy one.

There are several methods of making the turns for 'blood' knots which result in slightly different finished knots. In 1953, John Rowe, Major E. M. Stirling and I experimented to find the best and the results were published fully in the *Fishing Gazette*. Provided the tyer was thoroughly familiar with his knot, one version appeared as good as another.

Moistening the turns with saliva seems to result in smoother tightening of the knot.

Diagram 4.3   The four-turn water knot

The blood knot was unquestioned as the best knot for joining two strands of monofil until February 1970, when Dick Walker wrote in *Angling* that in the smaller sizes the four-turn water knot was slightly stronger. In the July issue Norman Simmonds published his test results and when several of us checked the water knot against the blood knot we found that we'd been using the weaker knot for a very long time.

I find the blood knot easier to tie, but in the lighter strands it is the water knot from now onwards for me.

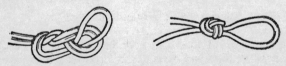

Diagram 4.4   The blood-bight loop

54

The 'blood-bight loop' is simple to make and is the only reliable loop-knot for nylon. It is important to note that it has one more half-turn than a 'figure-of-eight' knot. Care must be taken to draw up all strands evenly. I place the loop over a round nail and pull on both the long and short ends.

Although the 'blood-loop' is probably the strongest of the dropper knots, the dropper length, being attached to the loop by the 'tucked half-blood', it is a little clumsy in appearance.

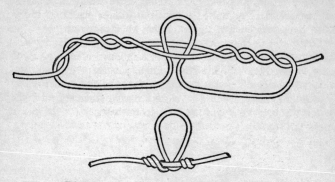

Diagram 4.5   The blood-loop dropper knot

With tapered leaders it is quite safe to attach the dropper length by means of a 'tucked half-blood' round the main cast immediately above a 'blood' knot. The dropper knot then jams down on to the leader knot. Hinging of the monofil can occur in casting, and frequently occurs when a fish on the dropper is played; the 'blood' knot should therefore be retied occasionally (See also diagram 9.3).

Diagram 4.6   The tucked half-blood

This knot is unbeatable. It first came to my notice in a list of knots given in *Field and Stream*, and it was stated to have a breaking strain of 98 per cent of that of the unknotted monofilament. I tied eighty specimens and tested them against other hitches used for the same purpose. In forty such tests against other knots, only twice was this knot beaten.

The knots which beat the 'tucked half-blood' could not repeat their victory, which must therefore be attributed to bad tying of the 'tucked half-blood'. A further forty tests against a spring balance gave four breakages in the strand, and an average breaking percentage of 93 per cent, with two freak breakages of 50 per cent and 58 per cent not included in the average. Apart from these two freaks the lowest result was 84 per cent.

It is essential when finishing this knot always to pass the working end of the monofil through the first turn of the half-blood as shown. Loss of strength occurs if the tuck is made around the standing part (the straight length of nylon in the diagram) before it passes through the eye of the fly. Provided you follow this procedure it matters not whether you pass the nylon through the eye of the hook from the back (as shown) or from the front.

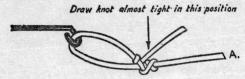

Diagram 4.7

It is usual to draw up the knot in front of the eye, as shown above, and then slide the knot down to the eye by pulling on the standing part A while holding the hook.

Since a 'blood' knot gives an average breaking strain of about 85 per cent, it will sometimes be found that when the fly is attached by means of the 'tucked half-blood' the point is lost when a break occurs. The remedy is to join your monofil with the four-turn water knot!

Many anglers still pass the nylon through the eye of the fly and tie their knot round the shank of the hook between the eye of the hook and the head of the fly. They allege that such knots, of which the Turle is the best-known example, give the fly a clean entry into the water and keep the hook shank in line with the cast. I believe that this is more important in theory than in practice and it is certain that with knots such as the Turle the nylon hinges where it passes over the ring of the eye when line and leader straighten before and behind during the act of casting. By knotting the cast to the eye itself this defect is entirely overcome, because the knot slips on the ring, and the cast, therefore, does not bend. Furthermore, when a fish is hooked it matters not from what direction the pull comes on the fish; there is no bending of the nylon with consequent weakening of the cast, for the knot slips round the ring as the direction of pull alters. I have not found in practice that the fly works any the less well for being attached to the cast in this way, but I did find when I first used this knot that the number of my breakages was reduced, a most important consideration.

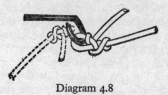

Diagram 4.8

This same knot is of course used to a secure a leader or a monofil shooting line to the 'no knot' terminal eyes described when we discussed fly lines, and has the same strength advantage for tying a monofil spinning line to a swivel or bait.

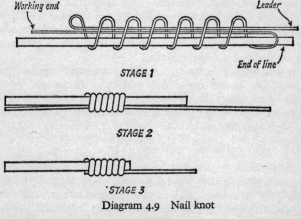

Diagram 4.9 Nail knot

Whenever the line/leader union is required to float, 'no-knot' (metal) eyes are out, so too are bulky wake-producing line-to-leader knots such as the sheet-bend line fastening to a blood-bight loop at the head of the leader.

Improbable as it may seem, the knot shown in diagram 4.9 is safe as well as inconspicuous and is destined to become as popular with reservoir fishermen as it has been for many years with coarse fishers who use it for tying fine nylon to spade-end hooks. I used it for the whole of 1968 on one of my lines and found it excellent.

Forming knots

Knotting is an art which is best divided into two separate parts: first the making of the turns, and secondly the forming of the finished knot. All anglers complete the first part more or less successfully, but few take trouble over the second and far more important part of the process.

Try this experiment. Make your turns for a blood-bight loop; hold the loop and the two ends, and draw tight. Now have a close look at your knot. It is an even chance that you will find that strands which should lie parallel are, in fact, crossing over one another, and have not tightened evenly. This sort of thing can occur with any knot, and is best avoided by tightening evenly and slowly on the standing part or parts, at the same time drawing up the two ends. Great care must be taken to avoid over-tightening, with consequent weakening of the monofilament in the knot itself. Soaking the monofil before knotting has been proved to give up to 5 per cent increase in the breaking strain (BS) of the knot – 'spit' is a good lubricant when you are tying hurriedly at the waterside!

It is a fact which I have proved in a series of experiments that your first twenty tyings of a new knot will have a lower average breaking strain than, say, the average BS of Nos 200 to 220. From this it follows that it pays to stick to a good knot when you find one, and avoid switching from knot to knot.

French and English measurements

It is still sometimes necessary to convert metric sizes to Anglo-Saxon sizes, and for the benefit of those who wish to construct tapers to the specifications given above, I give below a table for comparison purposes. The size-number of Continental nylons is the diameter expressed as hundredths of a millimetre. 1/100 mm = ·0003937 in; therefore, to obtain the equivalent size in inches, we multiply the Continental size by ·0003937. Thus 26/100 mm nylon is: 26 × ·0003937 in diameter, i.e. ·0102 in (or 1x as it was known when I used silkworm gut).

Size in inches	Size in millimetres (approx.)	
·008	22/100 approx.	
·009	24/100	,,
·010	26/100	,,
·011	28/100	,,
·012	30/100	,,
·013	32/100	,,
·014	35/100	,,
·015	38/100	,,
·016	40/100	,,
·017		
·018	45/100	,,
·019		
·020	50/100	,,

It is impossible to find exact metric equivalents for any size in Anglo-Saxon measurements, and in several of the larger sizes of nylon monofil no near metric equivalents are available.

The breaking strain of nylon monofilaments

It is an unfortunate fact that the breaking strains quoted for some monofils are gravely misleading. Nylon absorbs water, and when thoroughly soaked (100 per cent relative humidity, or '100 RH' as it is usually expressed) its BS may be 25 to 30 per cent lower than that stated on the spool. The apparently greater BS of certain monofils may reflect nothing more than their test in a relatively dry state.

During 1967 and 1968, a number of super-strength monofils were offered. These had remarkably little stretch and for a given diameter gave advantages of 40 per cent or so in breaking strain. All of those that I tried proved very brittle when knotted and I lost a number of fish with them, particularly fish that had taken the dropper fly. Returning to my standard materials, nylon monofils by Pezon & Michel, Platil or Gudebrod stopped the nonsense.

As with all new materials the early snags were soon ironed out. 1969 saw me using a new Pezon & Michel monofil 'Trilon'.

26/100 mm diameter gave no less than 9 lb BS, and it was supple and knotted surely using conventional knots. On one occasion I wound in sadly, certain that I had been broken all ends up by a smash take, only to find a no 4 long-shank lure hook had been all but straightened.

It is interesting to recall that we used to catch our trout at Hollowell in the late 1940s on 2x (·009 in) silkworm gut with an average BS of around 3 lb wet and knotted. Most of us found at first that we lost more fish on nylon than we ever had on gut; but this turned out to be due to inadequate knotting as often as defective nylon.

CHAPTER 5

Reaching out for distance

To refer in conversation with a river fly-fisherman to continuous casting of distances greater than 23 yards is to court disbelief. Few river anglers throw a fly so far, and then only when the wind happens to be just right and their timing is a little better than usual. And yet it is not untrue to say that the experienced reservoir fisherman thinks of 26 yards as commonplace and most can manage 30 today.

'Debunking' is always amusing for a writer, and whenever it can do good it is well justified. In a discourse on casting one cannot help but debunk the generally accepted methods.

How often we used to read of the book-under-the-elbow method of tuition, and how seldom did the counsellor refer to the necessity for keeping the line between the left hand and butt ring tight.

Let us examine what happens when the average caster is at work. He grips the line with his left thumb and forefinger and raises his rod to throw the line to the rear. The distance from his stationary left hand to the butt ring increases as the rod lifts. After pausing briefly to allow his line almost to straighten at the rear, he punches the rod forward, and in so doing he decreases the distance between his left hand and the butt ring. In other words, when he should be exerting a forward impulse against a tight line so as to gain maximum forward line speed, he is, in fact, punching against slack line, just as he would be were he to shoot line from his left hand as he made his forward punch.

The first step in improving your distance is to learn to follow the rod movements with the left hand so as to keep taut the line between the left hand and the butt ring. If in the past you have neglected to do this, you will be amazed at the difference in distance this small left-hand movement will make.

The tournament caster makes even greater use of his left hand, for he not only keeps his line tight as he punches, but also pulls on the line in time with his rod movements to accelerate the speed of his line. Earl Osten, the American caster, says that this style of casting developed on the west coast of America and was introduced into tournament casting by Marvin K. Hedge. That its use is important in distance work is demonstrated by the fact that it is everywhere the standard technique.

'Left-hand line acceleration', as it is best termed, gives the caster two great advantages. The first is that the line travels faster and therefore farther, and the second is that the pull on the line, exerting its effect slightly before that of the rod impulse, lifts the end of the straightening line and prevents it touching down either in front or at the rear.

As to the actual timing of the pull with the left hand, even the champions differ. Osten says rod and hand movements begin together, while Hedge and Gregory insist on hand movement just after the start of the rod movements. Edgar May pulled at the same time as he began his punch and kept the whole movement as smooth as possible so as to get even acceleration. It is quite possible that all methods are equally effective and are merely individual interpretations to suit the styles of the users. There is little doubt that the hand movement is the first to affect the fly because the forward or backward punch is first expressed as a curve thrown into the butt of the rod. This curve travels up the rod and at the time when the tip is moving fastest the butt is under no stress at all. Diagram 5.16 shows the rod flexed at the butt, while both diagram 5.5 and diagram 5.17 show how such a curve reaches the middle and top leaving the butt unflexed. Dick Walker believes that the curve which travels up the rod is reproduced in the line, and I would hazard a guess that he is right. If he is, he has accounted for the wide line loop associated with butt-actioned rods. Diagram 5.9 shows the interesting result of the butt, under the influence of its own momentum, curving backward before the rod has straightened.

I will not say that the method of casting shown in diagram 5.1–19 is easy to learn; few techniques worth mastering ever are; but it is well within the capacity of any angler who has been casting for two seasons and who has learned to keep his left hand moving so as to keep his line tight when punching. Mastery of left-hand line acceleration lifts the caster right out of the average class and puts him among the 30- to 35-yard men. If the angler goes after the occasional salmon on fairly big rivers

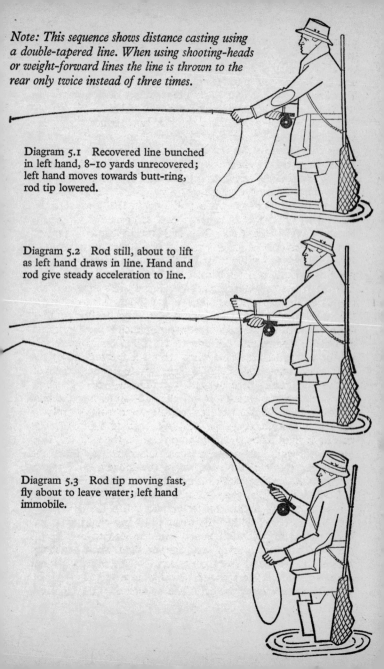

Note: This sequence shows distance casting using a double-tapered line. When using shooting-heads or weight-forward lines the line is thrown to the rear only twice instead of three times.

Diagram 5.1   Recovered line bunched in left hand, 8–10 yards unrecovered; left hand moves towards butt-ring, rod tip lowered.

Diagram 5.2   Rod still, about to lift as left hand draws in line. Hand and rod give steady acceleration to line.

Diagram 5.3   Rod tip moving fast, fly about to leave water; left hand immobile.

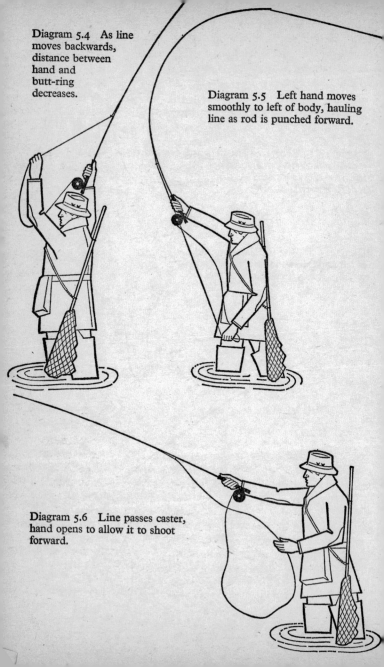

Diagram 5.4 As line moves backwards, distance between hand and butt-ring decreases.

Diagram 5.5 Left hand moves smoothly to left of body, hauling line as rod is punched forward.

Diagram 5.6 Line passes caster, hand opens to allow it to shoot forward.

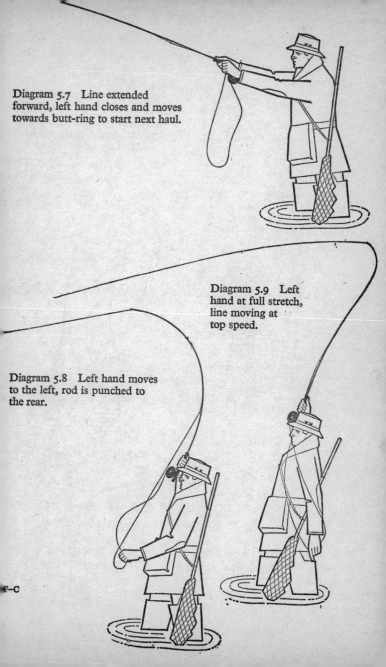

Diagram 5.7 Line extended forward, left hand closes and moves towards butt-ring to start next haul.

Diagram 5.9 Left hand at full stretch, line moving at top speed.

Diagram 5.8 Left hand moves to the left, rod is punched to the rear.

-C

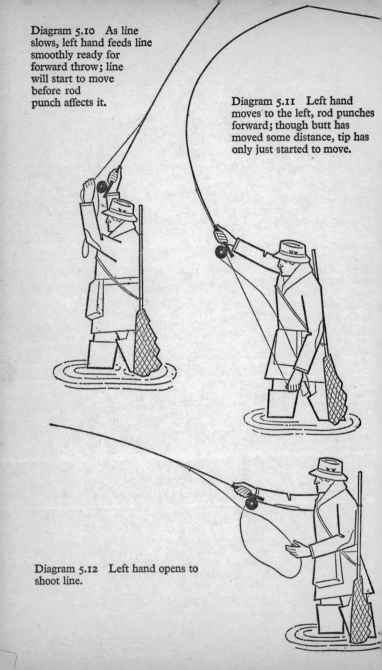

Diagram 5.10 As line slows, left hand feeds line smoothly ready for forward throw; line will start to move before rod punch affects it.

Diagram 5.11 Left hand moves to the left, rod punches forward; though butt has moved some distance, tip has only just started to move.

Diagram 5.12 Left hand opens to shoot line.

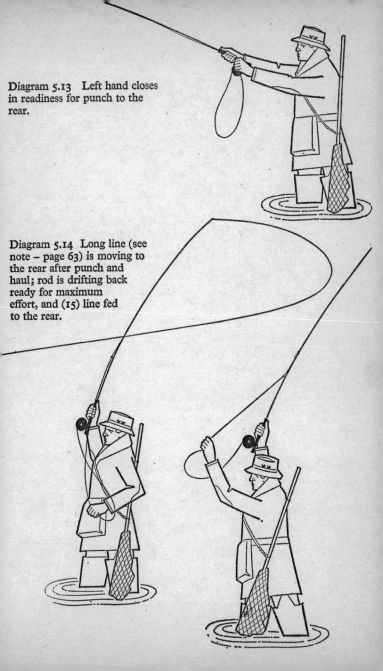

Diagram 5.13 Left hand closes in readiness for punch to the rear.

Diagram 5.14 Long line (see note – page 63) is moving to the rear after punch and haul; rod is drifting back ready for maximum effort, and (15) line fed to the rear.

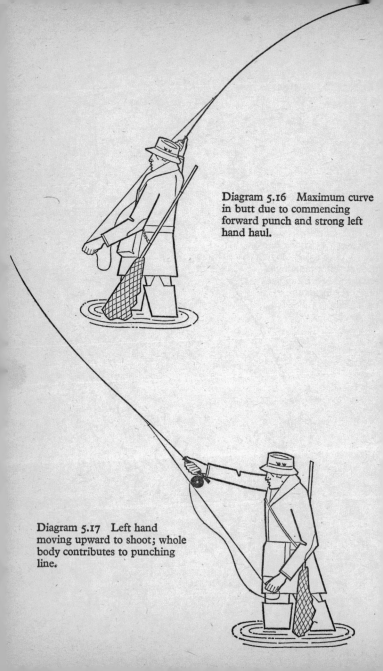

Diagram 5.16 Maximum curve in butt due to commencing forward punch and strong left hand haul.

Diagram 5.17 Left hand moving upward to shoot; whole body contributes to punching line.

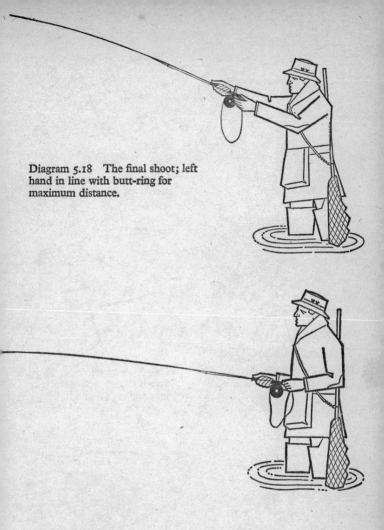

Diagram 5.18 The final shoot; left hand in line with butt-ring for maximum distance.

Diagram 5.19 Rod at correct fishing angle, line being recovered by left hand.

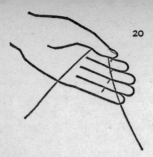

Diagram 5.20 Taking line to commence recovery.

Diagram 5.21 Finger closes over line; thumb and forefinger grip line at X.

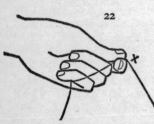

Diagram 5.22 Forefinger and thumb lifted to draw line.

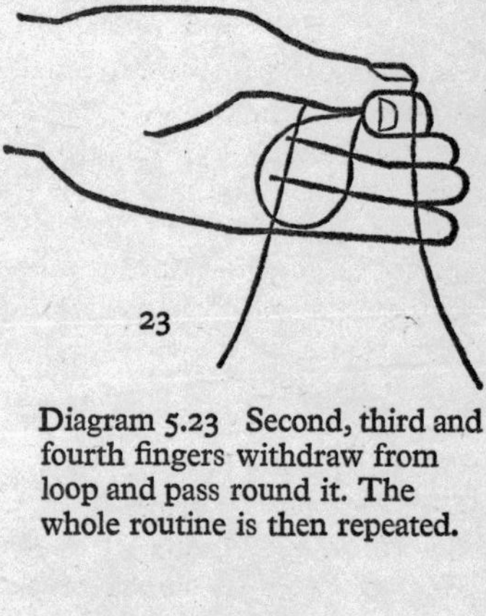

Diagram 5.23 Second, third and fourth fingers withdraw from loop and pass round it. The whole routine is then repeated.

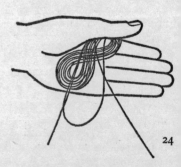

Diagram 5.24 The final result; a 'figure-of-eight' bunch.

he will find that he can cover quite as much water with a 10 ft rod as he can with his greased-line rod, though the 12-footer 'mends' line better.

I know that I have errors of style which limit my distance – most of us have unless we are practising every day under the eye of a good coach – but sometimes we try to correct supposed faults which are not really faults at all. I often find I am casting with my finger pointing up the rod. I did so once when casting from the Bedford Casting Club's platform. Afterwards I said jokingly to Edgar May, 'I suppose I get a reprimand for pointing both thumb and forefinger along the rod?'

'Why should you?' he replied. 'If you are comfortable casting that way, that is all that matters.'

More and more, the coaches of today are concerned that their protégés adopt body positions and styles of action which are comfortable. Most tournament casters get greater power by casting with the right foot forward, but both Godard and Osten cast 'open-body' style with left foot forward. Osten adopts this stance so that he can turn his head to watch his line at the rear, which, though once regarded here as a fault, can be most helpful in gusty weather and with obstructions behind. I do not suggest that all body or rod movements are correct if they are comfortable, but I do suggest that an uncomfortable position cannot be correct.

It is possible that many river anglers, who habitually cast with the right elbow well into the side, may have the idea that merely raising the arm and increasing the effective length of the rod will of itself increase the distance cast. I am afraid they are going to be disillusioned unless they appreciate that a longer rod, or should I say, rod plus extended arm requires greater muscular power, and the real purpose of raising the arm is to enable the muscles from toe to finger to be brought into play.

Throwing a long line demands muscular effort, but when the caster's movements are rhythmic, fatigue is negligible. There is, nevertheless, a limit to the number of false casts the angler can make between 'pick-up' and 'delivery'. Although in tournament casting it is the practice to false-cast until the line is working to the satisfaction of the caster, the fewer the number of false casts the greater the effort which goes into the final forward throw. Quite frequently the tournament caster is able to lift off and throw to the rear; throw forward; throw back, and then throw forward to deliver. It must be remembered, however, that he is using a line which is much heavier in the belly than an AFTM 6 double-taper line and with a very much lighter shooting line. I find that I achieve my best distance which is economical of effort by using the routine shown in the series; if I make an extra false cast my distance is no greater, and often it is rather less.

Line recovery

The easiest method is drawing the line over the hooked forefinger of the right hand and dropping it onto the water or the ground or into the bottom of the boat. Dropping it onto the water is fine if you are using a floater or a monofil shooting line; but, if yours is a sinking line, recasting and shooting will be a labour of Hercules. All in all this recovery method works well for a wading angler only if the line is dropped onto a floating line raft made fast to the straps of his thigh waders. More and more anglers are using them these days.

The coiling method of recovery is the fastest method of recovery when the line is held in the hand as opposed to being dropped. When, however, it is necessary to cast a long line and the left hand is used to accelerate, the coils throw over one another and make it difficult to shoot line. Again, it is a fairly frequent occurrence for the coils to jam at the butt ring when a newly-hooked fish runs.

The method shown in diagram 5.24 is infinitely superior. It is often referred to as 'W' bunching; but, since this name is also sometimes applied to a method of winding line between the little finger and thumb, I prefer to call it 'figure-of-eight bunching', since the small coils naturally assume that form. Twenty yards of line are easily held in the hand, and the line runs free, both when shooting and when a fish makes his first rush. In fact I have yet to lose a fish through a figure-of-eight bunched line jamming at the butt ring.

Diagrams 5.20–23 show the breakdown of the movement. Figure-of-eight bunching should never be attempted with a monofil shooting line!

Casting and fishing distances

In the correspondence of the *Fishing Gazette* of 30 August 1958, Mr H. Wells recorded that he cast up to 15 yards on alternate days of his twelve-day holiday at Chew Valley Reservoir, and over 20 yards on the other six days. His twelve fish, and another forty by neighbouring anglers, were all taken at over 20 yards' distance. Restricted to a short line Mr Wells would have returned 'clean'.

In 1954, Captain T. B. (Terry) Thomas and I used our own and each other's fishing rods with both double-taper lines and weight-forward lines (often called torpedo-head lines) and discovered that the torpedo-head gave us only a 2-yard advantage, which was unimportant since our shortest cast with the DT line was 32 yards and beyond effective striking distance.

If we ignore deep fishing with shooting heads, about 35 yards is still the greatest distance at which I have risen, hooked and landed a trout; but at the Ashmere Club, in Mr Homewood's presence, I recall breaking when I struck and hit a fish at least 36 yards away. I was using a $10\frac{1}{2}$ ft leader and the line-backing splice was well outside the tip ring. The strike, at a fish I had already missed twice, was perpetrated by pulling line with the left hand while swinging the rod upward and sideways. I have since used this strike successfully at medium range when fish are taking and quickly ejecting the fly, but a break is almost inevitable if a fish takes determinedly.

Whilst fishing a deep-sunk nymph upwind from a drifting boat, I have on several occasions caught fish at distances up to 50 yards but they have hooked themselves. Probably it is still true that the maximum distance for effective hooking is around 30 yards and a lot or even most of the fish that are risen at 35 or 40 yards by anglers using shooting heads shake themselves off early in the fight.

Photographing casting

There is no gainsaying that you can spot your faults more quickly by studying good action photographs than by any other means. I had always been under the impression that if you enlarged a few frames from a ciné film of casting you would be able to see your every movement and analyse each. In this I was quite wrong: enlargement of ciné shots gives a picture in which movement is blurred and definition very poor. Although I believed it impossible of achievement, Bill Finney soon showed me that a series could be compiled by photographing each required position separately. So good were the results that I asked him to complete some notes on technique, and this he most kindly did for me. The three paragraphs following summarize his conclusions.

A photographic analysis of a cast shows what is actually happening to a rod and line, and this may be different from what the fisherman thinks is happening, or what he hopes is happening. Such an analysis is well within the scope of any keen photographer.

In this case the choice of camera lay between a Rolleiflex at 1/500th, a Leica IIIb at 1/1,000th and a $3\frac{1}{2}$ in $\times$ $2\frac{1}{2}$ in Zeiss Microflex at 1/2,000th. Any of these would have done, but the Microflex was chosen, largely because its shutter speed was faster than the others and its negative was reasonable in size. The lens was a 135 mm Zeiss Tessar used at its full aperture of f3·5, and the photographs were taken on Kodak P1200 plates, tank developed in Kodak D61a.

It is quite essential that extremely detailed briefing is given to the photographer, so that he has a mental picture of what he is trying to photograph. Although a cast is quite fast, it is not in the least difficult to open the shutter at exactly the right moment. What is difficult is for a non-fishing photographer to recognize the right moment when he sees it. It was found that the only satisfactory method was for me to make small pencil sketches showing the position of the arms, rod and line at the various stages of the cast and once this technique was adopted it was quite easy to get the analysis made.

CHAPTER 6

Flies: a philosophy based on fish behaviour

Flies may, broadly speaking, be divided into two large families: exact imitations and attractors.

The chalk-stream anglers, few in numbers but strong in social and journalistic influence, wrote many books whose teachings were seldom applicable to other waters. They plugged the exact imitation dry fly. Some, I am told, regarded that truly great observer and angler, Skues, as little better than a poacher because he fished a sunken fly – albeit an exact imitation of the nymphs the fish were taking. Such was their bigotry!

Today, I have begun to question the truth of the exact imitation philosophy, even on its home ground, the chalk stream. On my first visit to a beat of the upper Test, the very well-known and highly skilled angler/keeper proffered a fly like a Treacle Parkin with a clipped hackle with the advice: 'I usually fish this and it works most of the time' . . . it did too!

Other outstandingly successful chalk-stream anglers have similarly rationalized approaches which add up to belief in general representations, and I am satisfied that chalk-stream fish are just as daft and, if you fish carelessly, just as cautious as reservoir trout. And this, is, after all, what we ought to expect because they are frequently bred in the same hatcheries and enjoy the same parents!

Now, if an angler imitates the natural to the extent of producing or aiming to produce a fly of the same size, form, translucency, flash and perhaps sex, and get enjoyment and satisfaction from his handiwork, by all means let him do so. He will undoubtedly catch fish. But let him not attempt to persuade me that he owes aught to a superior skill in fly tying.

Let us be honest about it. How many of us can ever be satisfied with our exact imitations, having seen the real thing? Do they not by their failings – however clever we may be – fill us with doubt as to whether or not the fish will sneer at them as they pass them by? Of course they do. How then can we fish well with them when we lack the first essential: complete faith in the fly we are using.

My views on fly design resolve themselves into a sort of Morton's fork from which there is no satisfactory escape.

Let us first suppose the trout to be imbued with the intelligence of Rutherford, the coordination, speed and judgement of Pelé or Charlton, and the retentive mind of an accountant. Such a creature would certainly perceive the difference between the natural insect and your attempt at imitation and particularly easily so if you threw the wretched object at him in the middle of a rise, when he had ample opportunity to make comparisons. This proposition begs the use of flies not intended as copies of natural insects – flies which might be a new kind of food.

Now let us suppose the trout to be what he probably is – an unreasoning creature without conscious memory process but with an insatiable appetite subjugated only when visual and/or vibratory stimuli induce a fear condition. Stupid, hungry and without memory – obviously within reason it doesn't matter what you throw at the creature: exact imitation is pointless.

The proof of the pudding is in the eating and so far as reservoirs are concerned, general representations are proven to be adequate. So too they are on rivers which are seldom fished, for North American writers make it quite clear that trout, grayling and char in the virgin waters of Alaska will hit anything thrown at them. Only when we consider the hard-fished river do we become aware of 'selective' rising and finicky rejection of carefully tied imitations.

I am going to suggest that a fish's cussedness varies in direct proportion to its experience of mankind. In rivers, the angler moving about the banks is a familiar sight and most fish of takeable size will have been clumsily covered by a line lying across the water and connected to the 'lump' kneeling on the bank. If it happens repeatedly, the sight of the angler will trigger off fear-of-line splash (or pricking) reaction and the fly will be refused. In time, oft-covered fish may become nonrisers.

When some twenty years ago at Hollowell or Ravensthorpe, only six or nine anglers a day fished the banks and only one or two boats were available, only those trout in the obvious 'holes' at the corners of dams were flogged hard. The vast majority of fish lived out their lives seeing only one fly – the one that killed them. They had little opportunity to 'learn' or absorb the man/line-splash/hook-prick association.

Today on most waters, the numerous bank anglers and the large number of drifting boats, mean that every fish rapidly acquires experience of man, and having done so becomes a different and more difficult animal to catch.

Tackle-shadows, line-wake, line-splash and pricking being part of a mature fish's experience, and each with a man-presence association, line-wake and line-splash will, today, trigger off flight reaction in every hard-fished water.

Once you accept this, *almost* every failure to catch fish becomes explicable without recourse to the fly-refusal or selective-feeding theory. Why after all should a trout discriminate against any pattern of fly when autopsies show us that they ingest twigs, small stones and other debris from time to time, unless the rejection is associated with man and the presence of his tackle? Richard Walker recently has found that there are occasions when trout will take a 'stationary' fly better than the same fly when moved to simulate life.

There is indeed overwhelming reason for us to fish with the confident belief that feeding trout will take and attempt to swallow anything with the general form and behaviour of food, and much that is neither ... provided always that no man-association triggers off the fear-flight reaction. (See Chapter 17 footnote, page 217).

The implication of these facts is clear: when trout refuse your fly it is because they sense your presence from one or several fear-inducing phenomena. Not only are they at that moment refusing *your* fly but most probably they are refusing nearby natural foods as well.

Often they continue to show themselves in the same area but remain uncatchable ... Salmon, too, often continue to lie in the same position after you have revealed yourself, but seldom will they take. And a flock of sheep will stop feeding and stand still and watch a fox until it is out of sight in much the same way.

The fault lies with the angler and not with the fly. To paraphrase the song, 'It ain't what you fish it's the way that you fish it'.

The logical deduction from that paraphrase is that the style of fishing is of paramount, and the fly of only secondary, importance. Continuing from this point we reach the conclusion that we cannot decide on a fly until we know by what method we are going to fish. In its turn the decision as to method depends upon such things as light, wind, season and the way the fish are seen to behave.

Most of us have at some time or other seen a wet fly cast made up with, say, an Alexandra on the tail and a nymph on the dropper. How can such a combination be effective? Only one of the flies can be fished at one time, for flies like the Alexandra are best fished fast, whilst nymph or spider should move only fast enough to appear alive.

We have arrived at a convenient point to differentiate between the two types of attractors, namely: the 'flashers' which include such patterns as Peter Ross, Butcher and Alexandra; and the 'deceivers' such as Greenwell's Glory, Tup's, and my Black and Peacock Spiders, all three of which bear a superficial resemblance to many insects and other water creatures.

I believe that although a trout may take a well-presented 'imitation', it will more readily accept a well-fished 'deceiver', accepting it unsuspectingly, as a different food species. How otherwise do we explain consistent refusal of an imitation followed by immediate and confident seizing of a great 'Fuzzy-Buzzy' which does not in the slightest resemble any God-created water animal? The experience is of too frequent occurrence to be ascribed entirely to the 'daft 'un' or the 'bloody-minded' fish.

The influence of light

Those who have fished with me through the years will know that the light condition I most abominate is what I term a 'milky' light.

It can occur at any month of the season and almost always coincides with a spell of balmy weather with light winds out of the south-west or west. I used to arrive at the water, grin in cocksure anticipation of the limit inevitably to be mine – maybe by lunch time, and recognize around 4 PM that something went wrong somewhere and wasn't it funny how this always seemed to happen when that haze of white cloud softened the highlights and reduced the shadows.

In more recent years I have recognized that milky light means hard work for markedly reduced bags; accepted the situation and wondered, idly, from time to time about the underlying causes. More often than not I rise a number of fish but fail to hook them or merely turn them over. Many follow the fly for yards without taking at all. It would be easy to deduce that the fly was wrong.

Reg Righyni's article, 'Sunshine and the Flyfisher' published in *Angling* in July 1968, supplied the answer, a blindingly obvious answer, only it never occurred to me.

Nor had it occurred to me how much we reservoir fishers lose by our inability to study living trout at very close quarters . . . we just don't have Righyni's opportunity to look over low stone walls and observe the reaction of trout to visual stimuli under various light intensities. Even where the occasional road bridge, as at Ravensthorpe Reservoir, provides an opportunity to peer into a fish-holding pool, the fish swim deep and are seldom to be seen. If you were able to see them each time you passed by they would seldom be the same fish.

Righyni's regular observation of a small group of trout in a pool in a roadside stream in Lunesdale showed him that in bright sunshine – provided no shadow fell on the water – he could approach them unseen far more closely than was the case in dull light. He reasoned, and I believe correctly, that in diffused light a trout's vision is more acute than in strong sunlight. He went on to illustrate his theory by reference to discrimination between one fly and another under dull light conditions and the readiness of trout to accept almost any pattern in brilliant light.

Probably we have further justification for the dull day – dull fly, bright day – bright fly rule.

Righyni believes pattern is of great importance under conditions of milky or diffused light. But I find this difficult to accept. My belief is that diffused light makes the presence of the angler or his associated tackle-shadow, line-splash, line-wake and so on apparent at much greater distance and the rejection of the fly is the predictable sequel.

No matter which viewpoint is right, the outcome is the same; in diffused light the fish are more easily alarmed and more difficult to catch. Righyni's observation is a most valuable contribution to our knowledge of trout; certainly it helps me to account for a most unusual experience at Grafham in 1968.

Sunday 30 June was one of those brilliant summer days when 'civilized' folk go down to the country or the sea, glory in the brilliant sunshine and get a tan. Such days are hell for anglers, and for boat fishers a doubled purgatory – a dose of ultra violet from the heavens and another reflected from the water.

Conrad and I left Hemel after a good lunch and went afloat at Grafham at 3.45 PM. It was a hopeless day and we were prepared to await the evening rise. By 5.30 PM we had had a sack of fish and I needed only one for my limit.

They were all rainbows and were taken on a size 8 Claret and Mallard fished medium to fast using a sinking tip to a floating line. The nylon leader was tapered to 28/100 mm and every fish took decisively and was securely hooked.

From 5.30 to 6.30 PM (by which time light intensity was falling fast) a number of fish short rose and were pricked or missed altogether, then activity ceased until the evening rise began.

The Claret and Mallard was put to several fish, they certainly saw the fly and as certainly they refused. Not until I was down to a 22/100 mm point and a very slowly fished size 14 Wickham did I hook two good fish ... which came unstuck during the fight, as also did a fish around 5 lb that took a double B & P Spider fished slow and deep in near darkness and which circled unendingly beneath the rod tip.

Recognizing the light problem is the first step to overcoming it. If we accept, as I think we should, that Righyni is right and our fish see too much that is wrong (man-associated) with our fly or terminal tackle in dull light, we clearly must adopt tactics that effect better concealment.

TV films have shown us that fish accept phenomena beneath the surface that scare the daylights out of them above the surface. Clearest evidence of this is the tolerance of fish to skin divers at their own depth, and their panic when humans walk by the water. Birds scurrying across the water and even sudden wind squalls induce the same panic, though the phenomena must be commonplace enough.

I start with the assumption that it is what the fish sees above or on the surface that will cause it to accept or reject the fly. Let us, as we start to fish, make the further assumption that the trout has neither seen you, the angler, nor felt the vibrations from your movements through its lateral line.

Let us examine what happens when the line and leader and the fly alight gently near to our confidently feeding trout.

If your unattached fly or nymph had roughly the same size,

shape and light-transmission qualities as a typical food form, any hungry trout would seize it as it sank through his feeding depth. True, he would usually eject it quickly afterwards.

But we know, from the fact that our sinking fly so often remains unaccepted, even when it drops near to a feeding fish, that something is preventing the fish from taking; either he hasn't seen it, or he doesn't like what he sees.

The latter is immediately explicable once we remember that the important difference between an unattached fly and the fly we fish with, is, if you will permit me to labour the obvious, a straight length of light-reflecting nylon leading from the eye of the fly directly to a circle of light in the trout's 'window' where the leader passes through the surface. As the fly sinks deeper the circle of light moves away from it along the surface . . . and nothing like that ever happened when our trout rose to a living creature, or an unattached artificial.

And now let us suppose the trout did seize the attached artificial and moved away with it. Immediately the circle of light would accelerate away and the unnatural phenomenon would almost certainly cause the trout to attempt to reject the fly. Were you to tighten, your hook would probably take only a light hold or the fish would be pricked and lost.

Let me emphasize that shy or short rising such as we have described seldom occurs in a ripple because a broken or moving surface causes light scatter in which the nylon's entry 'hole' is unlikely to be obvious to a feeding fish. Nor is such acute perception and rejection to be expected when strong sunlight swamps the retina of the fish's eye – trout have a fixed iris and cannot reduce the brilliance of a visual image as we do. Dazzlement must be their usual state near to the surface in open water on a sunny day.

In wet fly fishing as we usually practise it, there seem two obvious answers and both are effective. Either your fly should be fished virtually in the surface on a very fine leader, when the nylon between hook eye and surface might be no more than a leg of the insect trapped above the surface, or the whole leader, with perhaps part of the line, should be submerged and of such length that the entry point is so remote from the fly as not to be associated with it. Dapping is a third, very effective but seldom-employed technique, which we have probably neglected far too long.

The first of the two methods was by and large the means by which I killed many rainbow trout in the evening rise from June onwards at Grafham in 1968. With floating nylon so close to the fly, recovery must be sufficiently slow to eliminate wake from the leader and I sometimes take four to five minutes to recover 18 yards of line before recasting. (See also Chapter 7 for table of recovery speeds.)

The second method is customary when fish are feeding several feet below the surface, and the fly is being fished at the recovery speeds given in Chapter 7. Nylon is notoriously prone to float, and a sinking tip to your floating line is the only way to ensure that the whole of your nylon leader is submerged before you start to recover line. A 14 ft leader and 2 yards of no 5 sinker spliced to your floating line means that your fly is separated from line wake by some 23 ft (the sinking line drags down several feet of the floating line as well) and that, in practice, seems enough to deceive most fish.

Experienced reservoir anglers are generally agreed that the buzzer is a wonderfully effective pattern almost everywhere ... those same anglers would probably agree that they find buzzers most effective when fished at minimal speed ... how many might now further agree that absence of line- and leader-wake in the mellow all-revealing light of evening calm contributed as much to success as the bug itself!

As to dapping – I can only say that wherever it is legal the technique is certain to be more widely used for it provides – when the wind permits – the ultimate concealment of tackle by keeping it wholly off the surface.

The dry/wet controversy

Looking back over my 1947 to 1952 angling diary in which I recorded weather and light conditions, my takes and those of other anglers (and the blanks, too!), I find that I took only six fish on the dry fly over the six-year period. On many occasions I devoted the whole of a rise to testing the worth of dry flies; on others I fished wet near to another successful angler fishing dry. The results of tests, fairly conducted by several of us, prove that the wet fly is far and away more deadly than the dry fly, even in a rise.

Unlike river trout, reservoir fish do not take up a 'lie' and feed on creatures on or below the surface carried down to them by the current. In slack water, they are free to move about, and in fact spend their lives doing so, feeding as they move on a wide variety of food forms. These fish do not grow to be $2\frac{1}{2}$ lb* at as little as four years by feeding on surface fly; in fact, the wonder to me is that we see them rise to surface food at all. When we perform an autopsy, we find the gut full of snail (I have taken fish which rattled when you shook them) mixed with various larval insects, water-boatmen, and later in the season, sticklebacks in large numbers. There is little incentive to fish to rise when the bottom provides such rich feeding, so why persist in fishing dry, when for every creature taken at the surface at least forty must be taken below it. Again, although a dry fly can be worked, it soon loses its buoyancy, particularly in a ripple. Yet work the fly we must, in order to cover as much water as possible, for as we have said, the trout are not confined to a lie over which we can float the fly at will. However we look at the matter, the practical answer is the wet fly.

Do not let your attitude be clouded by the social and technical superiority quite wrongly arrogated by some dry fly men. In wet-fly work the angler is concerned with the things he cannot see, and his fly works in an extra dimension: depth. He must know, or find out by trial and error (or hunch based on experience), what speed of fishing and therefore what fly will give the best results at the required depth. I took my fastest Hollowell limit, four fish – 11 lb 10 oz – in thirty minutes without having seen a fish rise but having a shrewd idea where they were and what they were doing. Like John Moore's colonel who could think like a goose, we must try to think like our quarry, the trout.

It is no coincidence that all the outstanding reservoir fly fishers that I have met were or are outstandingly good coarse fishers.

My early references to dry fly fishing caused a great deal of perturbation and botheration. Significantly, most of the critics who felt dry fly had been unfairly condemned were men who lived in Wales. Many of the Welsh reservoirs are oligotrophic waters, deficient in bottom feed. Fish in such waters rise to fly relatively freely because the natural is an important part of their diet. It was most noticeable that men such as Ernest Phillips, Myles-Tonks, 'Mayfly' and others who knew Midland waters

---

* Such brownies are, of course, exceptional; in most waters the four-year-old will weigh about 1 lb 2 oz.

well, shared my views and endorsed the majority of my conclusions.

Of the many letters received, only one referred to a selective rise and this was stated to occur at Durleigh Reservoir to a Chironomus variety. Apart from a crazy two brace in fifteen minutes in May 1955, I certainly found Durleigh trout difficult to take ... but locals fared no better. Unfortunately, a few Silverhorns were up and it is possible that they, rather than Chironomids, were the cause of the trouts' cussedness.

The superiority of the wet fly is as true as ever ... while we are writing about brown trout, but as we shall learn in the chapters on Grafham there is a circumstance in which a radical change of philosophy is required. Briefly, it may be described as the predominating presence of rainbow trout, an animal of very different feeding habit.

Fly tying: an eye for beauty is a snare for ever

Although I have stressed the necessity for fishing the fly in an attractive manner, it is obvious that some patterns are more attractive than others. At one time I would cheerfully have gone out with only the Black and Peacock Spider dressed in several sizes. But the following season it failed badly and I had to evolve alternatives.

In 1951, I counted twenty-eight different patterns in my box. On only twelve of them had I caught fish, and according to my records four patterns had accounted for 85 per cent of my fish while eight patterns had accounted for just under 96 per cent. It is these eight patterns which I shall deal with in detail in my next chapter, together with several of the lures which have at times proved effective at Grafham, and my specials for the rainbow evening rise.

I often ask myself why I bother to tie other patterns, and the only answer, I fear, is vanity.

They do look so nice in the box; they satisfy my eye; they provide me with an opportunity to demonstrate a very little skill at fly tying. These non-fishing flies, by the way, were never created until I had passed the novice stage as a fly tyer, and I would suggest that when a fisherman reaches this stage he is in a very great danger of beginning to overdress his flies. I have avoided the danger by tying two sorts of flies, those for me and those for the fish, and it is not a bad principle.

And what of the hooks we use?

My preference through the years has been wide-gape Sproat hooks. Mrs Messeena used to describe them in her catalogues as 'Pattern 106'. Veniard's 'Wide-Gape Trout' appears the same pattern, and both are virtually identical with the Wide-Gape Sproat made by Partridge of Redditch. The wire is light, the point is sharp and short, the wide gape gives it a good deep hold (in flesh) and the tempering is perfect.

The trout is hard-mouthed, and long-pointed hooks often hit bone before they are 'in over the barb'. In lake fishing, the head of the taking fish may be pointing in almost any direction when the strike is made, and hooking in the 'scissors' of the jaws happens in only about 20 per cent of cases. For the remainder, the hook may be anywhere inside or outside the mouth and 'skin-nicking' is common, hence my insistence on short points. The short-pointed hook goes in over the barb, even in skin over a bony surface, and thus gives one a decided advantage.

The size of the hooks is of great importance. When a large fish heads for a weed bed there are four things which can happen. You can stop the fish, or more probably, the fish achieves his object. On the other hand your cast may part or your hook may tear free. It is this last possibility I am concerned with now.

Large hooks, being made of thicker wire than small hooks, have less tendency to cut the flesh and thus enlarge the hole; in addition their initial hold is much deeper. I have fished with small hooks and taken several fish on them, but I am worried from the moment I strike to the moment the fish is lost or netted, because I know that I can never apply full pressure and that every turn of the fish is loosening a hold which can never be truly secure unless it is in the 'scissors'. I lost the second largest trout I ever hooked (the fish mentioned in Chapter 3) solely, I believe, because I used a hook smaller than could reasonably be expected to hold for the duration of a long fight! The basic size of hook for use on reservoirs containing large fish is a size 8 (Redditch scale) during early spring, and a 9 from mid-May onwards when the light is more brilliant. The largest standard length hook I use is a 6 and the smallest under normal daytime conditions is a 12, though in the evening rise fishing to a shoal of rainbows I have, on several occasions, reduced to 14s and even 16s.

The biggest reservoir fish I have landed on a 14 hook was 3 lb 4 oz but I have had rainbows up to 4 lb 5 oz on dry fly when river fishing. I nonetheless still regard small hooks and fine nylon as unfair fishing except when you know yourself to be fishing to a shoal of rainbows and can be reasonably sure that they are all in the $1\frac{1}{2}$ to $2\frac{1}{2}$ lb bracket. Rising fish are sufficiently hard to find without decreasing their number by pricking and losing them, an experience which must tend to discourage fish from feeding near the surface.

A day when I rise fish galore and take a limit, perhaps pricking a dozen others as does sometimes happen, is not a satisfying day. We should all aim to hook and net every fish we rise, and we ought not to take risks which preclude the possibilities of doing this. I notice that at Chew a 7 lb BS leader is the officially recommended minimum. You cannot cast a large hook on a fine point, and a small hook will not work properly when constrained by a stout one, thus, you either must fish safely or take two risks: fine point *and* a small hook.

I believe that when waters are known to contain a large number of very heavy fish, the rules ought to lay down minimum sizes for both leader and flies, but until that happens our common sense and good sportsmanship must suffice. Unfortunately, the ill-effects of pricking, or hooking-playing-and-losing trout are not confined to conditioning them to be non-risers.

To avoid capture, wild creatures will frequently exert themselves to a point where physical collapse is followed by death. Several years ago an experienced angler fishing near by played out three under-sized fish of about 11 in and held them upright in the water until they swam strongly from his hand. An hour later as he waded ashore he found the three trout lying dead on the bottom. Examination by both of us showed, beyond all doubt, that the dead fish were those so recently released.

In high water temperatures, particularly, played-out trout die much more frequently than is supposed, even when they are released under water by holding the fly and letting them wriggle off the hook. On many waters the rules require that all fish caught must be retained and I feel the practice is to be generally recommended. It was adopted at Grafham in 1969 and undoubtedly reduced the deplorable practice, previously common on days when fish were feeding hard, of returning fish up to 2 or even 3 lb in order to bring in a limit of high average weight.

Among the inexcusable reasons for losing fish is the very common one of blunt hooks. A hook point should be so keen that it will grip and penetrate your thumb-nail rather than skid off. I carry a Carborundum file 4 in long and $\frac{5}{16}$ in $\times$ $\frac{5}{16}$ in section and find this the perfect hone.

CHAPTER 7

Useful fly-dressings

I started fly dressing for the very prosaic reason that I could not afford to lose flies at 9/6 per dozen, their price when I returned home at the end of the war. How grateful I am now that my pocket was not better filled, for I would have missed a lot of fun and the additional satisfaction of taking fish on my own handiwork. I would also have caught far fewer fish, and that is a point that concerns us all.

In 1951 I had killed a fish and was in the process of weighing him when E.G. came along to help me gloat over him. 'What did you get him on,' he asked, 'another one of your bare hook shanks? I'm damned if I know why the fish take 'em.'

I think his question and remark should be studied by every firm tying flies, particularly the Midlands and London fly dressers.

One famous London firm were the tyers of an Alexandra which was given to me some years ago. It had so much dressing on it that it would not sink until it was given a good sharp pull, and it was tied on a heavy-wire Limerick hook at that. The North Country fly dressers tie flies which will catch fish without prior removal of more than 25 per cent of the dressing, but it is much easier to dress your own flies and have them correct to start with.

Great skill is not necessary. Two very successful angler friends of mine tie the most horrible monstrosities I have ever seen – one dressing is known to us all as the 'Pregnant Nymph', and this is a pretty fair name and description. Nevertheless, crude as many of their dressings are, they catch fish, and that will always be the acid test of a fly.

Following Frank Sawyer's 'rationalized' chalkstream nymphs, the process of simplification seems everywhere to have been accepted as respectable and most of us now have a few grey-yellow wool-bodied objects in our boxes that can only be described as artificial maggots. They start life looking very similar to well-chewed rough olives – long recognized to be at their most effective when about to disintegrate.

The essentials of a good wet fly are that it shall sink readily, its hackle-fibres shall be soft and sparse, and its wing very narrow (if there at all) and tied to lie low over the body. The whole fly should be light and sparkling – never opaque – in silhouette against the trout's window.

It has been something of a disappointment to me that I have had so many inquiries about colours of herls and flosses, etc, and so few, relatively, on methods of fishing the flies. Yet manner of presentation has been emphasized by every sound angling writer for hundreds of years.

A number of my comments in my early articles were apparently very similar to those made in the 1851 edition of Pullman's *Vade Mecum of Fly-Fishing for Trout*. One of my readers noticed the similarity of outlook and sent me a copy. Having read in Pullman's Chapter VII of the follies of exact imitation I came across the following passage:

But supposing this to be otherwise – supposing even the angler to be an expert, and to have a good imitation of the fly at which the fish are rising well – say a fly of the dun tribe, prevalent on every water. He makes his cast admirably. In the gentle stickle which hugs the opposite bank, a line of trout are rising gloriously; but not one of them is attracted by his well-presented lure. He throws, and throws again, but still with the same result. He is at a loss to account for the cause, except that it must evidently be something or other wrong in his fly. No such thing. We admit the fly to be a good imitation, to be nicely cast over rising fish, repeatedly, time after time, and yet with not a rise is poor Piscator favoured. Well, how is this? Piscator does not see – he is so wrapped up in the make of his fly – that something more than make is necessary; that under certain circumstances an imitation of the action of the natural fly is indispensable, and that when that action is not supplied, as in the present case, success cannot be had.

We have seen astonishing, even terrifying changes in the last 120 years, but Mother Nature's trout have let time pass by them. Today, they behave much as they did in Pullman's time, though hatchery rearing, a process of domestication, must have bred out some of the behaviour patterns of wild fish.

The dressings that follow are now widely used. You will notice that they offer a wide range of tones, and varying degrees of reflection. Their profiles too are markedly varied. To the patterns given in earlier editions I have added several simplified dressings of old standards that have killed well at Grafham, and a very killing 'grub' and two tandem dressings.

The dressings themselves are, as I have suggested elsewhere, of little import unless taken in conjunction with the suggested methods of fishing them.

'It ain't what you fish . . .'

Diagram 7.1   The Black and Peacock Spider

Tie in three or four strands of bronze peacock herl and a strand of any dark silk floss at bend of hook, leaving the short end of 5 in of tying silk hanging. Wind the *long* end of the tying silk back to the head. Wind a floss underbody, slender at the tail and fairly thick in the thorax, and tie off the floss at head. Twist the strands of herl together in anti-clockwise direction and wind the body in clockwise direction; tie off. Now wind the short end of silk anti-clockwise to the head as a rib to hold down the herl and increase the wearing qualities of the fly. Tie in a relatively large, soft-fibred, black hen hackle by the stub, with the underside of the feather facing the bend of the hook; take two turns only and tie off. (Hackles for this and the following dressing should never be doubled.) The hackle should stand out as shown in the diagram. Whip finish and varnish. This pattern should be tied in sizes 12 to 6 (Redditch scale sizes are used throughout this edition). Sizes 9 and 8 are the most useful.

This fly is the best all-rounder in my box. I have taken fish on it under every type of weather condition. It should be fished very slowly at all times. When small black snails are seen on the stones of the dams it is particularly good (remember the snail comes to the surface and drifts with the foot uppermost while breathing). The fly also does very well when the fish first begin to feed on fry. In addition, it is my best pattern in the crazy Silverhorn rise.

During the evening rise, when the back fins of the fish break water as they take with little disturbance, the Black and Peacock Spider is very deadly fished on a cast greased down to the last 18 in. The fish themselves are often moving only about a foot below the surface, and it is essential that your fly shall fish between 2 in and 6 in from the surface. Because the wake of the cast will only be a foot or so from the fly, very slow line recovery is a must.

Many fishermen are afraid to draw slowly, so I will try to explain the theory of the practice.

If you watch a few square feet of clear shallow water you will notice that small water-creatures move a matter of only 3 in or 4 in in as many seconds. It is true that on a river your fly travels from A, across stream to B, downstream, quite quickly. But relative to the water which carries it, the fly moves scarcely at all (I presume the line was mended and that there has been no 'drag'). Perhaps the rapid travelling of the river fly is responsible for the idea that many lake fishermen have, that their flies should travel over the ground at a similarly high speed.

Remember always, that the deceiver patterns are intended to resemble in appearance and behaviour typical food forms. You ruin the illusion if you strip line like crazy with a nymph on the end!

I am convinced that it is easier by far to catch fish if you appeal to the instinct which is seldom dormant: the feeding instinct. Give a thorough trial always to deceiver patterns before you resort to the use of fast-fished flashers.

Flashers certainly have their uses as we shall show, but it will help if I explain now, that a fast and erratically moved lure probably relies for its effectiveness on that 'sick-fish' motion that seems to arouse the kill instinct in fish of all sizes and feeding pattern in both salt and fresh water.

It is fact that whilst flashers are sometimes very deadly, their use is accompanied by line and/or leader wake and more often the end result is to scare fish away.

Since Squadron Leader Mike Hunt and 'Mayfly' (W. J. Thomas) wrote to the *Fishing Gazette* about their excellent sport with the Black and Peacock Spider at Durleigh Reservoir in 1951, it has become a standard pattern for lake fishers over much of the English-speaking world. Letters testifying to its efficiency now number several hundreds.

Diagram 7.2   The Green Nymph

Tie in white floss and pale-green nylon monofilament at bend of hook (the nylon should be ·009 in for size 11 hooks increasing to ·014 in at size 7; the whitish nylons absorb dye very readily). The nylon strand is more easily tied in if the end is first notched between the teeth. Whip tying silk back to ⅛ in from eye. Wind floss under-body, making thorax slightly thicker, and tie off. Wind nylon closely to ⅛ in from eye, and tie off. Tie in brown partridge hackle and wind on two turns, then tie off. Now tie in two strands of bronze peacock herl: twist together as before; wind about four turns to form a largish head in front of the hackle and tie off. Whip finish and varnish. In very small sizes I usually omit the partridge hackle without, apparently, reducing the effectiveness of the fly.

This fly is heavy and is therefore ideal when deep sinking is required or when very small flies must be used. During May and June when big hatches of fly take place, there are many hours of the day when not a move is to be seen. This is particularly true on days of flat calm when no land insects are blown on to the water. The fish are there all right, and they are feeding, but not near the surface. They will be found wherever there is an open mud bottom with 4 ft to 8 ft of water over it, and they will be gorging nymph. Use as long a leader as you can handle, and ensure that the monofilament will sink readily by removing the grease with soap, or with a moistened pad on which a little household detergent has been sprinkled. Depending on the depth of the water, this may be one of the occasions when a length of L-5-S line could be added to the end of the floating line. I carry lengths from 1 yard up to 5 yards, each with a no-knot eye at either end, and it takes only a moment to tie one to the line-eye with 30/100 mm monofil.

Having made your cast and allowed the fly anything from fifteen to forty seconds to sink to the bottom, with rod point at half-past ten o'clock, or to one side and at an angle to the line, draw the line 6 in, and pause a second or so; repeat until ready to lift and cast again. Sometimes you will see the line draw; at others a slow drag will be the first indication of the presence of a fish. Frequently you will experience neither: the slight drag of the well-sunk leader and line will prick and panic the fish into action. He hooks himself and the rod all but leaves your hands as he begins his run. If you have been fishing with the rod pointing down the line the better to feel a light or cautious offer, a smash take by a fish over 3 lb will nearly always result in a break. By the way, the smash take seems always to come just when you have decided that there are no fish about, or when you are watching something other than your line.

It is easy to concentrate on a river, but the habit is difficult to acquire on still water. Lack of concentration will cost you many fish at first.

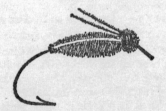

Diagram 7.3   The Brown Nymph

Strip the flue from two strands of green-dyed ostrich herl and tie in at bend of hook; tie in oval gold tinsel and one strand of brown-dyed ostrich herl; carry tying-silk back to ⅛ in from eye.

93

Wind ostrich herl body and tie off; rib with tinsel and tie off. Carry green quill direct from the bend, over the upper side of body to the head and tie off. Tie in two strands of peacock herl; twist together and wind about four turns behind the eye to form a head and tie down. Now separate the two strands and carry them backwards to form horns, and tie down in the position shown in diagram; tie off. Whip finish and varnish. This pattern may be simplified in size 12 down by omitting the green quill and leaving the clipped ends of the peacock herl sticking up $\frac{1}{8}$ in behind the head of the nymph. Again, in small sizes a brown-wool dubbed body, well teased out, will be found as effective as ostrich herl. (We are getting closer it seems to the maggot profile.)

This fly is lighter than the Green Nymph and consequently fishes in the middle or upper part of the water. It is excellent when fish are taking nymphs as they come to the surface, although I must admit I have had as great success with the Black and Peacock Spider when this is happening. Again, you must fish it slowly and be ready for smash takes well below the surface of the water. Both the Green and Brown Nymphs should be tied in sizes 12 to 7: sizes 10 and 9 being the most useful.

Diagram 7.4   The Green and Yellow Nymph

Tie in two strands of green-dyed swan herl at bend: carry silk back to halfway up the shank. Wind green herl to middle of shank and tie off. Tie in two strands of deep-yellow-dyed swan herl; carry silk to $\frac{1}{8}$ in from eye of hook. Wind yellow herl to $\frac{1}{8}$ in from eye and tie off. Tie in two strands of peacock herl; wind head as for Green Nymph; tie off; whip finish and varnish.

This fly should be tied in sizes 12 to 10; sizes 12 and 11 being most useful. The fly fishes high in the water, and should be used when fish are nymphing just beneath the surface or are taking the surface fly.

The smallest dressings of the Green and Yellow Nymph and the Brown Nymph have both proved effective fished right in the surface film on a leader greased down to the last 2 or 3 inches during the dusk stage of feeding of a shoal of rainbow trout ... the speed of line recovery for this purpose is virtually nil. The light air of an evening breeze provides more than enough movement to line and leader.

Diagram 7.5   The Brown and Green Nymph

Tie in four strands of peacock herl by their tips, leaving the tips pointing aft as a tail $\frac{1}{4}$ in long. Tie in one strand of green-dyed ostrich herl, one of brown-dyed ostrich herl, and oval gold tinsel at bend, and carry tying-silk back to $\frac{1}{8}$ in from eye. Wind green and brown herl together to form a segmented body of alternate colours and tie off. Rib with tinsel and tie off. Carry peacock herl direct to the head over the back and tie down. Now twist the strands of peacock herl together; wind three or four turns to form a bold head and tie off. Whip finish and varnish.

I tie this fly in sizes 10 to 6, leaded and unleaded. I use it as a change fly for the Green Nymph and the Brown Nymph and it has always killed well. I have also used it very successfully on 'stickle-backers', fished both slowly and fast, probably because the fly is somewhat minnowish in appearance. At Grafham in September 1967, Mike Brady enjoyed a fantastic success with this pattern in size 6 fished downwind from the boat and recovered fairly fast at about 5 ft depth. Sticklebacking brown trout up to $4\frac{1}{2}$ lb went crazy for it.

Diagram 7.6   The Gentile

When you drag a caddis grub out of its shuck you have a dirty-white maggot with a fringe of legs next to its head. The Gentile is a general representation of a caddis doing an imitation of a bluebottle maggot.

The body is a dubbed mixture of chopped white and yellow wools, wound to a maggot shape starting slender well back on the bend and thickening towards the head. The ginger hen hackle is clipped short as shown in the illustration. This nymph is tied in sizes 16 to 11.

It has been my most effective pattern for dealing with rainbow trout rising to little unidentifiable duddybugs near the surface and has been as good in brilliant sunlight as at dusk. It should be fished with infinite slowness through the area of general activity.

Diagram 7.7   The Cinnamon and Gold

This dressing is just another variation on Wickham's Fancy, and notwithstanding the flasher-type body, it is usually fished as a deceiver. Richard Aylott of Farlow's it was who demonstrated the effectiveness of this fly at Grafham.

Body: oval or flat gold tinsel; hackle: two turns of short-fibred, doubled, ginger cock hackle; wing: a bunch of fibres from the same cock hackle, or cinnamon partridge wing.

I tie this fly in sizes 15 to 9, omitting the wing in size 13 and smaller.

In June and July this fly has proved a good killer, particularly for brown trout, when fished medium-fast in coloured water on the lee shore. Sizes 9 and 10 are best for this purpose. In sizes 12 and 13 fished near the surface it killed well on several occasions from the boat in calm lanes and in flat calms. And in an evening rise in size 12 and smaller, it teased fish into taking when, with rod point high, line was recovered in short quick draws so that the fly gently furrowed the surface film. The technique is the same as fishing a Fuzzy-Buzzy dry fly as a 'wake' lure, and the belly of line between rod tip and water provides the same delayed contact that enables the fish to turn down before the tighten.

'The Buzzer' is the name given to the pupal stage of a large chironomid found in most Midland reservoirs and in many other still waters. It is a deceiver that seems to kill well almost everywhere.

The important feature of the dressing appears to be the starting of the body half way round the bend of the hook to simulate the hook-shaped body of the natural. Cyril Inwood reported in 1968 in *Angling* that he had found silk or wool bodies best and my own experience is that both are good, and wool is easier to tie.

Diagram 7.8   The Buzzer

Hook: size 9 or 10; body: a strand of black or claret or emerald-green wool, that is to say, one of the two or three strands that are twisted together to make knitting wool; rib: fine silver wire; wing case: a short tuft of white wool, hair, or feather fibre; head: two strands of peacock herl wound in the same manner as my Brown Nymph.

I have enjoyed most success fishing buzzers in mid water, say, from 2 to 6 ft down, the rate of line recovery being about the same as for nymphs, and always, of course, with complete absence of line wake. Cyril Inwood draws a foot of line at a time and dwells a pause between each pull so that the nymph will sink again. Afternoon or evening seem equally good for the buzzer. Be warned, the buzzer is a fly that is taken decisively and smash takes are common. Concentration is a must.

The Pretty-Pretty is a fly which seems to satisfy the eye of both fish and fisherman. The tying is quite orthodox.

Tag: silver tinsel; tail: small golden pheasant topping feather; underbody: floss silk; body: peacock herl and green-dyed

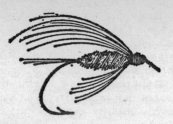

Diagram 7.9   The Pretty-Pretty

ostrich herl twisted together (the excellent effect of this mixture when wet has to be seen to be believed); ribbing: oval silver tinsel; hackle: two turns of green-dyed hen hackle; wing: goat hair dyed orange-yellow.

I tie this pattern in sizes 9 to 6, size 7 being the most useful size. This fly must be fished fast; too much goat hair will make it surface and render it useless. John Rowe and 'Jim' Robinson in the hot July of 1959 found it particularly effective for the rainbow trout at Chew Valley Reservoir, and I have since established beyond reasonable doubt that the Pretty-Pretty is much more effective with rainbows than browns.

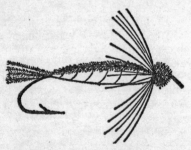

Diagram 7.10   The Jersey Herd

Take a size 6 long-shank trout hook (these can be obtained from Messrs Veniard) or alternatively a size 6 low-water salmon hook, though these do not drive home so easily as trout hooks. Tie in floss silk at bend and wind a bold underbody which thickens at the centre of the shank, fly-minnow fashion. Now tie in wide, copper-coloured, flat tinsel or alternatively a strip of milk-cap foil, and about twelve strands of bronze peacock herl, leaving the tips of the herl pointing aft to form a tail about $\frac{5}{16}$ in long. Carry your tying silk to $\frac{3}{16}$ in from the eye; wind your tinsel as for an Alexandra, and tie down at head. Carry the herl over the upper side of the body and tie down. Tie in a doubled, short-fibred cock hackle dyed a rich orange; take two turns and tie down. Now twist the strands of peacock herl together in an anti-clockwise direction and take two turns in front of the hackle to form a bold head. Tie off and whip finish.

This pattern should be tied both leaded and unleaded. I found that when using the leaded pattern it was necessary to use a point up to ·014 in in diameter for the sake of ease of control in casting. Although so thick a point would seem to be so conspicuous as to alarm fish, this does not occur in practice. The fly is best fished very fast though some success is reported for slow recovery at the bottom. Some idea of the speed at which the fly must be fished will be gathered by my statement that it is impossible to recover line fast enough by normal 'figure-of-eight' bunching in the left hand. Stripping through is the only way.

It may be said with some justice that 'stripping through' is nearer to spinning than it is to fly-fishing, but under difficult conditions on a reservoir you will never be blamed for using any method or fly which is within the rules. In any case, there is no denying that the Jersey Herd is a very minnowish creation: it certainly does not resemble a fly any more than do the Peter Ross and Alexandra.

There is an interesting history to this 'fly'. During Whit-week, 1951, I was on the water almost every day. The 1951 season was a crazy one, with fish migrations within the reservoir taking place three weeks later than is normal. In April instead of being off the dam, we found the fish were still in the marginal shallows. During Whit-week when they should have been back on the shallows they were feeding off the dam and the shallows were hopeless.

On Whit-Monday several anglers took fish off the dam while using Alexandras or other 'monstrosities', but I noticed that other anglers on the dam who fished with normal-sized flies caught nothing, and I concluded that it was a matter of using a fly which could be fished fast without its coming to the surface.

We had stiff northerly winds blowing straight into the dam

all the week. The usual 9 ft 6 in heavy-centre McClane taper leader would not cope with the conditions, and I resorted to one of 7 ft 6 in, tapered steeply from ·020 in down to ·011 in. Even size 6 Alexandras and Pretty-Pretties were too light to stay down and merely skated across the top, so severe was line-drag.

That evening I produced a really heavy large fly of a type which E. N. and A. L. had occasionally used in 1950. I used this fly to the exclusion of all else on the Wednesday, Thursday and Friday, and took a limit of two brace on each day. Other, and successful, anglers persisting with normal flasher patterns accounted for odd fish only. There was no question of superior skill: weather conditions demanded fast recovery, and my fly was heavy enough to stay submerged while I stripped through.

This fly is now a permanent addition to my box. I have used it on many occasions, under conditions varying from a heavy lop down to flat calm, and I have never failed to rise a fish with it. As you would expect, in July and August and during calms the fish tended to chase it without actually taking it, but that, too, can be turned to good account. On several occasions, having thus found a fish, I rested him, and then 'flogged' him and took him with a nymph fished deep.

The origin of the name? The fly was rush-tied with the only 'gold' tinsel available – foil from the top of a bottle of Channel Island milk.

The Alexandra is one of the most effective of the standard flashers, but the shop-bought versions are usually horribly over-dressed. I usually tie this fly with oval silver ribbing over the flat tinsel body to increase the flash. I never use more than eight strands of herl for winging large sizes, and only three or four strands for size 11 hooks. A Golden X Amherst Pheasant topping feather completes the dressing.

This fly is useful in all sizes from 11 to 6, and I have known it to be used successfully in size 15 and size 16, fished slowly near the surface in conditions of brilliant light.

Another 'standard' which is particularly good fished medium-fast towards dusk is the Butcher. My dressing employs the usual materials but I again rib with oval silver tinsel to increase flash and my wing is more slender than commercial tyings and is tied to lie over the body like a streamer wing.

Tie in the same sizes as the Alexandra.

Probably my most effective two-hook patterns are the Double

B & P Spider and its more flashy relative, my Black Knight sea-trout fly again dressed tandem.

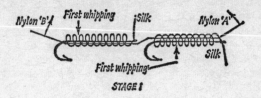

STAGE 1

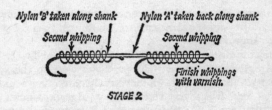

STAGE 2

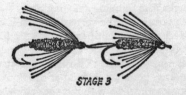

STAGE 3

Diagram 7.11   The B & P Tandem

The hooks used are wide-gape down-eyed Sproats whipped to double 20 lb BS nylon as shown in the diagram. The distance between the two hook shanks is about ⅜ in.

Once you have the chassis made, the two bodies are tied in completely orthodox manner. The dressing for the B & P Spider was given earlier in this chapter.

Tandem Black Knight

Body: oval gold or silver tinsel close-wound from tail to head (alternatively flat tinsel overribbed with oval tinsel for extra flash); hackle: three turns of dyed-black hen hackle.

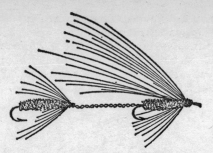

Diagram 7.12   The Streamer-type Tandem

Both patterns have also proved effective with a streamer-type wing of black-dyed polar bear hair mixed with strips of peacock herl as shown above.

Whilst these tandem-hooked flies have killed well when fished by stripping through fast, keeping them close to the surface, they have also yielded a number of large rainbows from the bank at dusk fished very slowly (figure of eight winding) right on the bottom. The fish have picked them up confidently and the 'take' has been a firm tighten exploding into a rocket take-off. They seem to do best when the surface feeding is coming to an end with the onset of dark. Nine-pound BS leader material is none too heavy for this style of fishing. The same method has also worked well fishing in 20 ft of water from a stationary boat.

Small trebles often get a better hold at the bony front of the jaw than two singles and I have found the following dressing a very useful variation.

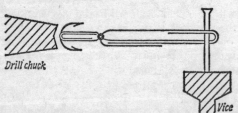

Diagram 7.13a   The Treble-hooked Lure: hook and wire before twisting

The body of the fly is tied of the same material as the tandem-hooked fly but the 'shank' of the hook is made from 14 lb BS Alasticum wire passed through the eye and between the hooks of the treble and then spun using a hand-drill until the four strands form a single firm but springy shaft. The diagram shows the manufacture of this type of lure.

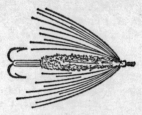

Diagram 7.13b   The Treble-hooked Lure: the finished fly

White flies have killed excellently at Grafham and during 1969 most of the limited mass-murder that occurred at Grafham could be traced to variations of a fly widely known as The Missionary. The origin of the fly is not known to me, but it is white and they eat it so maybe there is some justification.

Body materials include white fur, hair, wool and chenille, and the wing has varied from white swan fibres tied in at tail and head, to a loop of ram's wool or a white hackle feather or polar bear hair.

Diagram 7.14   The Polar Bear

My preferred dressing is polar bear wool body wound thick at the thorax, and ribbed over with flat silver tinsel. The wing is of polar bear fibres tied in streamer fashion! I tie this fly on long shank hooks sizes 4, 6 and 8 and on standard hooks size 6. I have used both bronze and nickel finished hooks.

Like the Double B & P Spider, the Polar Bear seems to kill

well fished deep and very slow, or stripped through at the surface. When wet the fly is translucent; almost transparent in fact. It also has flash and is as good a general representation of fry as I have encountered.

The chief limitation of flashers is that unless fished deep on a sunk line they have no application under conditions of flat calm: the use of the Jersey Herd for searching out a fish during July or August is exceptional. In the ordinary course of events flashers should be used only when there is sufficient ripple to break up the wake of the line. Small wonder the loch-fisherman, limited to the standard (flasher) loch flies and methods, prays for a stiff breeze and rippled surface.

Although the deceivers will always be my first choice, possibly because of the delicacy with which they are fished as much as the excellent bags they make possible, there is one occasion when flashers must be used.

In strong crosswinds a floating line will develop a deep belly downwind. This drawback can be overcome, in part, by putting the rod point over, but the only fully satisfactory remedy is to use flashers and fish fast to keep in touch with your fly. Throughout the book I have been using loose terms such as 'slow', 'fast', 'medium speed' and so on. Speed is important since it affects both the depth of a fly and its power to deceive. I have therefore carried out a series of time trials under actual fishing conditions to establish the speeds at which I use the patterns of flies given in this chapter. My line was marked at $21\frac{1}{2}$ yards and a $3\frac{1}{2}$-yard leader was attached making a total of 25 yards. The 10 ft 'Ivens Original' was used in the experiments and the pick-up was made when the cast loop was 6 in from the tip, that is, when the fly was 7 yards away from me. Thus 18 yards of line was recovered after making each 25-yard cast. The times for recovery given in the table below are the average of five separate recoveries for each pattern.

Speed	Fly Pattern	Method of Recovery	Time
Normal	All nymphs	Figure-of-eight bunching	2 m. 13 s.
Slow	All nymphs	Figure-of-eight-bunching	2 m. 40 s.
Normal	Black & Peacock Spider	Figure-of-eight bunching	1 m. 28 s.
Slow	Black & Peacock Spider	Figure-of-eight bunching	1 m. 42 s.
Normal	Alexandra & Pretty-Pretty	Figure-of-eight bunching	1 m. 2 s.
Fast	Alexandra & Pretty-Pretty	Figure-of-eight bunching	44 s.
Normal	Jersey Herd	Stripping through	35 s.
Fast	Jersey Herd	Stripping through	28 s.

The 'fishing out' of a cast when the line, leader and fly are all lying in the surface film is a very special case. In a light cross wind you may not recover line at all, the wind imparting all the movement necessary, while you watch where the fly is ready to tighten the moment the line stops.

In calms, to fish out the 30-yard cast desirable for maximum angler concealment may take anything from four to six minutes.

Dry flies

Whilst dry fly fishing for brown trout is, most of the time, only the second-best method, some people prefer it (for reasons that have nothing to do with catching fish) so a few words on suitable dressings will be appropriate. If you are fishing lakes where rainbow trout predominate then a good working knowledge of dry fly dressings for lakes is essential, for suitable dressings are almost impossible to buy.

Perhaps it is labouring the point to suggest that the primary requirement of a dry fly is that it shall float. Nevertheless there are many dry flies sold which are very deficient in this respect.

In river fishing, the fly, relative to the water, remains stationary; in still-water fishing the fly is worked, and normally dressed patterns readily become waterlogged.

Diagram 7.15   The Fuzzy-Buzzy

Flies dressed as in the diagram float much better than the single-hackled patterns. If necessary you can tell yourself that you are dressing the 'knotted' imago. Tie in two stiff hackles from a Brown Leghorn cock neck at the bend of the hook. Wind to form a good bushy hackle and tie off. Tie in a piece of oval gold tinsel and wind it as a body to about $\frac{3}{16}$ in from the eye. Tie in two more hackle feathers and wind the front hackle; tie off. Whip finish and varnish head.

If you prefer it, the front hackle can be of another colour and your fly thus becomes a type of 'Bi-visible'.

These dry flies can be dressed on hooks from size 12 to 7. The floating powers seem to be improved by clipping the hackle as shown in the right-hand part of the above diagram. Such Fuzzy-Buzzy dressings in large sizes can be used as 'wake' flies in the gloaming and John Rowe, of Northampton, has fished a large buff Fuzzy-Buzzy, sometimes motionless, sometimes gently worked to achieve good results in silverhorns rises.

Small dry flies of conventional pattern but dressed with super-quality hackles and usually with wings omitted were used regularly at Grafham from June 1968 onwards during the rainbow evening rise. Sometimes, as I found myself on two occasions, small dry flies would bring an offer when rainbows were difficult in the mid afternoon. Not that this proved anything, for on both occasions immediately afterwards Mike hooked fish on a big Black Pennell fished fast about 5 ft down.

For sea trout and salmon, too

Early in spring, 1953, on the Deveron, I tried out the Black and Peacock Spider during hatches of March Browns. Using an artificial March Brown on the same cast, I found the trout preferred the Black and Peacock Spider whether fished as tail fly or dropper. So, too, did a clean salmon of about 8 lb which leapt and broke away as the hook drew home. In the *Fishing Gazette* on 26 September 1953, 'Lemon Grey' reported hooking two salmon in fifteen minutes on his Torridge water. Both took my Green Nymph which sank so readily in the low and almost still pool.

I have now used my flies for eighteen years for sea-trout fishing. The Black and Peacock Spider has proved a wonderful killer on dark nights used either plain or with an oval silver tinsel rib, and has taken a number of salmon from shallow runs in the gloaming of a summer's evening. In the dawn rise, I have found the Green Nymph, Brown Nymph and Brown and Green Nymph quite as killing as any conventional sea-trout pattern and the Jersey Herd has again rendered valuable shock treatment.

The figure-of-eight method of line recovery is that recommended when working flies in those deep, slow-moving holding pools, and at the fast-moving tails when it is necessary to avoid the fly washing down over the 'lip' as it swims across.

Fly-dressing materials

It is seldom necessary to buy expensive plumage. Many highly coloured feathers are a chalky white in reverse and nowhere nearly so efficient as dyed material. When dyeing, plumage should be stripped of soft fibre and down feathers, tied in small bundles and thoroughly cleansed of grease in warm soapy water. Cleaning should be followed by thorough rinsing and the feathers should be wet when placed in the dye-bath to ensure even dyeing. The dyes I use are household 'Fairy' or 'Drummer' dyes and I use them at about 180°F. The colour should be checked frequently by lifting the bundle by the attached cotton and rinsing in clean water. If you are dyeing to a pattern, wet the pattern thoroughly so as to make a fair comparison.

Nylon is dyed in the same way, but after the soap washing requires thirty minutes' soaking in warm water. It will then readily absorb the dye.

Ostrich herl and other plumage used for body making should always be dyed on the quill.

Hackle feathers should be obtained on the skin whenever possible: they are thus already graded for size. If you see a bird with the required neck plumage hanging at a poulterer's shop ask him to cut the neck skin off for you. At home open the skin and tack it stretched on to a board with the flesh side uppermost. Scrape off as much fat and flesh as you can and merely leave the skin to dry. I have read of rubbing alum into the skins but I have never done so myself and I have two neck skins over twenty years old in my box of plumage and in perfect preservation . . . though a bit short of feathers!

Some sellers of tying materials supply herl, hair and the like as a shapeless mixture packed loose in an envelope. Why they do it I do not know, but I loathe the practice. Materials of this type should always be supplied on the quill or on the skin.

Hair has largely replaced feather as a winging material for many patterns, and there is every reason to suppose the result is a better fly. Hair wings 'work' in a wonderfully life-like manner and are translucent, polar bear hair, plain or dyed, being particularly valuable in this respect.

When you start to use hair a whole new field of sources of supply is opened up. I recall that a few years ago I found an excellent 'Brown and Grizzled' mixture for low-water March

Brown wings, on the flanks of a good-looking collie. The dog didn't mind and the owner never knew.

Part Two

CHAPTER 8

Raw spring days

I have always attempted to elevate fishing to the plane of an exact science. The man who *thinks* 'fish and fishing' must ultimately succeed in catching more fish than the man who believes in leaving it to luck. And yet, until the middle of May, the element of chance in reservoir trout fishing cannot be relegated to a back seat.

The whole of the trouble appears to me to centre around the fact that when the season opens some fish are in good condition, others barely recovered from spawning, while some are still heavy with spawn. In other words the fish as a whole have not settled down to a predictable pattern of behaviour.

May I quote some results which illustrate my point. Tuesday, 11 May 1948. Four fish taken, 1 lb 4 oz, 1 lb 6 oz, 1 lb 12 oz, and 2 lb 8 oz. The first three were fat as butter and were probably fish which had spawned for the first time. Scale-readings of similar fish taken in 1951 tend to support this conclusion. The first spawning of brown trout is seldom an exhausting process. The $2\frac{1}{2}$ lb fish was 18 in long and had a girth of $10\frac{1}{2}$ in. The ovaries were well developed and there were two or three unabsorbed ova in the abdominal cavity, proving she had spawned during the previous winter. Her flesh was pink and firm. At 2 PM on the same day, E.N. took a hen fish weighing 5 lb 8 oz and which contained about $1\frac{1}{2}$ lb of unshed ova.

Saturday 9 April 1949, I took one fish of 2 lb 15 oz which was $22\frac{1}{2}$ in long. She came ashore writhing like an eel and was promptly returned to the water. The fish, by the way, was smutting and I took her on a size 4 Black and Peacock Spider. Strange what fish will do!

At this time rainbows were not stocked in the Northampton reservoirs so, confused as the behaviour pattern was, it was still simple by comparison with what occurs when there is a mixed stock of brown and rainbow trout.

As we shall show later, rainbows are of two distinct races or strains so far as spawning date is concerned and I have no doubt the strains have become mixed so that maturity can occur from mid-November through to the following summer. A 3 lb 4 oz rainbow taken on 25 April 1967 had large but ripe ovaries and her flesh ate badly. A fish of exactly the same weight on 5 May 1968, was a picture of quality, a short deep body, silver, tinged with lilac, and flesh deep orange-red when cut. It is by no means uncommon to unhook cock rainbows in July that squirt a milk-like stream of milt over hands and clothing.

I suggest we go fishing on a really bleak opening day and solve our problems as we meet them.

The first thing we notice as we get our permits and sign-in is that the water is about 11 ft higher than it was when we left it last season. In fact, with a 15 mph to 20 mph wind setting towards the outflow, water is pouring over, as waves nearly 2 ft high break against its concrete and brickwork lip.*

As usual we tackle-up down by the boathouse. We seem to be

* By contrast, the opening day of the 1952 season saw the beginning of an unseasonably warm spell. In spite of water temperature of only 44°F, we had a series of evening rises such as the water keeper had not seen so early in the season during his twenty-five years' experience. Fish refused a fly sunk more than 2 in and many wet fly fishermen, not realizing what was happening, and unable to get fish on a wet fly 12 in or more below the surface, changed to dry fly and then took fish. I found the answer to their behaviour when my first three fish of the season were taken on a dropper. Fishing greased leader from then onwards proved a complete answer.

the first arrivals, which is just as well, or we would have been yarning till 10 AM of last year's notable deeds.

We meet with no snags assembling our gear, nor should we after six long 'black' months, with time and to spare for tackle repairs.

The sky is leaden, and what is more important, the water is very rough, so we shall fish fast and use flashers of size 8 or larger.

This is not the kind of day for the heights of casting finesse – so we put up a reel holding an AFTM WF-8-F line terminating in 2 yards of level sinker and a no-knot eye. Our leader will be short, a Platil taper to 30/100 mm with a 2½ ft 28/100 mm point – about 9½ ft in all.

In absence of marginal weed in the early season I frequently fish a dropper, but in this high wind a dropper would increase wind resistance, and generally make casting more hazardous so it shall be a tail fly only.

Nor, I think, over deep water does a dropper provide real advantage, for a fish that sees the dropper will as easily see the tail fly. Much better he rise to a fly at the end of the tackle than come to a dropper with a length of leader lying close by. Long experience shows that one gets far fewer abortive plucks when using a single fly. But more on this later.

I suggest we give them an alternative diet: you try a Pretty-Pretty and I will use an Alexandra. There is usually a fish in the corner where dam and bank meet, and we may as well start there.

So close to the dam; if we drop our flies about 80 ft from the margin they will be over 6 ft to 8 ft of water – a useful depth at this time of year. Fishing this spot will help us to deal with one of the problems of wind.

Diagram 8.1 shows our position relative to the corner of the dam.

As we cast from X, at 90° to the bank, the wind is blowing at 60° to the line and forming a deep belly, so we hold our rods parallel to the water and at 110° to the line, as in diagram 8.2, to cut out the belly of line between rod-tip and water. The belly of line on the water, plus the rod at an angle to the line, will prevent a breakage if we have a heavy take.

Fanning our casts enables us to cover all the water within reach, but after half an hour has passed we have not seen, felt or heard anything of a fish, and so, having got the 'feel' of our

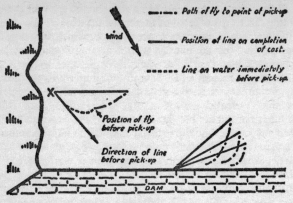

Diagram 8.1

rods again, we decide to tackle the difficult conditions of the dam.

Early in the season when most brown trout are regaining condition after spawning, they lie in deep water where there is an abundance of snail. The steep gradient of the dam offers us our readiest method of reaching deep water. In addition, the crevices between the granite blocks offer cover to many small food creatures such as sticklebacks and loaches.

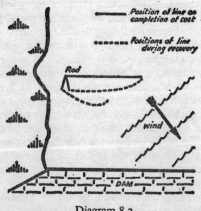

Diagram 8.2

The granite blocks today are wet with spray, so off come the waders, and on go rope-soled shoes and a pair of nylon and Vinyl waterproof trousers to keep out the wind. Where smooth concrete 'batters' protect the face of the dam, water authorities often prohibit angling, so denying the bank fisher an opportunity to cover really deep water. It would be so easy to render them safe for angling if only a little thought and money were made available during construction. And why, in any case, should there not be timbers bolted to the face of the concrete here and there to provide safe footholds at intervals along the smoothest of concrete faces?

The wind here is much stronger than it was in the corner sheltered by the land, and 18 yards will be our longest cast; a longer line would soon be drowned. With the dam rising at the back, and the wind blowing almost straight in, we compromise by casting as shown in diagram 8.1. Casting 18 yards of line at 40° to the dam, our flies drop $11\frac{1}{2}$ yards from the margin, and are over 12 ft to 16 ft of water, depending on the slope of the dam. The second and third casts are made at 30° and 20° respectively. The last cast does not fish much new water, but it takes a lot of fish, namely those that followed in the first two casts. Of course it doesn't matter a jot if you cast at 42°, 28°, and 20°. But it is essential to realize that the angle or gap between each cast must bear some relationship to the size of the trout's window at the depth he is lying.

The relationship between the width of the window and the depth at which the fish is lying is approximately as 7 is to 4 (see diagram 8.3).

In 12 ft of water the window would be 21 ft across, and theoretically speaking, provided the casts were never wider apart than 21 ft all fish within reach of the caster must see the fly at least once, while they continue to lie at 12 ft depth.

But if the fish lie at 6 ft and their window is narrowed to 10 ft 6 in, then casts separated by a distance of 21 ft may escape the fishes' vision altogether. But please do not conclude that a fish can only see objects in his window; he can and often does see a fly which is a long way outside it. Under conditions of poor light, however, he will undoubtedly see the fly in the window more distinctly.

Even here on the dam the wind is causing a deep belly in the line and we put the rod tip down to the water to gain closer

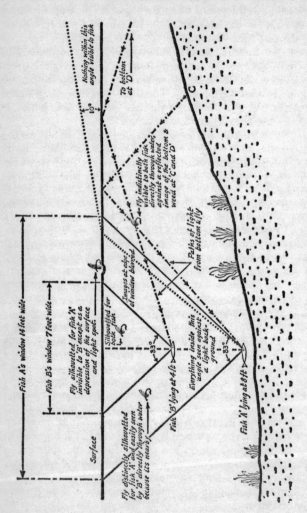

Diagram 8.3

Fish A's window 14 feet wide

Fish B's window 7 feet wide

Nothing within this angle visible to fish

10°

To bottom at 'D'

Fly indistinctly visible to both fishes directly through water against a reflected image of the bottom & weed at 'C' and 'D'

Paths of light from bottom & fly

Images at edges of window blurred

Silhouetted for both fish

Fly silhouetted for fish 'A' invisible to 'B' except as a depression of the surface and light speck

Fish 'B' lying at 4½ ft

83°

Everything inside this angle seen against a light back-ground

83°

Fly distinctly silhouetted for fish 'A' and easily seen by 'B' directly through water because its nearby

Surface

C

Fish 'A' lying at 8 ft

114

contact with the fly. As the line comes round to the side we begin the lift, and the fly leaves the water not 2 ft from the edge. By reaching well forward when we begin the pick-up we throw our line high at the back, so as to clear the low wall that flanks the path that runs from one end to the other.

Have you noticed yet that although your line leads straight away from you, the fly as you pick up seems to leave the water away over to the left? If you will glance back to diagram 8.1 you will see what is happening. The thick lines show the position on casting. As you recover, your line bellies, until it lies as shown by the dotted line in the diagram.

All this means that it is no use looking down your line for the expected rise, for it is going to occur over to the left where the fly is. Try to imagine the path of your fly and keep your eyes fixed on the general area of water where this analysis tells you the fly is fishing.

After fishing out the three casts move down two paces; repeat the 'performance' *ad infinitum*. So short a move ensures that a fish sees the fly at least twice. Fine! I am going to fish down 30 yards behind you. 'When does something happen?' you ask.

'Perhaps now, perhaps in two hours' time, perhaps not . . . but anyway, keep your mind on the job.'

Forty minutes later we are some 80 yards farther down the dam and gloom reigns supreme. Conversation regarding lunch reveals a state of mind which is not conducive to good fishing. Just as you turn to speak, there is a wild commotion at the surface *not 3 yards from the side* and you are into the first fish. Luckily he is only about 1¼ lb or there would have been a break 'on the take'. As you play him, boredom quite gone, the pressure of the wind on your rod is giving trouble. Under these conditions, I often find that when the wind gusts I lose the 'feel' of the fish altogether: another argument for strong leaders. Your large net makes child's play of the netting and having killed your fish, which actually weighed 1 lb 6 oz, you ask yourself whether or not to carry on down the dam.

In your position I would stay put. Possibly because the remains of old weed beds provide feed for tubifex, snail and nymph, the fish appear to be very localized along the dam, particularly in the early season. Having picked up one fish I would 'flog' 10 yards either side of the spot for at least forty minutes before moving on down. I am aware that river etiquette demands that you move down, but we normally invite the chap behind to go in front. He will not mind provided you indicate to him what you intend to do. This sort of thing is the logical result of the fact that our fish behave differently from river fish.

You're going to fish it out? Splendid! I will go below you and look for a lie of my own.

Half an hour later, the wind has veered so as to blow straight into the dam at 20 mph to 25 mph. This is where a sunken line comes into its own, so off comes the one reel and on goes a reel with a no 7 weight-forward rapid sinker. The much greater weight for diameter of a sinker greatly aids casting into a wind and a no 7 will go out at least as well as the no 8 floater. Nor shall we now have trouble with line belly.

The same leader will do excellently, but my fly will now be a size 6 B & P Spider.

Despite the wind, casting is noticeably easier and tackle control returns with the line quickly sinking several feet below the surface. Recovery speeds and techniques can now be varied from figure-of-eight to draw and pause and stripping-through.

The latter method, unless you coil recovered line, means that you will probably drop line to the dam as you fish out each cast. Be warned now. Place your feet comfortably before you start stripping line, and step forward *after* making your cast, being certain first that you did shoot all the line that was on the ground. Whether the shooting line is of monofil or of dressed nylon, treading on it will usually cause serious damage and may even cut it clean through.

Twenty minutes later with hands wet and cold and thoughts turning to a cup of something hot from the flask, the commencement of another pull on the line in the stripping-through process is met by firm resistance and the irresistible drag of a very big fish. In shocked surprise we fail to release line; the rod tip is under water and everything is as suddenly slack. Only another angler can ever know your feelings as you wind in and find the fly gone.

This kind of disaster is particularly likely to occur when you are fishing deep over very deep water. Nothing is seen of the approach of the fish to the fly and a downwards pull on your rod-tip as he sounds after taking is instinctively resisted where you would yield line to a side pull from a fish running near the surface.

Disappointment aggravates the fatigue of continuous casting into the wind and we decide on a change of scenery.

The spring migration

Most reservoir anglers will be aware that the first few weeks of April often provide excellent sport with brown trout under vile weather conditions, and that as May approaches and the weather improves, sport paradoxically deteriorates. This was the common experience at Hollowell and Ravensthorpe and we usually attributed it to the fish becoming educated to the regular presence of anglers in the marginal waters.

Wading anglers, particularly in great numbers, certainly do upset margin-feeding trout, but I was most interested to find strong evidence of an early spring movement of brown trout from the shallows quite independent of anglers.

As part of the diagnostic fishing programme by a Northern Water Board, which plans to open its reservoirs, to which end I was retained with others to represent fishing interests, a netting programme was carried out by the river authority in spring 1968. We wanted a quick check on the size, age, food and condition of the indigenous population of trout.

Nettings in April and early May yielded good results; there were clearly plenty of trout in the margins. In mid-May and onward netting results were suddenly very much reduced. The same net was operated by the same team in the same areas but the fish were no longer present.

Spring comes late to that bleak moorland area and for living things mid-May is the equivalent of mid-April in the softer climate of the Midland Plain. The odds, I feel, favour an outward migration as the true cause of a fall-off of bank fishing sport in late April. Nonetheless, the population of trout in our shallow marginal waters in early April is seldom as large as it will be in June when the weed beds are well grown and provide cover for fish and food alike.

But we have decided to fish shallow water off the point of the bay on the far bank and from now, 11.30 AM to 1 PM should be the best part of the day.

Fishing over 8 ft or so of water we shall not need our fast-sinking line and we change to a floater and add 2 ft of 35/100 mm nylon to the stout end of our Platil tapered cast to give us a leader of 12½ ft with a double-taper profile. There will now be

20 to 22 ft of sunken tackle between the fly, an Alexandra, and any line wake.

Trout usually cruise along a certain depth-line. Having

Diagram 8.4

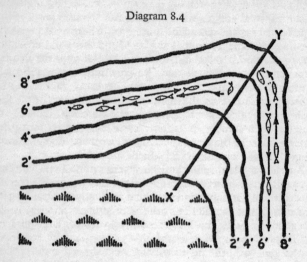

reached a position such as that represented by the line XY in the above diagram of a typical point, the fish find the water deepening and turn around. Thus from the point we are able to fish to two groups of fish.

We enter the water slowly, making as little disturbance as possible, casting ahead of us in case there is a fish lying close in.

We commence fishing about 20 yards apart: in these water conditions two lines close together will not worry the fish. By the way, an approach to 30 yards from another angler is seldom resented provided you wade very quietly and do not cast to fish which he can reach and is, in fact, fishing for.

Casting here, with the wind blowing from behind onto my right shoulder, is anything but comfortable. I used to cast over my left shoulder with a wind from the right, but it reduced my distance and most of us are well able to throw the line clear of our bodies, anyway. But however competent a caster you are, a gusting wind can destroy your control of a long aerialized line – and I will not disguise the fact I wear Polaroids in all but the dullest conditions and feel the extra eye-protection is worthwhile.

And while on this subject of safety, may I urge that you keep well to the rear when walking the bank past a wading angler and shout 'Passing' and 'Clear' in case he has not seen you.

After fishing for some fifteen minutes, I hear what may have been a rise some 25 yards away, so I move up and cover the area. I continue fishing fast to keep in touch with the fly, and after some twenty minutes have a heavy pull; only the rod well over as in diagram 8.2 saves me from a break. There was no warning swirl, just a pull which was in fact the start of the first rush and I have not yet driven home the hook. Despite the heavy take, a number of fish are lost if you neglect to tighten hard as soon as the rush slackens, so, with rod high, at arm's length, I make sure of the hookhold.

I used to say that striking twice offered no advantage and that it could loosen a secure hold. Probably this was true when we used silk lines and gut leaders with comparatively little stretch. But today's lines and leaders are full of stretch and large hooks often fail to go home. I reduced my losses on large flies by 80 per cent at Grafham from mid-1967 onward by striking a second time after the first rush was over.

The fight is a fast one and pace soon slackens. I unclip the net and rest it in front of me. Two minutes later the fish is brought within reach; it rolls, for a moment off balance – the fight is over. I put on strain – never mess about with fish at this stage – slide him head on the surface towards me with net ready, submerged, and lift without haste as he comes over it. On the balance he goes 3 lb 2 oz; in two months' time he would be 6 oz heavier, but nevertheless, he is in reasonably good condition.

Some twenty minutes later I receive another pull but do not connect. A further twenty minutes yields nothing and, it being 1.15 PM, we leave the water and have lunch. Two fish by lunch is good going at this time of year.

Sandwiches gone, we move up to the top end. The walk warms us up, but apart from that gives us little satisfaction, for no fish are moving. The afternoon is seldom a good period, but it is too cold to sit about and we came to fish after all. It is only about 4 ft deep up here, and we may come across some of the four-year-old well-mended fish which will already be feeding on nymph: even in this cold weather small hatches of fly do take place and many nymphs are active. After fishing for half an hour using Black and Peacock Spider and Brown Nymph (at the upwind end of the reservoir the water is much calmer and the wind less troublesome, making it possible to fish slowly) we both hook fish within a matter of seconds of one another. They fight, weight for weight, far better than the three-pounder and both weigh 1 lb 3 oz. Obviously, several fish moved by us and will probably return, so without wasting time we get back to work.

One and a half hours later, having paused only to change flies – an effective means of ensuring that you are not fishing with a leader which has 'hinged' at the fly – we have had no further offer and decide that a spot of something warm is indicated. The wind by now has moderated and veered, the air is slightly warmer and it begins to rain.

Thermos flasks emptied, we move back to the dam and find that the wind is blowing along it, having veered through 130° since the forenoon.

Fishing hard, with flashers of size 6 and 7 we move along the dam, casting as in the morning but working from the opposite end of the dam. Fading light finds us with no more fish and we pack up. We have made the most of our opportunities and have a brace apiece for our efforts. What of the others ?

One angler has taken two fish from the dam: he apparently fished hard there after we had given it up as hopeless, and took both fish just where we took our first. The others are blank, having fished where it was comfortable to cast rather than where the fish were likely to be.

Had it been a warm spring day, with the water temperature customary in mid-May, we would have fished much as we would for that time of year, except that we would have concentrated on the deep water and fished our flies deep if the fish were not on top.

Many anglers consider the early-season fishing as time wasted but you are getting in practice, and when the good fishing does come you are in trim to make the most of it.

We fishermen can find excuses for every kind of madness we indulge in.

CHAPTER 9

The cream of the season's sport

Were I asked what part of the season gave limit bags most frequently, I would unhesitatingly reply, 'mid-May to mid-June'. Yet, when I look at my records I find that in some years the period in question has been quite poor: 1950 saw excellent (by standards then) sport – sixteen fish in my ten outings from 11 May to 10 June in a season when top score was thirty-five fish. 1949, on the other hand, was one of the bad years mentioned above – only eight fish in my twelve outings from 7 May to 25 June. My diary entry for Wednesday, 25 May, reads as follows:

'Fished from 9 AM to 9 PM Wind W force 4 to 5 (Beaufort Scale). Cold. Leaden Sky. Six anglers on water; all blank. No fish have been taken on this water for 14 days.' It was during this period that I took one fish in five outings.

While on this dismal topic of blanks, I feel it might be some encouragement to the reservoir novice 'enjoying' a sticky period to read that I once had a period of twelve outings with only one fish. That was on the Northampton Reservoirs after the war and before their restocking programme was begun. There was also a morale-destroying period of five consecutive blanks in August 1966, fishing the bank at Grafham . . . wholly and solely because I persisted in fishing a shallow bay that had been very good indeed in July, but from which by August the fish had moved elsewhere.

Reservoir fishing is something you have to stick at and master. One should never write-off a water after only three or four blank visits. Men who know the water still have blanks and many of them. I feel the newcomer should be prepared to make six visits before becoming downhearted about his lack of *luck*.

If you find that you will be able to fish twice during a given week, I most strongly suggest that you fish on two consecutive days. On the second day you will be able to exploit with advantage what you learned on the previous day. On the other hand, to fish, say, on the Monday and again on the Friday, means that on the Friday you will have a completely different set of problems to solve, for a change of wind and weather will have altered the whole picture.

It is in May that we begin to feel that we are truly fly-fishing. Hatches of the natural take take place almost every day and the fish readily take near the surface.

In years like 1951 and 1958, of course, prolonged wet and cold weather persisting into the summer cause the whole pattern of behaviour of the fish to go haywire. To be strictly accurate, the cycle remains much the same but local migrations occur later or earlier depending on water temperature, weed growth and other natural phenomena.

The cold northerly winds which plagued us on our last visit to the water at 'Floganper Spire' are changed to light south-westerly breezes; rushes are springing up along the margins, and the water weed is beginning to show beneath the surface in the shallows. The air, too, is warm, and one is filled with a sense of Nature's exuberant activity. Today, we ought to be able to see the fish move and it will be well worth our while to look for rising fish.

As we tackle-up at the boathouse, a keen watch on the water reveals several rises on the edge of the ripple a hundred yards or so up the bank.

We shall not fish deep water today, for by now the majority of the fish are feeding in the marginal shallows, or in offshore water less than 12 ft deep, where sunlight at the bottom is strong enough to support strong growths of water weed.

The water is very clear – its usual state in calm weather – and we decide to use 12 ft leaders consisting of a Platil knotless taper to 30/100 mm ending in 1 ft of 28/100 and $3\frac{1}{2}$ ft of 26/100 mm monofil. Too heavy you think? Perhaps, but these are fish that average $2\frac{1}{4}$ lb with a number well over 5 lb. Provided we achieve good concealment and presentation the leader diameter will matter little.

Today is a 'Black and Peacock Spider day', and size 8 will do nicely to start with.

We make our way along the bank and find the fish still moving. The rises are taking place over a distance of 35 yards along the edge of the ripple, and an occasional hump or swirl in the calm water 20 yards from the shore reveals the presence of at least one other fish nymphing hard.

After watching carefully for several moments we notice that the rises occur in definite sequence: one up on the left, followed by one in front, then another a little to our right, and then the order is reversed. The rises follow one another quickly and it is hard to realize that they are made by one fish moving fast. The nearer nymphing fish will be the easier to take, and in any case it would be folly to cast across them in order to take the more distant fish.

We enter the water a few feet and hold the fly underwater, squeezing it to expel air from the body and ensure its ready sinking. Without moving any farther from the shore and ignoring the individual swirls, we begin dropping our fly just short of the area of activity. There is no point in fanning the casts: we are fishing in water the fish are using.

We have slowly increased our length of line and the fly is now dropping well inside the target area. As we lift the rod point and take the line in the left hand preparatory to recovering line, we are taken heavily and broken. A bad start! It happens now and again and we just have to face it: there must always be a brief instant after delivering the fly when the line and rod are not fully controlled.

Somewhat shakily we tie on another Spider, and having soaked it, again cover the same spot, recovering line slowly to

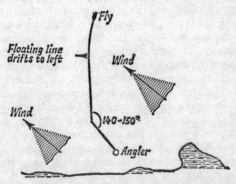

Diagram 9.1   Light wind from right, rod points slightly left. With wind from left, rod points slightly right.

avoid wake. Because the fish are moving fairly close to the surface, we grease the last 3 ft of our double-taper floater (most floaters have short tips that are just heavier than water and which therefore sink very slightly) and the 2 or 3 ft at the upper end of the leader so that the fly is being fished 15 in to 18 in deep. After half a dozen casts we are taken. There is no tighten, but the cast is suddenly seen to 'disappear through a hole in the water'. I am not being facetious; that is exactly what appears to happen. We drive home the barb smoothly and easily by a firm but essentially smooth and short movement to one side.

The days of upward striking are over for me. I fish right-handed and with breeze from the right or in a following wind I point the rod to my left as nearly as possible at an angle of 140° to 150° to the line. With a wind from the left I point the rod right a little to try to maintain the same angle. A heavy pull must always be against the spring of the rod. The theory behind this avoidance of upward striking is that upward movement of the rod merely results in most of its power being absorbed in lifting an inert line from the surface. Sideways striking permits the water to continue to support the line so that rod power is directed into moving the line laterally against water drag and driving home the hook. It is the difference between rowing a boat and throwing it!

Certainly this sideways strike was to some purpose. And what a difference in the strength of the fish since opening day. Warmer water has speeded up the rate of conversion of food into energy and flesh, and the fish are much stronger. In no time our backing-line is disappearing. The rod held high exerts little strain on the fish, but towing an increasingly long line will stop him eventually. The line is leading directly away from us, and we are somewhat surprised when the fish suddenly jumps once, twice . . . six times in all, about 50 yards out; but away over to the right. He loses much of his steam after this effort, and although we cannot feel the fish, line comes in easily enough. Thankfully, we see the splice pass down the rings, and a few seconds later we see the fish swimming across our front just beneath the surface and 18 yards away. The net is quietly unshipped, and then he sees us and is off again at tremendous speed, straight into a weed bed on the left.

Satisfied that he is still on, we put down the rod point and pull steadily on the line. No luck: he's in the thick of it. We

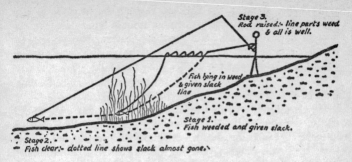

Diagram 9.2   Clearing fish from weed bed

pull off a few yards of line; leave it slack on the water and wait. About five minutes later the slack commences to move, and we strip off a few more yards. Just before it is all gone, we raise the rod and arm above the head and tighten on the fish once more. He is now on the far side of the weed bed; the tight line has parted the weed and all is well again.

This method works for me in nine out of ten cases: it is very seldom a fish is lost, though I confess there have been occasions of dismay all round, and one case of most unladylike hilarity when I have been caught up to my naked middle trying to free a fish from a submerged branch!

Again we bring the very tired fish close in, but he is still on balance and we must be prepared for more fun and games. Yes, I thought so. He makes a sudden rush and we see the cast begin to lengthen: he's coming out. Quickly we lower the rod-tip sideways and down to the water; he turns down leaving only a swirl where might have been a smother of spray followed by catastrophe when the hookhold gave. A few moments later he is led to the net and we administer last rites. Three pounds twelve ounces he goes: a beautifully conditioned fish. We open his mouth and find it full of the inevitable olive nymphs.

Perhaps you wonder why we did not lower the rod when he jumped after that first rush. Most of the classic angler/writers of the early twentieth century seem to dwell on dropping the rod point, but I see very little use in it. By far the greatest strain on the leader and on the hookhold was caused by the long length of submerged line which was being towed. Slack line at the rod end would have made no difference whatsoever if the fish had fallen back on the leader.

If you find that fish go into a succession of wild gymnastics in the first few seconds you are probably holding them too hard, although it sometimes betokens a light hookhold.

We wade back into the water to tackle the surface-feeding fish: he is still rising despite all the commotion.

He rises some 15 yards on the left, moving our way, so we cast to the edge of the ripple some 5 yards to our right: it pays to make sure of being ahead. We recover line slowly and see his shoulder break water 3 yards to the left of the fly and almost immediately afterwards he rises again to the right of the fly. A refusal? Perhaps, but the shoulder rise indicated that he was moving very near the surface and possibly he passed over the fly and is only interested in what appears in his window. Here is a case for greasing the leader down to the last 18 in, so that the fly fishes only about 3 in below the surface. A size 11 fly will be plenty big enough. Again we cast well ahead of him and several moments later he takes while moving fast, feels the point immediately, and shoots clean out of the water. The rod takes the shock nicely and he is played out without incident, and inspected on shore. He is markedly a different fish from our first. He is thicker for his length, silvery like a sea trout and black spotted. He is obviously of a different race of fish. Only occasionally do we take fish of this type, and more often than not they are surface-feeding at the time they are caught.

Undoubtedly, some of our fish are wild bred, and in the fry stage would be plankton feeders, a habit which Hewitt tells us artificially fed hatchery-fish probably fail to acquire. I think he could be right for brown trout, but I have caught too many artificially reared and released rainbow trout whose stomachs were a grey slime of part-digested water fleas to accept this as more than partly true.

If Hewitt is right where brown trout are concerned it is possible that fry stocking might result in more surface-feeding fish since a fly does represent a good mouthful to a small fish in the wild state, and the habit once acquired would persist. Alternatively we need far more brownies reared in the compensation-water system discussed in Chapter 21.

But what of our fishing? There is no more activity that we can see – there probably are several more fish feeding down below – but today we shall cast to rising fish while they are to be found.

We walk about half a mile along the shore and see nothing, so we decide to return to our old spot. There too the surface is undisturbed and a change of tactics is indicated. Off comes the leader; a 2-yard length of level sinker is attached to the line end, and the same leader is reknotted. We now have terminal tackle for medium-depth fishing.

The stout-end of the leader is cut 3 ft from the line eye and joined, using a blood knot. This is merely a stop knot for a dropper length which is then made fast by the tucked half-blood round the upper part of the leader.

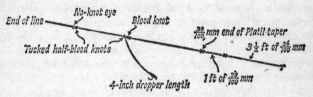

Diagram 9.3   Attachment of dropper to leader.

As dropper we tie on a Brown Nymph and as tail fly we continue with a B & P Spider, but this time a leaded version (fine lead wire replacing silk floss as an underbody). Had we not taken a fish earlier on the Spider we should probably have used a Green Nymph. We none of us care to change a winning team!

The whole of our present tactics is based on the fact that we do not know at what depth fish are feeding, and we therefore propose to improve our chances by fishing at two depths.

Having moved 20 yards away from that weed bed we commence casting. The flies are allowed to sink deep before we begin to recover line; in fact the tail fly should be allowed to sink to the bottom, when the pull-and-pause recovery recommended for the Green Nymph will cause disturbance of the mud, and attract the attention of fish. The dropper is fishing some 2 ft to 3 ft above the bottom and is thus serving a real purpose. After casting for half an hour, the line is drawn sharply and we tighten into our third fish, and presently land him.

This method will usually pay off at this time of year, but it does require enormous concentration.

Still nothing showing anywhere! This seems as good an opportunity for eating as is likely to occur today. We have taken three fish; all is well with the world, and we decide to take a nap rather than risk catching our fourth and last fish too early in the day.

This is an excellent way of missing a 'limit'!

Friend, if you want a limit – and we all do now and again – then you must catch it while you may; in an hour's time it may be too late.

Nevertheless, on this occasion we decide 'things are different'. 'This is the time of year when fish feed all day,' we tell ourselves.

At three o'clock we waken, and picking up our rod and net wade confidently into the water to catch that last fish. With luck we shall be home in time for tea, and come what may we shall certainly be home early enough to take our wife out for the evening. We have promised – albeit vaguely – a film and late supper.

By four o'clock we are resigned to missing tea. By five o'clock we have walked round to the other side of the water to cover some easier fish: fish that have not been flogged all day.

By six o'clock, our wife has missed her outing; that limit is as far away as ever, and we are fishing in deadly earnest.

Twenty minutes before we are due back at the boathouse to weigh in, a fool of a fish, the first we have seen since the morning, rises 20 yards on our left at the edge of a weed bed.

Despairingly we throw a nymph at him; and miraculously he takes.

'It is too much of a "gift" to be so easy,' you tell yourself, and are very relieved when the fish is safely netted.

Of course you were never really in doubt as to your ability to get that fourth fish, but it's too bad it had to come so late in the day.

When you get home, no one will accuse you of having a good day out without so much as a thought for your wife or children. No. The television marital comedy has taught them far more effective techniques. She will be so damned sweet about the whole thing, that you'll feel guilty as hell!

Plea for orthodox fly-fishing

To return, however, to the matter of the day's sport. We recall that the three fish taken before lunch were taken in flat-calm water, water which many anglers avoid, yet, like most problems in fishing, there was an answer requiring only a little thought. More importantly, we found an answer within orthodox methods of fly fishing.

There is little doubt that the use of monofilament lines in calm and brilliant weather would enable us to catch more fish than our all-too-obvious fly lines. In connection with long casting, several anglers pointed out in 1958, in letters to the *Fishing Gazette*, that it is quite simple to cast out a fly and bubble float (Wanless's controller is much the same thing) by using a fixed-spool reel and thereby achieve distance and tackle concealment. Without, I would add, having to bother to develop very much technical skill.

I believe the matter was put into perspective by Mr Philip Benton and also by 'Robin Hill' who wrote in May 1958: 'One of the curses of our age is the demand by mediocre performers, whether at work or play, for a levelling down so that those having little ability can compete on level terms with skilled craftsmen. In this case the answer to the controller addicts is: Get out on the water (any pond will do) and practise until you can cast a decent line.'

My own preference for the kind of fishing that goes with light double-taper lines and small flies in no way blinds me to the validity of shooting heads and fast-action rods when great distance is necessary and it is seldom I go to the water without the no 3 outfit described in Chapter 2, all ready for use when occasion demands. But this kind of outfit remains recognizable the world over as fly tackle – and fixed-spool outfits, no matter what you tie on the end, are equally obviously part of a different technique ... as is well established by their exclusion from tournament fly-casting events.

Part of the fun of fly-fishing is the gradual accumulation of the necessary skills. There is certainly much more to fly-fishing than killing fish.

CHAPTER 10

High summer

Mid-July to mid-August is, for many of us, a heart-breaking period. From dawn to sunset the sun beats down mercilessly out of a clear sky on the mirror-like surface of the reservoir, the water of which, needless to say, is crystal clear. Well, maybe! It is as likely that it will be dull with occasional showers, and blowing half a gale to boot. Whatever the weather, we must not blame it too much: it is not the primary cause of small bags. On mature reservoirs the worst enemy for bank fishers is weed, and only slightly less provoking is the changed feeding pattern of the fish. Gone are the days of heavy feeding. The fish are now in good condition, and do not need to feed continuously as they did in May. In addition, the ova are by now well developed, and perhaps beginning to cause the fish some discomfort.

In an average year the water will have dropped some 7 ft by mid-July, and the bottom over which we took fish earlier in the year will be now be dry land. Extending to some 30 yards from the margin and seemingly continuing in an unbroken stretch right round the water is the weed. Do not let it scare you: it is nowhere nearly so dense as it appears at first sight. Move round the water and you will find open bays in the weed, and in other places you will be able to wade out far enough to reach the open water beyond it.

Like the fisherman, the trout prefers open water, and you can be quite certain that if you fish these bays you will be covering trout, which is 90 per cent of the battle. If you find fish rising, then fish for them with a size 9 or 10 Black and Peacock Spider or Brown Nymph. Remember to grease your leader for there may be weed a foot below the surface. If you catch-up on weed as you recover line and the fish still rises, put on a big Fuzzy-Buzzy dry fly and cast so as to lay the nylon across the weed, with the fly 6 in from the edge, in open water. Allow it to sit there until you are quite certain the fish has passed it and refused or until you become bored. If he refuses the sitting fly, try twitching it next time he comes by and be ready for a violent take. By that I mean be ready *NOT* to strike violently as he breaks water or you will almost certainly miss him or break.

This is not the only approach to dry fly angling which the reservoir affords, but it is the approach which is most commonly used and it can be quite effective. It has often taken brown trout which would not look at a wet fly, and particularly those wily birds that feed near the lodge or boat house and which are thrown at every day by perhaps a dozen different anglers. Probably the method succeeds because the fish see nothing of the line.

Ernest Phillips, in a letter to *Fishing Gazette* on 1 December 1951, wrote of a 'school' of dry fly men who fished a reservoir, presumably Thrybergh, near Doncaster. He described how these anglers cast out their flies and sat down to await results, which deservedly were slow to come, for trout abhor lines: they kept out of range of those 'telegraph poles' lying across an otherwise unbroken surface.

I have seen this method in use many times, often enough while the fisherman is eating his sandwiches. Occasionally a fish is taken, and it is surprising how proud the captor becomes of his success fishing 'dry', though what he has done to earn his fish it is hard to say. Naturally, this is not the method used by men such as the late 'Ernie' Kench who studied dry fly tactics in much the same way that I study the wet fly. They present a fly to a rising fish when possible, or cast their dry fly around the edges of weed beds and work the fly very much as a wet fly is worked. Certainly they get fish, but few of them would claim that they take anywhere near so many fish as the wet fly man.

One of my severest critics, an enthusiastic reservoir dry fly fisherman, writing in *Fishing Gazette* stated: 'It is evident Mr Ivens is a wet-fly man, by which means I agree more fish are taken out of still water.' Those words sum up my case. When, as once happened on one of our waters, the season's top score was only thirty-five fish representing twenty-seven days hard fishing with a wet fly, the further handicap which the dry fly places upon the angler is quite unwarranted. Where fish are easy to take the whole situation is changed and a 'dry fly only' rule might be reasonable. Where rainbows are very numerous the dry fly *at times* is as effective as the wet fly.

A few moments ago I referred to dry fly fishing as a luncheon interlude, and it brought to my mind a striking case of the operation of the long arm of coincidence.

During a sweltering July morning of 1950, three of us, old friends, foregathered for lunch at the bridge-hole on a nearby water. The reservoir is divided into two parts by a dam carrying a public roadway. The apparently separated stretches of water are connected by means of a bridge under the roadway.

The bridge-hole, like all bridge-holes, has a good reputation as a holding spot and there are many stories connected with it.

As we ate, Jim recalled how, many years before, an angler had sat where we were, his fly dangling in the water below his feet. The inevitable happened, a trout took the fly; and rod, reel and line were pulled into the water.

Now all three of us had fished the hole at varying times during the morning and not one of us had seen a fish. On hearing the story, my second companion unhitched his fly from the cork of the butt and dropped it into the water. We carried on eating. Some ten minutes later a light breeze through the bridge lifted the line, and immediately an explosion in the water announced a 'take'. My friend grabbed at his rod; the trout – a fish at least 4 lb – bolted through the bridge and broke the leader.

That was the only fish anyone moved that day!

Fishing is full of such surprises.

In these July days few rising fish will be seen after 10 AM and with no fish showing and in brilliant light the best method is 'short-lining'. Find a stretch of the weed with pockets leading to open water, or alternatively a stretch where you can wade to within 8 yards of the edge of the weed and cast beyond and along the edge. Use a point of at least ·010 in and a leaded Alexandra of size 7 or 8. Using a maximum of 15 yards of line, drop your fly in open water; allow it to sink about 15 in and take the line *lightly* between thumb and forefinger below the first ring. Draw the line evenly by carrying the left hand away to the left side of the body, at the same time slowly raising the rod tip as though you were making a very slow pick-up. When the left arm is almost fully extended and the rod is at half past eleven, the rod is accelerated and the fly leaves the water. The spare line is shot out on the forward punch. The line should travel well to the side and low, on the lift, and overhead on the forward punch. The cast is very similar to the downward-cut cast for shooting into wind, except that the low punch is not required. The essential is a continuous motion. The line length remains constant. You deliver the fly; pause; pull with left hand and lift off and throw back; throw forward and shoot to redeliver the fly. Each time the fly drops in a different spot and you search every inch of the open water, particularly the edges of the weed, with a very fast-moving flasher. Fully 50 per cent of takes occur as you lift off, so again, never hold the line tightly. Move fast and cover a lot of water.

As an alternative to the Alexandra, you might find it profitable to use a Jersey Herd until you are followed and then, having found a fish, try for him with a nymph as outlined in Chapter 7.

Fish taken while short-lining are usually big cannibals, and landing them is a problem. Fortunately, most fish make for open water. I tire them, away out, whenever I can, and then when they quieten off I apply pressure and bring them straight to the net. If I am weeded, I merely give them slack and proceed as mentioned in my last chapter. More than once I have skidded a fish across the top of a weed bed, on his tail. It is a dangerous thing to do at any time, but with a tip-actioned rod it would be downright silly.

Since we have mentioned the short-line method of fishing, I would like to deal with its further application.

Fish tend to move into the wind and it usually pays to fish the upwind side of the water. But when the wind is strong and waves beat upon the lee-shore the water there becomes coloured and fish will be found feeding on the creatures stirred from the bottom by the action of the water. The extent to which fish feed in turbid water differs markedly. Over sandy or gravel bottoms brown trout remain close in and will take well. Where, as at Grafham, much of the bottom is clay, the margins can become a thick yellow cloud visible hundreds of yards away and seemingly deserted by fish.

Use an 8 ft steep-taper cast or a Platil knotless taper with a Black and Peacock Spider: black is far more easily seen by the fish in murky water than is any other colour. Assuming that you have a few yards of open water close in at the side, wade well out and move along, dropping the fly about 2 yards from the margin, casting and lifting as you go. It is surprising how close the fish are to the shore in rough water. Fight down your disbelief, and remember that bass fishermen often take good fish by casting their tackle into the surf where the bass are feeding on creatures washed off the bottom by the breakers. I scarcely dare to mention it, but you can create murky water in calm weather by wading backwards, doing a Charleston as you go. You short-line the water you have waded.

Sometimes having found fish feeding well at the surface on the upwind shore, you arrive on the water on the following day to find the wind has veered through 180° and is blowing off the opposite shore. I like to fish the upwind shore, but now and again, and usually immediately following a sudden change in the wind such as that just mentioned, fishing the upwind shore fails to give results. The answer may lie in the fact that the fish have not yet adjusted themselves to the change in the wind. After all, the surface drift in the new wind direction takes some little time to develop, and until it develops and the instinct of the fish to head into the current is triggered off, there is little reason for the fish to move over to the new upwind shore. Again there may well have been good feeding grounds where you were fishing yesterday and many fish will continue to feed there no matter from where the wind may blow.

I think it unlikely that creatures blown on to the water from the upwind shore have much to do with an upwind migration, for surface food has little attraction for the vast majority of our fish. The surface current shown in the diagram is more likely to cause migration.

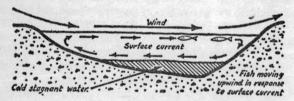

Diagram 10.1

Perhaps the most striking illustration in my experience of this tendency to delay migration for some time after a change in wind direction occurred on 22 May 1948. On the previous day I had taken a limit in shallow water at the narrow, upper end of

Hollowell Reservoir, the wind being east-north-east. On the morning of the 22nd the wind was west-north-west and I fished from 9 AM to 11 AM at a point immediately opposite the spot I had fished on the previous day, without an offer. I moved round to my old spot and within thirty minutes had my limit, short-lining both the margin and the open water. Of course it was my birthday!

These uses of the short line are not confined to high summer; they can be applied at any time in the season.

And now to our friend the 'sticklebacker'.

This thug appears when the fry are seen as patches of black needles on the surface of the water near the dam and round the weed beds. The fry appear in their millions about the middle of July and the fish go mad in an orgy of feastings.

When the fish first become aware, as it were, of this new food form, their attack is somewhat haphazard; but later it has all the markings of a planned military operation. The fish cruise slowly behind the shoal of fry, shepherding it towards the dam or into a bay in the weed. Suddenly you see the fry begin to skitter along the surface; a furrow appears behind the fry, and then the water is broken by a series of slashing sallies on the part of the trout as he takes his toll. It is sometimes said that the fish dashes in with his mouth wide open, but though I have watched a trout do it hundreds of times, often at a distance of only 6 ft, I still have not been able to see just how he takes. He moves like lightning on roller-skates and can only just be seen through the flurry of spray he throws up. It is the most exciting thing in fishing.

For the first week of the sticklebacking season the trout are easy to take, but it is no use casting continuously. Spot your fish, check up on his beat and lay your line out on the water well away from the fish. As soon as you see the fry skitter at the surface, pick up line and throw ahead of them and across their path if possible; recover line slowly. Usually you will be taken within three seconds, but if the fish ignores you, keep drawing; he may take you as he turns away from the shoal when your fly will be the only moving object in sight. I usually find the Black and Peacock Spider ideal for this fishing, as it fishes high in the water. However, if you are refused several times, change to a big fly, an Alexandra or a Green and Brown Nymph, and fish it fast across his nose as he furrows the water. If he still refuses –

give up. You are fishing for a laddie who knows all the answers. I shall deal with these fish in my next chapter, but since in the early part of this form of feeding the feeding period may last only thirty minutes, you have no time to waste and should look for another fish. Late in August, many fish feed on sticklebacks for the whole day, and then you will have time to plan a campaign.

Remember then, that this is one occasion when a single well-placed and well-timed cast will do more good than two hours' flogging.

In July and August there are very few reservoirs and lakes where the 'buzzer' correctly fished will not kill well. The essentials are an area of water known to hold fish, although they remain unseen, great persistence and concentration and the ultimate in quiet presentation.

The late afternoon and early evening are the best periods but when buzzers are about, fish are probably feeding on the nymph most of the day. Buzzer fishing is for me a calm-weather pursuit. Provided you can reach the known feeding area with a double-taper line let that be your choice. Use a one-yard sinking tip to your line and as long a leader as you can handle. Whilst you want the terminal tackle submerged, you also need the greatest distance possible between the all too obvious line and your flies.

First choice is the Black Buzzer to a size 10 hook, the dropper being 3 ft from the line and the tail up to 12 ft behind the dropper. Wade with extreme quiet; keep your feet still; cast without splash; allow the line-tip and leader to sink and commence drawing when you judge the tail fly to be about 3 ft down.

I find it best to figure-of-eight wind as slowly as will just keep the flies moving. Line wake is entirely absent. Cyril Inwood draws the line perhaps a foot, which tends to bring the flies upward in the water, and his brief pause before the next draw allows them to sink – a common swimming action of many forms of aquatic life.

The take is usually a quiet, decisive, slow draw of the line which, if the fish is large, will surely break you if your rod is pointing down the line – as mine was twice one day in 1968 when I was fishing Two Lakes in Hampshire. I broke on each occasion on what felt rather like ocean-going submarines. The method is so peaceful, seemingly so little is happening, that the result of lost concentration is nearly always disaster, not least because fish that take the buzzer seem to be above average weight. Keep your rod tip at an angle to the line . . . always.

Second choice for me is the 'claret' version of the buzzer if the black fails, and sometimes I fish a cast with two colours at a time. It really doesn't matter very much; the realistic shape and size of your dressings and the slow disturbance-free fishing technique together achieve the prime essential of angler concealment.

The buzzer may continue effective through the evening and the late-evening rise, but most of us prefer to throw at rising fish when it is possible to do so and about two hours before dark we move from the marginal shallows towards deep water.

Provided that the fish have not fed hard all day, there should be good fishing in the evening rise. You may have daytime and evening feeding of course; but it is unlikely.

Taken by and large, the dam is usually as productive as any spot in the evening. Often it is the only place where fish rise within reach before nightfall.

The method of fishing to brown trout in the evening rise is simple. Using a size 9 Black and Peacock Spider or any other wet fly which will fish high in the water, cast to the rising fish exactly as though you were presenting a dry fly, and draw slowly. If you have no success, you must assume the fish are moving fast and that you are not covering them quickly enough. Your best method then, is to ignore the rises and fish slowly through the area of activity. If you still remain fishless, change to a size 11 fly; cast; let it sink, and watch your leader carefully. Very often fish which refuse a horizontally-moving fly will readily seize a sinking one. This behaviour is not confined to the evening rise, but occurs more often then. The take, as I have said before, may appear as a straightening of the leader, or the disappearance of the leader 'through a hole in the water'.

Fish which head-and-tail are hard to hit, largely because we train ourselves to tighten the moment we see, feel, hear or sense anything happening. The head and tailer takes on the way down and we usually strike as he breaks water, which is much too soon.

For reasons that will be discussed in Chapter 17, trout tend to swim and take ever closer to the surface as the light fails. Where one hour before dark the whole of the leader will probably be sunk, at dusk the fish will be so close to the surface that the leader will need to be greased over most if not all of its length to keep the fly high in the water and in the trout's window. At last light, fish may show continually and as the intensity of rising increases so offers seem to become fewer.

At this point Mike finds a large Butcher fished fast will often take a fish or two, whilst my preference is for a tandem-dressed B & P Spider fished very slow and deep or very deep on the sunken line. Certainly, as darkness falls, I swear by this method and in high summer hook into good and very good fish on perhaps every other outing during the ten minutes' fishing immediately after the dramatic cessation of surface feeding as night falls.

This use of the sunken line is by no means confined to late-evening fishing. At any time of the day sunk lines may be used to get beetle-type lures and nymphs, including small ones (sizes 10 to 12), down to the bottom from the dam. It is astonishing too how often good bags can be taken when on burningly hot days there is not a fish to be seen at the surface. Usually, fish hook themselves against the drag of the sunk line and can often be felt to nip the fly several times before finally getting hold of it. In wet fly fishing it is the manner in which the fish takes that determines whether you hook him or not . . . the angler influences the outcome very little.

May I repeat an earlier word of warning? Always roll a sunken line onto the surface before you attempt to lift off to recast.

The effects of high water temperatures

High water temperatures tend to sicken trout, and above 70°F brown trout are unlikely to be caught. During the period 20 to 29 July 1959, 73°F was recorded at Chew Valley Reservoir when, despite the very intensive fishing customary there, very few trout were caught and those, almost without exception, were rainbows just over 1 lb in weight.

During this period, John Hodges and I had the good fortune on 28 July to fish a nearby closely preserved and seldom-fished private lake. Although the water temperature was 70½°F, our five hours' fishing produced twenty-two trout from 1 lb to 2 lb 2 oz and we returned another eight or nine fish only slightly smaller. Rainbows and brownies were about equally represented. From 7 to 9.30 PM activity was as intensive as anything I have ever experienced, and most of the fish fought much harder than one would expect with such a high temperature.

By contrast with Chew Valley Reservoir, the water was almost pea-green in colour indicative of an enormous algal crop. Photosynthetic action of the algae could have produced an oxygen concentration higher than that normal for the water temperature and this is the only satisfying explanation I can find for the excellent sport we enjoyed.

Three-quarters of our fish were caught in flat calm on the Green Nymph. Most fish took while the nymph was deeply sunk and moving slowly, but others took either while it was sinking, or, occasionally, as it was lifted after being allowed to sink; that is to say without any line being recovered.

The nocturnal trout

In high summer when sea-trout fishing is at its best, we depart for the river after a leisurely dinner and start to fish perhaps an hour after sunset, at any time up to 11.30 PM in the North. From then until an hour after dawn, sport can be continuous and the bag may weigh 30 lb or more by 4 AM. The fish we have caught are *Salmo trutta*, the surviving migratory form of the same *Salmo trutta* (brown trout) of our reservoirs and lakes.

I have touched briefly in earlier chapters on the usefulness of reservoir techniques, flies, rods and so on when fishing for sea trout and salmon. It is high time that we reversed the process and examined the application of sea-trout philosophies to reservoir brown trout.

It is overwhelmingly evident that brown trout and particularly big brown trout in high summer, behave like sea trout and may best be caught in sea-trout manner. In short, by night fishing.

Obviously the rules of the water may be a limiting factor, but there are many lakes on which there is no night-fishing prohibition. West Loch, Coldingham, in Berwickshire is typical of these, and is famous for the numerous trout over 10 lb which are regularly taken when the big sedge flies are on the water on a still summer night.

Several of my Yorkshire friends fish Windermere to good effect in April and May but give it never a thought in July and August, and I have no doubt they are right so far as daytime fishing is concerned. But can they say, from knowledge, that it fishes badly on a warm summer night? Is it not probable that by adopting the night fly they would take those 'ferox' which at present are caught only on the troll?

There are, of course, several West Country reservoirs where night fishing is proscribed, but where the rule is not noticeably enforced, probably because the waters have become inland resorts and wise authority turns a blind eye while fishing methods are fair, to the advantage of many visitors who would otherwise go home blank during very hot spells.

On these waters, night tactics have evolved. One of the most successful exponents used to stand on the shore, a few yards back from the water and lightly throw a short line to search the shallow margins of the lake. The fish were caught in water only inches deep, and apart from my preference for kneeling on the bank he could be said to have been using probably the most successful technique for taking sea trout lying in the thin water at the tail of a pool. It only remains to add that he was not a night sea-trout angler: he developed the method to suit reservoir brown trout. Regrettably he died a few months after I introduced him to night fishing on the Torridge at which he quickly achieved the same mastery that attended all his fishing.

Since sea trout and brown trout are the same fish, it is illogical while stocks are well maintained to allow night fishing for the one and prohibit it for the other. During July and August night fishing could well be permitted for reservoir brown trout, subject to fair fishing. This, after all, is but a small extension of bank-fishing rules at several waters which already permit fishing from one hour before sunrise to one hour after sunset. In midsummer this excludes only three to four hours of the night!

CHAPTER 11

Late August and the backend

For the last two weeks of August, and possibly the first two weeks of September as well, the sticklebacker will provide most of the sport for the bank fisher. Few other fish move during the day, and the sticklebacker makes his presence so obvious that it is not surprising that most of these fish are 'flogged' very heavily.

By the time the trout have been feeding on fry for a fortnight most of them know that there is an unpleasant connection between the man on the bank and the line which drops on the water. Having recognized the connection, the fish continue to feed as though the angler and his gear were not there at all. Their heavy feeding among the fry continues unabated, often within feet of the angler, but they very seldom make a mistake and take the fly. It is essential that the angler recognize when he is up against an educated fish, and change his tactics before too much time has been lost. If I may generalize again, I would say that any sticklebacker which has its beat in a frequently fished position requires special treatment, as does also any fish which has refused a well-presented fly three times.

I had an excellent example of the futility of fishing for these smart operators by orthodox methods on 24 September 1949. The fish were mad-on from 9 AM to 6 PM. There must have been forty fish working the shoals of fry along the first 200 yards of the dam, and all six of us flogged these fish until we were reduced to incoherent, impotent bewilderment. The ultimate in frustration, the nadir of self confidence.

At about 2 PM I moved away from the others, and threw at a solitary fish down by the valve tower. Three times I cast; three times he rose, and three times I missed him. That fish was the first that anyone had risen that day. I sat down for a moment to smoke a cigarette, calm down and think things over. I was a full 20 yards from the fish when I rose it, and I was certain that no one else had fished for it that day; perhaps that was the answer.

I moved on down to the shallow bay at the far end of the dam, and immediately noticed several fish working the fry not more than 5 yards from the margin. I knelt down well back from the water and waited for the fish to move towards me. To cut a short story shorter, in twenty minutes I made three casts, and took three fish. I was then joined by two other anglers who, seeing the fish still feeding confidently, flogged away at them. The fish were not at all put out by lines and flies flopping all over the place: they continued operations among the fry; but none of them made a mistake from that moment. I left the water early, but so far as I know, no other fish were taken that day. I learnt later that the sticklebackers went down at about 6 PM and as was only to be expected after such heavy daytime feeding, there was no evening rise despite a quantity of fly on the water.

Whenever I find myself up against an educated fish, I follow certain definite tactics based on two fundamental necessities. Firstly, the fish must never see me until he is hooked; and secondly, he must see the fly before he sees the leader or line.

Before fishing, I watch the fish carefully to find the limits of his beat. If he is more than 10 yards from the shore, I wade out; place myself 20 yards from the end of his beat, and wait for him to work towards me. I usually use a Brown and Green Nymph, size 7 or 8 (remember its minnowish appearance?) for this work, and drop it *well ahead* of the fish and along the line of his beat. I draw slowly until he either takes or passes it. If the latter, I continue drawing until I can pick up the line with no possibility

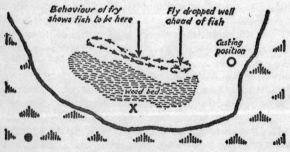

Diagram 11.1

of the fish being near to the inevitable slight disturbance of the surface which occurs on picking up.

This diagram shows the beat of a typical sticklebacker, and my probable approach to a fish in such a position. Unless it is quite impossible to fish the ends of the beat, I never cast across the line of advance of the fish. All too often when I do cast from a position such as 'X' in the diagram, the leader drops very near to the fish, and the chance of taking him after such treatment is almost nil. True, there is always a daft'un.

On several occasions, having failed with a large Green and Brown Nymph, I have changed to a size 11 Brown Nymph and taken the fish first cast. Which again argues the pointlessness of the exact or close imitation. To further bewilder the reader as to what goes on in the minds of these fish of ours, let us place it on record that E.K. took a number of difficult fish each year by floating a dry fly on their beat. Often enough fish taken in this way are very large.

Surely, if ever proof were needed of the fact that fish will take anything which might be food once the urge to feed is upon them, it is supplied by the 5 lb trout which having fed for hours on fry, suddenly dashes at a Coch-y-bondhu and seizes it.

Nevertheless, these occurrences are exceptions and E.K.'s success should not persuade you that the method is anything but a last resort to be used when all other methods have failed.

It is not, of course, solely the attractions of the fry and stickleback shoals that bring the brown trout back into the shallows in September though it is reasonable to suppose that the fish are likely to congregate where the food supply is best, the onset of spawning is probably the dominant factor in the migration to shallow water – the autumn counterpart of the outward migration in spring.

Whilst a fish's maturity season is fairly closely determined by genetic inheritance, the actual date of spawning is influenced among other things by water temperature, spawning occurring earlier in cold autumns. In the Midlands brown-trout spawning will be in full swing in an average year from early November to mid-December and odd pairs may spawn as early as mid-October or as late as February though many 'late' fish will retain and absorb their ova. In a cold summer and autumn the whole cycle may be a fortnight earlier. And the North will be similarly earlier than the Midlands.

Although some of the nutrients for the enlargement and maturing of ova and milt derive from the body's store of proteins, fats and salts, heavy feeding at the backend also contributes. Trout in this respect are rather like mammals: appetite increases markedly as a mother-to-be feeds to support two ... or more.

The striking fact is that the inshore migration to which we fish on most reservoirs is solely that of the brown trout. Our season, ending everywhere on 30 September, or 15 October, has closed too early to get the benefit of the rainbow-trout inward migration which at Grafham appears, from bankside walks in winter 1968, to occur in late November.

The important fact that the backend angler must not lose sight of is that the presence of the fish in the shallows stems from a biological need to be there. The pre-spawning urge to go shallow, and maybe to seek suitable bottom on which to spawn, appears to over-ride the impulse to flee, but not the feelings of fear if the cessation of feeding in the presence of an angler is anything to go by.

When trout are swimming at the margins the need for concealment and special fishing tactics, limiting wading perhaps, are greater than ever.

From July to September, the silverhorns fly appears in great numbers. My knowledge of entomology is strictly limited and the scientific name *Athripsodes cinereus* may perhaps convey as little to you as to me; but if I describe it as a small grey-brown sedge with antennae about ½ in long, you will probably know what insect I refer to as a 'silverhorns'. If this fly is going to appear on the water in the evening you will usually find them lying-up in the grasses during the daytime. At dusk, provided the wind is not more than 8 mph to 10 mph, they fly over the water, knot, and tumble on to the surface where the trout are waiting for them.

I know of no other fly which will cause the wild surface-activity occasioned by the silverhorns. I have seen a stretch of unbroken surface become a seething maelstrom in two minutes: where not one fish was to be seen, hundreds appeared as the first flies fluttered across the surface.

The rise is usually very localized. Perhaps 100 yards of the marginal shallows will be boiling with fish while the remainder

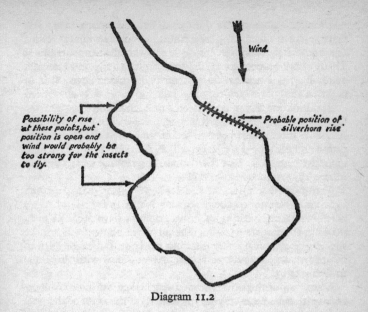

Diagram 11.2

of the water continues undisturbed. Fortunately, it is possible to make a fairly accurate guess as to where it will take place.

The rise always occurs on the upwind shore and usually at a point where the wind is blowing off and slightly along the shore as in diagram 11.2.

In choosing your spot, you should remember that the wind usually drops to light airs at dusk, and that the edge of the ripple which is within reach at 7 PM may be 200 yards away at 8.30 PM. Where the wind blows off-and-along the shore, the edge of the ripple should remain within reach. The edge of the ripple is very important for it is the point at which the wind strikes the water, and the flies are being carried by that wind.

Having found silverhorns in the grasses during the day, I spend the time after 7 PM preparing for the evening rise. If several of us are fishing together, we spread out and watch the water over a 400 yards stretch. When the rise starts, we all hasten to the spot and fish within yards of one another. When it is all over, we wade ashore slowly and try to think up a few new reasons for having failed to land a fish, despite having had many offers. Therein lies the point of this discourse: very few fish are taken during the fifteen to thirty crazy minutes which the rise usually occupies. I have in front of me at this moment a diary entry which records that from 8 PM to 9 PM on 16 August 1948, I rose, pricked and lost no fewer than eleven fish in addition to those which rose and failed to connect at all. I tried everything: rod point down, rod horizontal and at 90° to the line, striking at the rise, waiting for the pull . . . all to no purpose. A friend, fishing dry, fared no better: he rose fish but failed to connect. This type of experience is so common that I have long toyed with the idea that the fish are not feeding at all, but are merely sporting.

At this point it becomes necessary to say that the 1948 experience mentioned above remains as true today . . . while we are thinking and writing of brown trout. I have at times been very much more successful fishing to rainbow trout in the silverhorns rise using very different methods, but there seem to be special factors involved and I prefer to deal with this topic in Chapter 17.

Almost all of the brown trout I have taken during the silverhorns rise have been very lightly hooked at the front of the jaws and, more often than not, the fly has fallen out when the fish was in the net. However, it is great fun provided your mental stability is not in question, and you do sometimes pick up a brace of fish to compensate for other disappointments.

I have noticed that immediately the rise starts I often land a fish, and, again, during the period between the end of the rise and darkness when all is quiet I sometimes take a second fish. During the peak of the rise I merely miss fish galore.

During the rise I find the Black and Peacock Spider my most effective fly, and size 10 is quite large enough. I usually fish greased leader so that the fly fishes shallow, and I see as much as possible of the take. I entirely ignore the individual rises (the fish are moving very fast and in no predictable direction) and merely cast and draw my fly through the area of activity.

Stick to the Black and Peacock Spider, even if it does not produce a rise straightway, and keep on fishing over the same water after the rise is over, sinking the leader and perhaps using a line with a sinking tip so as to get the fly down deep.

This rapid change of style of fishing in the critically valuable last minutes of the day can be accomplished without loss of time only if you have the other outfit ready assembled. It has become noticeable in recent years that most of the regulars tackle up two rods at the beginning of the day and switch from one to the other to alternate from deep to surface fishing as frequently as fish behaviour or personal inclination demands.

May I say it again: during the last few casts of the day you will be tired and mentally relaxed after the excitement of the evening rise. Keep your rod point at an angle to the line in readiness for a smash take.

John Rowe has always refused to accept my hypothesis that trout were not feeding but sporting during the silverhorns rise. He believes they are actually taking a large buff sedge which is on the water at the same time, and has fished effectively with a large buff Fuzzy-Buzzy dry fly. His usual method is to leave it stationary on the water and give it a twitch, or draw it as a 'wake' lure when a trout rises near by.

In contrast with John's dry fly technique, Jim Robinson catches fish on a big fly stripped fast through the area of activity ... You pays your money and you takes your pick!

Look at it as you may, the silverhorns rise remains an enigma.

There is a tendency amongst anglers to fish larger flies because it is getting dark. I have experimented on this point and my conclusion is that it pays to continue using the same size of fly as was successful before darkness fell, for brown trout can see a small fly quite as well as sea trout do. This is not to say that there is no point in changing to a tandem-dressed Black & Peacock Spider or Black Knight ... these obviously represent something entirely different in the way of food.

The last fortnight of the season sees the fish reverting to their daytime surface-feeding habits of May and June. If you can get away from the work-bench or office during this period, you are almost certain to find good sport and perhaps a 'case fish', though being heavy with spawn the fight is a trial of strength rather than a thrilling, dashing affair. Small nymphs are sometimes astonishingly successful with the portly matrons which tend perhaps to prefer a delicate titbit rather than meat-and-two-veg. Most of us have encountered this at some time or other in our private lives too!

CHAPTER 12

Some observations on surface feeding

The trout's sporadic surface foraging has caused him to be widely regarded as a surface-feeding fish. But you and I know better, and when we fish a lake or reservoir we concentrate on the things we cannot see and try to fish our flies at the depth at which most trout are feeding, sometimes to the extent of ignoring fish rising near by. Usually we prosper, but now and then there appears at the keeper's hut some fugitive from the Deep South who has not read the best books on lakes, but is nevertheless carrying the only brace of fish of the day – fish caught on a dry fly. Needless to say, being a gentleman, he will be infuriatingly modest about his achievement and will forget all those occasions when the situation was far, far different.

Surface-feeding fish are a problem of their own, and since the first edition appeared I have given them a great deal of thought. The number of fish which will habitually feed at the surface depends principally on the type of lake in which they live. Deep, rocky-bedded lakes produce a less abundant crop of subsurface food than shallow lakes with a rich mud bottom. Where there is a paucity of snail, mussel and shrimp, trout much more readily incline to a diet of insects, and in deep and possibly acid waters surface feeding is an important activity. Conversely, in shallow lakes with an abundance of bulky, appetite-satisfying creatures to be found in weed beds and mud, the trout tend to ignore surface food; a general rise is, in fact, of sufficiently infrequent occurrence in daytime to justify the basing of one's whole technique on deep fishing with the wet fly. Nonetheless, individual fish will rise persistently throughout the whole day. Why they do so, I do not know; sufficient is it that they exist and can be caught at times when our customary methods of wet fly fishing have failed to produce results. I have often found it well worth while to walk the banks until I locate one of these conveniently abnormal trout. Sometimes he will be the only fish taken that day.

Where are rising trout likely to be found? The best way to answer that question is to tell you what I can about surface food in lakes.

The flies which seem to bring on the boldest surface feeding are lake-olives, silverhorns, sedges, flying ants, midges, craneflies and, where the beasts occur, mayflies. Flying ants appear only for a few hours every season so we can ignore them in this generalized comment.

Few lake anglers will quarrel with my statement that the occurrence or non-occurrence of a general rise does not primarily depend on the quantity of fly on the water. The deciding factor appears to be the strength of the wind, calms, or near-calms being conducive to trout feeding at the surface. I incline to the belief that this has much to do with the fact that trout can see a fly at the surface more readily than they can see it in a lop. Rising in rough weather is usually to the larger flies more readily seen from below – the olives, damsel flies, sedges, craneflies and mayflies.

But for most of the season the only flies present can be classified as small, very small and completely inimitable. On windy days you may fish without seeing a rise, then with a drop in the wind, large areas of calm water appear and a few fish will then show themselves.

At one time I felt that the calm had made visible rises which previously had been undetected in the broken surface. I am now convinced that this conclusion was wrong for I have often, when wading, found nearby water become calm and fish begin to rise so close to me that I must have seen or heard them had they risen when the surface was rippled.

The explanation appears to lie in the fact that over calm water lies almost calm air – air which will not deter feeble flying insects (and these are usually the small insects) from forsaking shelter to fly out over the water. I have already touched on this point in my references to the silverhorns in Chapter 11.

That we regularly observe trout to feed enthusiastically at the surface in the evening, results, I am sure, from the fact that calms then occur more frequently than at any other time of the day with the possible exception of the dawn period. Encouraged by the calm, insects leave their hide-outs or cease hovering in the shelter of rushes and trees and fly out to lay their eggs. If the calm persists the rise may continue for an hour or more, but it usually ceases before dark, though it may begin again during darkness. The return of the breeze, dispelling the calm, brings the rise rapidly to an end, though individual fish may continue to show. Again, as we all know, the failure of a wind to drop at dusk means that chances of a general rise are remote.

You may have noticed that during daytime calms a very few insects will attempt to lay their eggs only to be blown out of control across the water, victim of the wind's caprices. It is easy to see that the wind's action selects-out insects with a daytime-laying tendency leaving the species as a whole instinctively evening egg-layers.

Fishing for surface feeders

In the early-morning calm, the lee shore, to which all spinners trapped in the surface film will have drifted during the night, is likely to be worth a search. It pays to cast only when a fish has risen and revealed his line of advance so that you can place a fly ahead of him with reasonable chance of his seeing and taking it. The first airs of the day will disperse the scum and you must then look elsewhere for a riser.

No matter how featureless the surroundings of a lake may be, there is always some irregularity of the terrain, a promontory, or a tree or copse which will divide the wind and cause it to approach the water in two streams which continue their separate paths leaving a lane of calm air *and calm water* between them. It is seldom that fish cannot be found surface feeding somewhere along these lanes.

Calm lanes which run directly out from the margins are of little help to the bank angler, for the fish may be hundreds of yards from the shore. But by going to a part of the water where the wind is blowing along and slightly offshore, you will often find that a lane can be covered for several hundred yards of its length and it is then up to you to locate your fish. Fish feeding in the lanes will usually rise time and again in roughly the same position: they have no need to go hunting when the wind, like the current in a river, carries their food to them. The parts of the lane to watch are the rippled edges of the calm – fully 90 per cent of the rises occur there and the fish, which are usually very close to the surface, will frequently ignore (or perhaps fail to see) flies that alight off the line of their beat.

It is impossible to over-emphasize the importance of calm lanes to the angler. Drifting down one of them in a boat will produce far more rises than a drift through rippled or rough water ten or a hundred yards to one side. Since it is practically impossible to fish a fly really deep from a drifting boat the advantage of fishing where trout are near the surface is obvious. It has been my daytime experience that most takes occur as the boat approaches the downwind shore and shallower water. Not all lanes are equally productive of fish; some will pass through areas where subsurface food is plentiful and where the stocks are therefore greater.

Observation plus thought equals fish

The significance of calm lanes first became apparent to me on 27 August 1953. It struck me when I returned home that I had never seen anything published on the subject, so when the experience was repeated, I wrote this account of that first day, and it was published in the *Fishing Gazette* under the same title as I now use for a sub-heading.

> I arrived at Hollowell reservoir at noon to find the wind setting straight down the water and into the dam. I hold no brief for any creed regarding desirable wind directions* but it so happens that this reservoir lying north to south often becomes so rough in a north wind as to make deep fishing with a nymph impossible and slow working of the fly most difficult over the whole bank except for the three short stretches which lie east to west.
>
> There were waves 2 ft high breaking against the dam and I decided to cross over to the other side and walk up to the top end where the water would be calmer. Like most good intentions mine were destined not to be realized for I found myself unable to pass by the many good spots on the way up to the narrows. It was perhaps as well that I did wade out into the water at one of my favourite spots and cover the nearby deeps with a fast-moving flasher.

* Poor sport during east winds at Grafham tempts me to modify this opinion.

After casting for some minutes I found myself listening hard to identify and locate the source of the sounds for which the wind and wave would not entirely account. No matter how intently I looked for the tell-tale swirl which persists for several seconds after a rise I could see no sign of a movement and somewhat puzzled I waded ashore. After watching carefully for some twenty minutes, I slowly walked along the bank fully alert for signs of fish feeding, though I well knew that in such rough water my only hope lay in seeing the fish as he rose.

It was then I became fully aware of narrow lanes of calm water amid the general tumult. I had seen them stretching the whole length of the reservoir as I walked across the dam, but somehow their significance had failed to register.

As I stood, on this stormy afternoon, watching the near edge of a lane running almost parallel with the shore I at last saw a rise and having seen one immediately began to see several others. These then were the fish I had heard but which I had failed to see when wading.

I entered the water and began casting. It was no easy matter reaching the necessary 25 yards with a strong wind on my right shoulder and it was not long before I dropped my line heavily and the fish stopped rising. I wasted no time, but went ashore and walked 200 yards up the bank to the next small promontory from which vantage point the lane was within easy reach.

As I waded out a fish rose quietly and I covered him immediately. He swirled in the vicinity of the fly and I felt nothing and neither was there any line movement: clearly, a refusal. I changed to a Black and Peacock Spider and a few moments later was again refused. Could this be one of those rare occasions when only a dry fly would prove acceptable? I changed to a Fuzzy-Buzzy: the fish continued rising all around it, but made no mistake. I changed to a small hackled olive in case the fish were only to be interested in a fly resembling those on the water, but this too was ignored. There was far too much line drag outside the lane of calm water to make deep-and-slow tactics possible and I had no alternative but to wade quietly ashore and think things out.

The fish appeared to be swimming high in the water but judging from the seldom varying position of the rises were not cruising. I decided to employ calm-water-and-sunshine tactics, that is to say, a light leader with as fine a point as was safe, and a very lightly dressed Alexandra on a size 12 hook. I greased all but the last few inches of the cast, soaked the tiny fly to ensure its ready sinking, and moved up the water to the next point.

Here, the lane was about 12 yards from the bank and wading would have been folly, for fish as close to the margin as that often cruise right into and along the side in search of food.

I sat down well back from the water and presently a fish rose on the near edge of the lane 20 yards to my right. I moved up and knelt down opposite the fish and about 6 yards from the water. I made a few false casts to adjust my distance and dropped the line on to the margin water to my left and, as I trusted, well away from the fish. I waited. Presently he rose and as he did so I lifted the line from the water, made one false cast to change direction, and covered him. In all probability it took longer to read about than to do. The moment I began to recover line and move the fly he took me confidently and was duly played out and netted.

Another fish now rose 30 yards higher up. Over-sure of myself I bungled the cast badly and the fly hit the water like a careless coarse-fish-angler's plummet. The fish, as was only to be expected, stopped rising.

I walked down to the fish which had refused me earlier, and saw a rise straight away. Apart from the fact that I had to wade in order to reach the lane I adopted exactly the same tactics as had proved successful only a few minutes before. He rose; I lifted my line and covered him; he took the fly, was hooked, played out and landed. I had visions of an easy limit but it was not to be: for these were the only two sizeable fish taken that day.

Two friends were using the boat when all this happened. Seeing that I had moved away to look for another fish, they drifted down the lane in which I had taken my brace. Although there were still several fish rising – I later took three there which were undersized – they saw never a fin. It is easy to fail to see rises from a boat, particularly when it is drifting fast.

Perhaps those who so often represent lake-trouting as being

mere long-distance casting and high-speed recovery of the fly will ponder the manner of the taking of these two fish.

Fishing for surface feeders

Surface-feeding fish can often be found at the ripple margin on the upwind shore, but fishing under these conditions has been adequately covered elsewhere.

If you intend to fish the dry fly you will find Fuzzy-Buzzies and Palmer dressings preferable since they float excellently and are visible in a ripple even at the distances customary when bank fishing. The dry fly is, nevertheless, seldom so effective as the wet, because, as autopsies prove conclusively, the rising trout is also feeding hard below the surface. Examine the oesophagus of the fish you kill and you will find an amazingly wide selection of food creatures, the surface insects few in number and well mixed with the subsurface forms. It remains fact, over twenty years after writing my comments on the silverhorns rise as a time of sporting rather than feeding, that I have never identified a silverhorns in the stomach contents of a fish taken in the silverhorns rise.

Generally, a deeply sunk fly will prove less effective than one near the surface because the fish is high in the water and may actually swim over the top of a deep fly. Greasing the upper part of the leader so that the fly fishes only inches below the surface, is a sound policy, or alternatively, in absence of weed you could fish a dropper and thus fish both shallow and deep water at the same time. The number of surface-feeding fish which will take the dropper is high. Taken by and large, flies used near the surface should be more lightly dressed than those for deep fishing. To put the dressing customary on a size 12 hook on to a hook three sizes larger will give you a surface-fishing wet fly with a hookhold adequate for a prolonged fight.

The most difficult information to obtain about a rising fish, and the most necessary, is his speed of movement. On 13 June 1953, I threw for an hour at fish which were rising in leisurely manner and apparently swimming quite slowly. I had not an offer. At about 8.30 PM it became almost calm and immediately after a slow rolling rise, well out of casting range, I saw a furrow shoot across the water to be followed by a second lazy rise 25 yards from the first. I had thought it impossible that the fish were cruising at such high speed, and equally impossible for so violent a checking of speed not to be accompanied by swirl at the surface. Shortly afterwards, a fish rose 40 yards to my left while moving towards me and I threw about 25 yards in the general direction of his advance, my fly being taken almost as soon as it hit the water. Exactly the same thing happened half an hour later. The stomachs of both fish were crammed with tiny larvae, two or three sedge pupa being present in the oesophagus.

The pattern of rapid movement seems to come to an end from thirty to forty-five minutes after sundown. If you are fortunate enough at dusk to be fishing a part of the marginal waters into which several fish have moved, the most likely fly to be taken is that which drops bang in the centre of the ring. Particularly is this so with fish that rise behind you only feet from the bank.

Often on these occasions, there is no pluck or draw to tell you when to tighten; your almost stationary fly is taken as it sinks and before you commence to recover line. The only indication of the take may be a slight swirl, where you think your fly is and you should tighten and hope that this was the take and not, as is sometimes the case, the purposive movement of the trout towards your fly!

Chucking and chancing

Apart from the calculated campaigns against rising fish which we have just discussed is the matter of surface fishing in areas where no fish are to be seen moving. By and large it is not effective, but, paradoxically, appears to give its best results over very deep water. A dry fly here will probably give as good results as a wet fly, particularly in flat calms since it will sit up like a haystack and can be left motionless; in other words it can be fished without line-wake.

Conclusions

Coping for several years with the problems associated with fishing for persistent risers has made it possible to reach the following conclusions.

(i) Ripple-edge or bottom feed may hold fish poised almost stationary when they may be taken by dropping the fly in the ring of the rise.

(ii) In calm water with no ripple-edge fish may cruise at high speed over a wide area frequently changing course, when throwing ahead of them becomes very much a matter of chance.

(iii) In deep water, fish may cruise at depth and will then observe a wide expanse of surface. Fish may then see and take even flies which land astern of them.

(iv) Slow, rolling rises with back-fin showing can occur with both slow- and fast-moving trout: a tail-wagging disappearance is, however, usually indicative of leisurely advance.

(v) Splashy rising may indicate sporting rather than feeding and is usually evident in fish of less than 2 lb. Splashy risers are frequently seen to miss naturals to which they have risen, and may rise again and again to the same fly, or 'knot' of flies, before finally taking or leaving it/them unharmed.

(vi) Relatively few fish in an area show at the surface: many remain feeding unseen below and will take flies fished even at the bottom.

(vii) Choice of pattern seems to have little bearing on results: style of fishing is, as ever, the governing factor.

(viii) A sinking but otherwise motionless fly will sometimes take fish when other methods fail.

(ix) It will be noticeable that fish taken in the evening rise are usually in above-average condition.

(x) An evening rise is never dull, merely gloriously infuriating.

CHAPTER 13

Stalking big trout:
a discussion with Barrie Welham

In the last few years Barrie Welham has probably taken more really big trout than any other British angler. What follows is an edited transcription of a taped discussion lasting nearly two hours one evening in February 1969.

TOM: *How many fish over 6 lb have you taken?*

BARRIE: Without looking it up I am not sure; but I think about seven or eight.

TOM: *And have all these been from Two Lakes?*

BARRIE: No, I had a 6 lb brown out of Chew, and another from Grafham, plus a third in Ireland; but all the others came from Two Lakes.

TOM: *Clearly, Two Lakes is a water you fish a lot. Just how long have you been fishing there?*

BARRIE: I think I am in my seventh or eighth season; but I had one year when I didn't fish.

TOM: *Were you always so successful?*

BARRIE: No. When I started there I couldn't catch anything. I took a rod in June, just after the cream had gone. I fished most weeks until the end of the season, and never touched a fish. Never had a pull. Just nothing! And that was the year a great friend of mine took the biggest bag ever of fish from Two Lakes on a dry fly. He took five fish weighing 20 lb 14 oz only about a fortnight before I joined; in fact that was *why* I joined and there was I at the end of the season blank!

TOM: *A lot of people say that Two Lakes is rather like fishing in a goldfish bowl hopelessly overstocked: a duffer's water made easy and so on. Do you agree with that?*

BARRIE: That kind of remark possibly comes about because guest-days are limited, and most members tend to invite their guests early in the season – after all, any host likes his guest to catch fish. Afterwards such visitors perhaps think it is the same throughout the season. If one thinks what the fishing is like in (say) the first or even the third or fourth weeks in April, it can surely be very easy; but that is true of most still-water fisheries. I have been a member of the Enton club and it can happen there; and with reasonable weather on opening day, Chew and Grafham are not difficult. Sometimes you get your limit in under two hours, and have to pack up and go home. It's true of most places – on opening day nearly everyone catches a lot of fish.

TOM: *I fished Two Lakes as you know in the late summer last year and found it very difficult on the second occasion. Your comment on Enton struck an echo too, because I can remember one occasion when my host and I rowed up to the top, and we each had two fish in five minutes. We were then faced with taking our time to get our remaining brace and avoid going home almost as soon as we arrived. I wonder how your bag of big fish compares with that of other people at Two Lakes?*

BARRIE: I have not found the answer to catching large numbers of fish at Two Lakes; but I was reasonably successful with individual big fish. The difference between catching a 4 lb and a 6 lb fish is mostly luck. I am fishing for fish that I can see and, while I know that they are big, whether they turn out to be 4, 5, 6 or even 7 lb is luck. I just concentrate on the biggest fish I can find and mark down. On one occasion I saw two fish swimming together, the smaller being the most active. The big one looked about 3 lb and the small one about 2 lb. I got the small one out and he went 5 lb 10 oz. Heaven only knows what the other one weighed.

In the past a number of anglers at Two Lakes have consistently taken limit bags, and then as they got older, or through ill health, lost their power to concentrate. One of the most successful anglers ever at Two Lakes took up salmon fishing immediately his trout catches dropped. He told me he couldn't concentrate and think about trout the way he used to.

TOM: *You mentioned people getting older. What effect does this have on their fishing?*

BARRIE: I think as their eyesight deteriorates they seem to lose the knack. I am still fortunate to have very good eyesight, and hope to keep after big fish for some time; but I think the ability will fall off in time.

TOM: *I agree with you very definitely that fitness, youthful concentration, the devotion of a great deal of thought and energy are prerequisites to success in fishing, particularly when it comes to specimen hunting. Lake fishing is often regarded as chucking-and-chancing; but you clearly have made it a matter of stalking. You refer to seeing fish and concentrating on catching them; how do you set about this?*

BARRIE: Two Lakes is in some ways unique. It is a small fishery and it is very hard fished; but waders and boats are not used. At Two Lakes you have limited access from the fishing piers and from one or two bits of open banking; but you also have a lot of bank that is inaccessible. It is possible to stalk undisturbed fish with a real chance of success; but such tactics are hopeless where people are tramping all over the place. I am fishing for individual fish and, because the brown trout stay very much in one place, I catch mainly browns. Rainbows are rovers, so you can't be sure where they are.

TOM: *This has been very much my own experience on other waters and it is one of the points that I have been making.* Still Water Fly-Fishing, *when it was first written, was written about brown trout reservoirs, whereas at Grafham we are really fishing to a dominant population of rainbow trout. Our techniques have varied enormously in the last two or three years.*

How much does local knowledge come into your success?

BARRIE: I now live near Two Lakes, and I have seen every one of the lakes drained. I made sketch-maps when the lakes were dry and I know where the deep water is, where you have those steeply cut banks, the sort of places that big chub are so fond of. Big browns also like water underneath them so they can just sink out of danger. So I go round when the water is clear and look in all the places that I think should be good. I look in the place where I saw fish last year, or the year before, or last week, and by about May I have probably got about eight or ten worthwhile fish catalogued. Then every week I go round and call on all eight or ten. Sometimes one of them is in a slightly different position, a foot closer than expected, and he sees you and bolts. In another place, you cannot see because the light is not right; the next fish is not there at all, perhaps because he has been caught. But whenever possible I have a cast and just occasionally I catch one and he should be a good one. But all the time I am building up my list of fish. Lots of these fish, mind you, are old stagers that have been known for two or three years; but you keep on at them, and a lot of other people also try for them. Once in a while, one makes a mistake . . .

TOM: *One of the points I have noticed on the occasions I have been down at Two Lakes is that we have not known you were there or, at least, we have not seen you there until sometime about midday when you have suddenly appeared with a fairly large fish. Is your shunning, as it were, of human companionship while you are fishing something quite deliberate?*

BARRIE: The places where visitors tend to go at Two Lakes are the well-trodden places where they can find some elbow-room. No one in their right mind would go to a new water and poke himself into a tiny little hole where he has no reason to think there are fish, and where he makes life miserable for himself because he is all the time caught up in the bushes. I get my fun from stalking and it is a case of getting away from other people because, however quiet they are, they can spoil your fishing. Two people more than double the chance of putting a fish down, so I tend to sneak off where I can indulge my own sort of nonsense.

TOM: *You have stressed getting caught up at the back, and casting difficulties generally for someone not used to the water or to the particular position from which he is casting. Good casting obviously plays quite a big part in your success. Have you got any general advice for other anglers on this subject of casting? How can they set about achieving this same proficiency?*

BARRIE: I think casting is important. I think the first time the fish sees a fly there is a fair chance he will take it, and every time he sees it from then on the chances diminish. I think good entry is perhaps more important than pattern. Remember, you are not drawing line for a moment or two, and the fly must enter the water cleanly to make this fish that you can just barely see in the water, move decisively so that you know when to strike.

The problem always is one of seeing into the water. The Large Lake is nearly always coloured and, although it's a good place for big fish, it is not a place you can see-in, and it does not produce for me. The sort of technique I seem to have success with demands me seeing-in, actually being able to see the fish or know it is there. Once I can see the fish there's no time to waste; I like to put the fly to him quickly, for any moment he may see me and move off.

I remember those leader designs you gave in your first edition. I think they were good, for it is important to use a leader that will straighten and put the fly down cleanly and accurately. I don't want a leader for nymph fishing that lets the fly down five minutes afterwards: I want something that will turn it over and lay it down. For the same reason I sometimes shorten the point of the line to make it turn over more positively. I use leaders of up to 11 ft; but when you are short casting round the back of a bush you really want a leader of about 6 ft. I usually have a long leader and a short leader, and another of medium length, wound round my hat, and I spend a lot of time changing things to get my terminal gear right for each fish and each casting position.

TOM: *You have been for very many years a member of the British Casting Association. Do you think this plays any large part in your success?*

BARRIE: Well, I was a long-distance caster with some things but not with a trout-fly rod. I can throw a longer line than most; but I am not in the 45- to 50-yard class of the top international casters. I think the ability to change direction fast has proved my greatest advantage, particularly when fishing for rainbows in open water.

I have sat by Home Pool for a couple of hours without casting, and eventually have seen the fish I am after moving along, sometimes very close in. I often sit on one of those three-legged shooting sticks; they are just about the right height for seeing-in. If the fish is very close, I think the best thing to do is to sit tight and let him go by, and hope he will come back. Sometimes he comes back in five minutes; sometimes it is an hour; sometimes never. But when he does come, the ability to pick up line, change direction very fast, and cover the fish as soon as you see him, is all-important.

This was something tournament casting taught me. In recent years the order in which you take the targets in the fly accuracy event means you have to change direction over quite a wide arc without a false cast. There are ways of positioning your rod just before you pick up your line that will help you to do this, whereas if you pick up the line and then try to change direction, often your line will catch up. If you have been sitting there for hours waiting to see a fish and then, as you make your one and only cast, your fly catches on the line or the rod, you feel like taking up Bingo.

TOM: *I think, Barrie, this is where we get to the matter of wet or dry. Clearly you fish both. What governs your method, wet or dry, when you come to tackle a fish you have marked down?*

BARRIE: At Two Lakes, we are fairly near the Test and when the wind blows from the river we seem to get a lot of extra fly; in addition we get a lot of lake olives, and David Jacques has identified about fifty-three or so different species of sedges.

Sometimes in April or May when the lakes are well stocked and the water temperature is such that the fishing is a bit easier over a longer period of the day, a lot of the members fish dry right through the day, purely to spread the day out a bit. It is noticeable that the fish caught in April on a dry fly are nearly all fish in good condition, whereas some of the rainbows that are caught on nymphs fished deep are the dark black cocks: kelts really.

TOM: *It has been very noticeable in my reservoir fishing that fish seen to be surface-feeding fish are nearly always found to be of above-average quality.*

BARRIE: I fish a dry fly a lot at Two Lakes because I enjoy the thrill of the visual take. I very often try a dry fly in places where I know or believe a fish to be, and just let it sit there. Sometimes the fish appears and very slowly moves over towards the fly, and suddenly you realize he is right underneath it, rather like a chub. And then he just tips up and takes it, and is the most surprised creature in the world when he finds he has a hook in his mouth.

TOM: *You mention chub, and of course this is the right parallel. It has been my experience that very skilled trout fishers usually have had long and successful experience of coarse fishing too. Is this true of you, too?*

BARRIE: I don't know whether I have been all that successful; but I certainly started off as a coarse fisherman. I used to be secretary of a coarse-fishing club and did a lot of match fishing, too.

TOM: *In other words, you learned about fish before you started fishing for trout.*

Can we now turn to tackle generally: your rod, reel and line?

I am particularly interested by the fact that you use an automatic reel. A friend of mine with whom I was fishing at Hollowell reservoir way back in 1940–50, while using an American automatic reel, hooked one of the very large Hollowell trout, one about 5–5½ lb. This fish took line until all of a sudden everything was bang up tight and the fish was gone. What are your comments on this?

BARRIE: When I first took up trout fly-fishing it tended to be still water, because this was obtainable: Blagdon, Durleigh and so on. I just threw out a line and I pulled it in again, and I was always very worried when I had possibly 15 yards of line in my hand and a fish of perhaps 1 to 2 lb going round in a nice big arc, and I was still left with all this line in my hand. It was always a relief to get the line on the reel, otherwise I had to drop the line to get the net off my back and netted the fish through a great mass of line round my feet.

The same thing applied when you were fishing upstream wet or dry fly on a swift river like the Usk. You hooked a fish about ½ lb to ¾ lb which would come bouncing down the stream towards you and had to be netted through a great loop of line that had floated away downstream.

I tried American automatics first and went to a lot of bother and expense in getting friends to send me reels that I had read about in magazines like *Field and Stream*. They all had the deficiency that you mentioned – that they used to wind up ever tighter, rather like a clock spring. They also had very small line capacity. Some would not even hold a full HCH line and those that did would very rarely hold any backing. So I gave them up.

But I have always been interested in self-wind reels because they seemed to do something that I wanted, if only one could find a reel that would do it properly. I first became interested in my present reel because it is made by the company that I represent (Mitchell) and it was then I found it had none of the deficiencies that I have mentioned. It holds 80 yards of 20 lb Terylene backing and an HCF line, and of course with monofilament you could have nearly 200 yards of backing if you wanted it.

TOM: *What strength of monofil shooting line do you use when you are using a shooting head?*

BARRIE: I use about 22 lb or 25 lb. There is no point in using very fine monofil; you only get a lot of tangles.

TOM: *I find the weight of 25 lb and heavier monofil helps to turn the line over.*

BARRIE: At Two Lakes the fish do not usually run great distances because some of the lakes are narrow, particularly Home Pool, and you can run along the bank and follow. On Large Lake, of course, it is different. A fish that goes across there is about 100 yards away and I once had a man on a pier opposite me trying to net out one of my fish. He thought it was a sick fish swirling around his feet. Eventually I got it out on my own bank. With the 710 reel there is no danger when fish run a long way: I have used it for sea trout and a friend of mine uses one for very big Lune sea trout.

TOM: *If you get a fish run 90 yards, as happens at Grafham when you get in a fish over 6 lb, and he heads for the middle, is there none of this business of the spring tightening up until she goes bang simply because there is far too much strain on the far end?*

BARRIE: The spring is fully wound when you have stripped off about 18 to 20 yards of line but the fish can run as far as it likes without increasing the tension.

TOM: *Is there in fact a friction clutch so that when the tension on the spring reaches a certain level she just slips?*

BARRIE: That's right; and there is no need to adjust it, for it is set at the factory. What you do have to remember is that when a fish runs 90 yards your spring was fully wound at (say) 18 and thereafter the clutch was slipping. So when the reel has recovered 18 yards of line and the fish is still 70-odd yards away you have to recharge your rewind spring by turning a milled wheel on the right-hand side. It is no worse than turning a handle on an ordinary fly reel, because one turn winds up a lot of spring, and with five or six turns it is wound.

TOM: *Do you believe in special flies, or do you use the good old standards that everybody else uses from time to time?*

BARRIE: When you say the good old standards, do you mean the traditional Scottish wet fly?

TOM: *No, more the standard lake fly we have known for the last twenty or thirty years in the South; standard reservoir flies or nymphs.*

BARRIE: Well, if you are talking about what I call the standard reservoir fly like the Mallard & Claret, or Peter Ross, or even Alexandra, my answer would be, no, I don't. I haven't fished with what I call a traditional winged wet fly at Two Lakes for many seasons. I do use the flies you wrote about in the first edition of *Still Water Fly-Fishing*, such as the Black & Peacock Spider and the Amber Nymph ... (TOM: *Not one of mine, Barrie*) ... and that sort of thing but I am no great fly tyer. I make up a few of what I call my little brown nymph, which is very simple. But I am much more conscious of its underwater behaviour than pattern accuracy. I colour-code my nymphs according to weight, by using different colour tying-silk at the butt or head so as to recognize the ones that just hang in the surface, those that sink slowly, and the ones that will go in and sink fast. I probably have in my fly box a dozen flies all of the same pattern and size but dressed to behave differently. I try them out in a glass of water to be certain they will do what I want when I am fishing.

Often, I grease the leader to within about 4 in of the fly so as to hang the fly in the surface. If the fly is too heavy it pulls the greased leader down and the technique won't work. What I sometimes do is to have a knotless-taper leader, then cut it so as to make a 4 in point before greasing heavily right up to the knot. The knot then holds the grease and acts almost like a float, keeping the fly just where I want it while I retrieve very slowly.

TOM: *Your slow retrieve, of course, means pulling very much more slowly than most people would understand. How long do you think it takes you to recover (say) 20 yards of line?*

BARRIE: Well, I have never done anything so exact as you did when you actually timed your recovery rates, but it's a hell of a long while: perhaps five minutes.

TOM: *Does tackle shyness feature in your philosophy? The flash of your rod, the glint of the nylon, or the thickness of your nylon. 'Tackle' rather than the human being at the far end of the line. Incidentally, do you believe that the human being is the biggest of the fish scarers?*

BARRIE: Trout certainly go away pretty quickly from humans and it is quite interesting that though they go away from Alex

(Behrendt)'s dogs, they don't seem to go away quite as quickly, although I will say the dogs have put fish down for me before now. I have also seen fish at Two Lakes go down when a bird flies over.

As far as nylon is concerned, it is not often that I have anything, more than the last inch or so, actually sunk. Most of it is on the surface and because I have got it smothered in grease it looks pretty thick. But I am not too worried about what is on the surface; but I certainly fish quite fine points. Several of those 6 lb fish were caught on 5x leader points.

TOM: *Are we taking about a strong monofilament like Stren? What breaking strain are you actually fishing?*

BARRIE: I very often fish with 'super-strength' nylons, but often I am fishing with $3\frac{1}{4}$ lb test when dry, so it must be pretty weak when it is knotted twice.

TOM: *Do you think that fishing fine has made the difference between rising the fish and not rising it?*

BARRIE: I don't know; it is like when you're shooting and missing. You try all sorts of things and when it comes right you think 'that is what helped me!' I think I only fish very fine, either to a fish I have repeatedly failed to catch, or when I have had a very difficult day, or in certain types of light. Somehow I don't think plus or minus a 1,000th of an inch really makes much difference to the fish, but it does give me confidence when the going's rough.

TOM: *I had an amusing experience of this, years ago at Ravensthorpe reservoir. Jim Robinson and I were fishing for a trout which was lying in the bay just by the overflow at the far end of Ravensthorpe Dam. I put a fly across him perhaps a dozen times and failed to take him, and began reducing the strength of the point (it was silkworm gut in those days) till eventually I was down to somewhere around 3x or 4x (·0075 in). This time the fish came up, looked once, and went away, so I came to the conclusion that if I had been fishing fine to start with I would have caught him.*

I walked across the dam towards the boathouse and there in the corner was a fish which had been thrown at pretty frequently during the day. I put my fly to him and he took straight away. I got him out and twenty minutes later Jim Robinson walked along the dam, and I said 'Going fine did it', and he held up a fish and said he'd got one too . . . the one at the far end, and look what he'd caught it on. This turned out to be the leader he used when he was salmon fishing the previous week!

What is the secret of your success, Barrie, if you will permit that hackneyed expression?

BARRIE: All I have done in fishing is to find out what is successful for me with my present physical ability. If your eyesight deteriorates you have to change your technique if you are going to continue to catch fish, because you will not be able to continue with a purely visual technique.

What we have been talking about so far applies, given a season when the water is fairly clear and when you have a fair number of brown trout that will take up a station. But this year we will probably have fewer brown trout, because, with UDN in the Test Valley, we are all worried about their susceptibility. With fewer browns in the water I think we are going to have to vary our tactics, and I don't think my present techniques will work so well.

Most of my fish this year have been browns. I had very few good rainbows, even though there were more big rainbows caught at Two Lakes than there were browns. Most of the big browns that were caught at Two Lakes, I think I caught. My technique is unfortunately very narrow in that it only really seems to suit browns. If there are fewer browns, and the water is murky, preventing me 'seeing in', or if my eyesight begins to fall off, my results might drop seriously.

TOM: *You have stressed this business of eyesight. Are you, like Frank Sawyer, able to see when a trout closes its mouth on a fly and strike at that moment?*

BARRIE: No, I have never been able to see that well, but I seem to see a little better than most people. Not so well as the famous Alf Lunn on the Test. He and others like him are so used to spotting fish, they know what they are looking for and where to look. But they too sometimes make mistakes and think a clump of weed is a fish.

TOM: *It is, of course, better to see something and think it's a fish and throw at it, than to walk by and see it swim away.*

BARRIE: The point that some people find strange is that at Two Lakes my fly is in the water only a very short time. There was a time when I used to arrive at 9 AM and leave after dark, having flogged the water all day except for lunch. The maxim that the man who has his fly longest in the water gets most fish, does not apply as far as I am concerned. But in fairness, I don't catch the most fish at Two Lakes. I catch my share of large fish but I don't catch the most, numerically. Many people catch many more. I catch one fish, maybe a good one, but not always, whereas other people catch three or four. That sort of result suits me but it would not necessarily suit all anglers. Some enjoy casting rather like some golfers enjoy the walking as much as hitting the ball. Many anglers at Two Lakes want to be doing something; they don't want to sit on a stick just watching the water: they have been sitting in an office all week. My technique would not suit them, even though afterwards they may say they envy my big fish.

Although I don't have my fly in the water very much I think I am, nonetheless, fishing hard and I come away very tired, often with a headache caused by the strain of looking in, which I do all the time there is a chance of a fish. When I am fishing I still watch the leader very intently because I am retrieving line so slowly that there is virtually no pull when a fish takes. I must see the leader draw.

TOM: *Do you mean by this that the fish takes with such confidence that he merely closes his mouth on it and gently swims on his way?*

BARRIE: Very often when you are fishing a nymph right *in* the surface they come along and just tip-up, rather like taking a dry fly, and then tip as quietly down again. Often they spit it out again without having moved on with it at all. Sometimes of course you get one that takes with such a smash that you are broken all ends up.

TOM: *This is the sort of thing you get in reservoir fishing with sticklebackers where the fish will actually charge up to the fly, or where you think your fly is, and he will stop. You can see his mouth opening and closing as he sort of chews the thing and it is anybody's guess when to strike, or whether you hit him if you do strike.*

BARRIE: Two Lakes also lends itself to my technique because being small there is nearly always a lake where you can find flat calm. This greased-leader technique does not work if there is anything more than a slight ripple, for the leader will sink.

To sum up, I am sitting and scanning the water fast all the time, finding a fish and then covering it, rather like dry-fly men, even though I may be fishing with a nymph. If you see a fish rise you stand a very good chance of catching him if you can put your fly over him properly. You may not know which way he is going; but on average you can only be three-quarters wrong, and now and again you must be in the right place. My experience is the same as Alf Lunn's. He says 'Let the fish see it go on', and very often he will put his brakes on, tip-up and take it. Whereas if you cast too far in front no matter how nicely, often the fish will pass it by! Sometimes on my day's fishing each week there is very little fishing at all. Rather like a very bad day on the Test when you never see a fish rise, never tie a fly on, and never even cast.

TOM: *Well, I chuck it and chance it on the Test when fish aren't rising, the same as I do anywhere else, except that I fish upstream. Interestingly enough, in mid-afternoon, the first time I went to Two Lakes in late June, I was fishing a Buzzer and was broken twice while using a ·010 in point. God knows what they were but they felt like submarines.*

BARRIE: They could well have been very big rainbows going past.

TOM: *These were the very slow tightens of fish not going any place. The rod tip went down under the water and, bang! That was it! Of course I wasn't paying attention.*

BARRIE: I agree. My attention wanders if I just stand and retrieve aimlessly. That's why I prefer very short periods of deep concentration. I just can't concentrate for very long periods. I get too tired.

TOM: *You are almost like a cat watching a mouse-hole when you fish, aren't you? And you have got to have this kind of approach to big fish, presumably. What is your recipe for success in angling?*

BARRIE: I'm not conscious of having a recipe, but in the fishing-tackle business I am lucky enough to have the opportunity to fish with experts in many fields. I don't think it is possible to be good at all branches of angling. To be a very good bass fisherman is half a lifetime's work; to be a very good salmon fisherman is certainly three-quarters of a lifetime's work. You may be good at two sorts of fishing; but there are very few anglers I know who are very good at more than one.

When somebody says to me 'Come along and catch a bass from our local beach,' I need him to hold my hand, so to speak; to let me look in his fly box if you like. I am quite prepared to imitate him parrot fashion, if I am with someone who is an accepted expert and, as I say, being in the business I meet many who have given above average thought to their fishing. When I am fishing with them in their own specialized areas and for the species they have studied, I mimic their techniques. What I know about salmon fishing I learned through watching people who were good salmon fishers. Probably this is true about any sport. It happens in athletics. When you have a top performer in the country you have a crop of good ones for several years, because others have something to aim at and someone to copy.

TOM: *This is the story of Northampton. I suppose fully half of the really good shallow-reservoir fishermen in the country live in the Northampton area and from what I can glean, this all goes back to a chap by the name of Stan Manchip who lived at North-ampton. I never met him but he was a brilliant fisherman and influenced people like Cyril Inwood, Edgar Nutt, and so on, and they in turn had their influence on other people. There has been a core, a nucleus as it were, which other people were able to imitate. But the other factor, I am sure you will agree, is 'purpose'.*

BARRIE: Yes, that's true. Knowing the whereabouts of the fish you want and then really setting out to catch it.

CHAPTER 14

Boats, basic boat-handling, weather clothing and food

Much as I enjoy bank fishing, I am by no means so stupidly dogmatic as to stay ashore when there is every indication that the fish are out in the middle, or when bank fishing is hopeless.

In late May 1955 I visited Durleigh Reservoir. The water was high and crystal clear; we 'enjoyed' brilliant sunshine every day, and there were no fish to be seen in the margins until sundown. In fact, apart from four fish weighing 5 lb 5 oz taken in the last fifteen minutes before closing time on 28 May, I rose not another fish from the bank during the whole of my stay.

In 1955 we had a late spring and marginal weed growth was still sparse in early June. Cover and food supply feature large in any Utopian philosophy that might be written by a trout, and absence of weed from the margins very commonly (but by no means always) results in the trout population's preference for deep water way out in the middle.

So at Durleigh, as on similar occasions elsewhere, I fished from a boat, a sturdy keel-boat which would have been safe in a moderate sea. Each boat was equipped with a concrete sinker secured by several fathoms of 1-inch rubber belting permitting the sinker to be lowered and recovered much more quietly than is possible with chain. But, as usual with round-bottomed craft with high freeboard, there was a good deal of swing to be coped with when at anchor in a breeze, and rolling was very pronounced when I was long casting. Drifting, even in light winds, resulted in a walking pace drift (there were no drogues) making it practically impossible to throw twice at the same rise and be on target. Mooring the boat was the general practice at Durleigh, and it seemed only natural when fishing from a 'platform' to look upon it as an extension of the bank and stand up to cast and fish ... as the local anglers had been doing for years.

Keel-boats are probably very necessary on large lakes, or on waters where dangerous squalls may occur; but on Midland waters up to even two hundred acres the punt is much the better proposition.

In the last ten or so years, glass-reinforced plastics have become much cheaper, and most of the new boats purchased by water boards are of this type. They are light and easy to row, they are very strong indeed, unsinkable, having moulded-in buoyancy tanks and are far easier to clean than timber craft. Painting maintenance, too, is unnecessary.

Unfortunately many of them have been designed and finished to appeal to saltwater-sailor owners who prefer the finish of varnished timber. Thus we have boats moulded to look like clinker construction, even to the point of painting their hulls after fabrication. We have mahogany gunwales, and knees, and seats, and timber deckboards secured by timber turnbuckles. From an angler's point of view they are a nightmare of line and tackle-catching traps.

Early in 1968, in collaboration with 'Thanetcraft', I set out to clean the whole thing up. We took as the basic boat the hull of the well-tried 'Thanet'.

The buoyancy tanks down each side were all that was necessary to hold the deck-boards in position and we stepped up the boards' thickness to withstand wear and tear from the anchors and weights that boat anglers seem to conceal about their persons before going afloat. We were immediately free from 90 per cent of the snagging-up of lines dropped onto the boat bottom whilst fishing out a cast.

Then there were the seats. Except when you are rowing and need a seat and stretcher positioned so that your knees do not foul the oars as you pull, fishing boats should have their seats at gunwale height to provide a comfortable sitting position akin to that on a dining chair. The Thanetcraft boat has this advantage. In the ordinary boat of course, you sit with your bottom 6 in above the deck and your knees under your chin and the discomfort after several hours can be acute. Worse, it is a damn bad fishing position.

We then moved the seats apart to give maximum clearance between the casters whilst preserving space for line handling. Where outboards were to be fitted, provision was made amidships for oars to be properly secured but available quickly when, with a dicky engine, you drift rapidly onto a wave-beaten lee shore. Finally, we provided rings for securing the sinker and/or drogue *outside* the hull at two points on each side, and at the bow. Total extra cost was about £10 per hull which resulted from the work being non-standard. In quantity production the same boat should be cheaper since it is much simpler than the listed model. It is the old question of the chicken or the egg – you need the order book before high production brings down cost, and you have to bring down cost before you attract the big order book.

The Thanetcraft 'Stillwater' Boat is available from Thanetcraft Ltd, of 2 Crown Road, New Malden, Surrey.

Boat handling

If you can row well enough to make progress against wind and waves on a large reservoir, you know enough about boats to need no further instruction. If you cannot handle a boat in a wind, the usual reason is inability to keep the boat's head on a steady course.

Here's how it is done. Sit amidship with your feet correctly and comfortably braced against the stretcher. Having pulled the boat round to the desired course, note an object on the far bank directly in line with the centre of the transom (the board at the blunt end of the boat). From now on keep your eyes fixed on it and row so as to keep it on the line. Remember that a boat drifts downwind while you are rowing and that you must aim for a spot *upwind* of where you want to land or start fishing.

In rough weather, rowing can take a lot of steam and by midafternoon, unless you are young or very fit, the hard effort will reduce your enjoyment and the effectiveness of your casting. An outboard then becomes advisable; a boat like the 'Stillwater' should be served by at least 5 hp.

Most regretfully I have to tell you that I still find most outboards are occasionally prone to starting difficulties and the British-made engines are noticeably trickier than American engines.

The shafts of outboard engines are available in several lengths to fit the depth of the transom and ensure that the propeller is immersed to a depth sufficient to avoid cavitation (churning air instead of water).

The biggest problem of outboard handling is failure of the

angler to follow exactly and every time the starting instructions on the plate on the engine, even when the engine has only been stopped for a second or two.

The other problem concerns the shear-pin. In order to avoid damage to the shaft and the engine when a boat goes aground – or when the drogue or anchor line gets in the screw – the makers secure the propeller to the shaft by a pin about $\frac{1}{8}$ in thick. If the propeller is suddenly stopped, the pin shears and the unloaded engine revs to a shriek but remains undamaged. The trouble is best prevented by tilting the engine forward in shallow water, cutting it and lifting the screw clear of the water as you run ashore.

It is the simplest thing in the world to replace a broken shear-pin ... all you require is a pair of pliers to remove the split-pin, a new shear-pin and a spare split-pin in case you break the other. I know of no water where any of these is provided in the boat!

Demand them before going afloat. A rapid repair could prevent serious damage to a drifting boat – or worse.

Long or short casting?

It is certainly true that fish rise very close to the boat occasionally, just as they will rise within arms' length when one is wading, but the circumstances are usually exceptional, and probably include near-darkness, mad-on rises to a surface insect, and turbid or very choppy water. There exists, however, the phenomenon of the rise which is not a rise at all. A drifting boat frequently scares surface-swimming fish, causing them to go down with a violent swirl or splash. I feel sure that this is the explanation of a high percentage of 'rises' which occur in the path of a drifting boat. Similarly, I have seen surface-swimming trout go down in alarm when their line of advance brought them close to an anchored boat.

No, for most of the time you are afloat you will need a long line to achieve concealment. A seated boat-angler, particularly on a box seat, is as high or higher above water than a wading angler, and he has no bank, trees or dam at his rear to conceal his outline. There he sits, silhouetted on the skyline and often without a weed screen in front of him too. In calm weather, seated, I find it necessary to throw a minimum of 20 yards; and, in that period of the evening just before sunset when a trout's perception is at its keenest, I frequently use a weight-forward line to reach 30 and more yards. At times even that is not enough and one must stand and achieve maximum distance.

Standing not only facilitates casting, it gives one a much better view of the line while fishing: that twitch at the remote end is often unseen from a sitting position. It also permits a much more effective strike. I still find it difficult to strike firmly yet safely when sitting, particularly if, as in some boats, I am sitting on a thwart perhaps a foot below the gunwale so that the rod is cocked up at an awkward and tiring angle. Standing, it is possible to put the rod-tip to one side and low over the water and compensate for the small boat movements which otherwise cause line-drag and nullify one's efforts to control the fishing speed of the fly. And here lies a major problem: I have never been able to control a slowly fished fly so well from a boat as I can with both feet on the lake bed.

Look at it how you will, a boat is merely a fishing platform which can be moved so as to place the angler within distance of offshore feeding grounds. Inshore or offshore the feeding habits of the fish are much the same, so why change your style of angling. The paramount need is a means of mooring a boat within casting distance of a known feeding ground in such a way that it does not swing. This can never be achieved by one weight or anchor but diagram 14.1 shows how it can be done with two.

The boat approaches the feeding area across wind. The engine is cut; weight B is dropped and anchor cable is paid out freely. At point A the second weight is dropped. By hauling on line A made fast to the stern and paying out on B at the bow, the boat lies tightly to both weights and will not swing.

When, then, should we drift?

Always and never are dangerous words in angling, for there are likely to be a dozen right answers to any problem and the best generalizations are likely to be true in not more than 50 per cent of cases. So it is with boat fishing.

While the anchored boat permits more accurate fishing, there are times when drifting is a wise procedure. When, for instance, those calm lanes that I mentioned in Chapter 12 appear midst ripple it pays to drift down them because they are a focal point for actively rising fish.

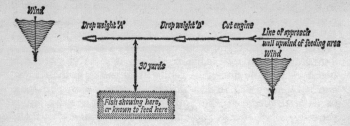

Diagram 14.1a   Approaching an anchorage

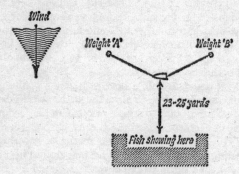

Diagram 14.1b   Boat moored

But the drift must be controlled; a leisurely advance, allowing up to four casts at any rise. Despite the creak of rowlocks, a boat pulled by a skilled boatman is the best answer, and you will also find his local knowledge most helpful on a strange water. Lacking a boatman, reduce the rate of drift by towing a sea anchor or drogue. An excellent drogue is supplied by Tratman & Lowther (Bristol), but an effective one can be made from a sack with the mouth held open by, and secured to, a barrel-hoop. The drogue should be made fast by lines leading to either end of the boat so that by shortening or lengthening at one or the other end the boat can be held at a steady angle across the wind.*

* Where anchoring is forbidden, drogues have been known to foul a weed bed and bring a boat to a standstill! I have also known a boat's painter to be tied direct to the stems of the more substantial water weeds to achieve a similar result.

Other occasions when drifting might be the better course are provided by the coincidence of the wind blowing parallel to the margin of the inshore weed-bed, or the need to cover as much water as possible when an unbroken weed bed several acres in extent lies a foot or so below the surface. In the former case the drift should only be made if there are no anglers fishing the margin waters, for to interfere with the sport of others is a serious breach of angling etiquette. For the same reason, you should not cut in and drift down ahead of another boat; you drift down behind him just as you would enter a pool on a river at a generous distance behind an angler already there.

Trolling, which I understand to mean trailing a fly or bait from a boat which is in motion induced by other than wind action, is forbidden on many waters. There is no clear division to the onlooker between casting and fishing from a boat that is being rowed and where the flies have the same motion through the water as when an outboard motor is set at trolling speed, and the fairly common and quite legal use of oars by a boatman to check the rate of drift.

Bow or beam to the wind

Most boats are drifted beam to the wind with a steadying drogue trailed behind. The two anglers straddle the seats and cast before

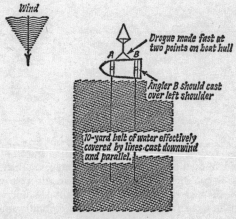

Wind

Drogue made fast at two points on boat hull

A B

Angler B should cast over left shoulder

10-yard belt of water effectively covered by lines cast downwind and parallel.

Diagram 14.2

them downwind, recovering line at sufficient speed to keep the flies working. My partner and I have caught a lot of fish this way at all seasons of the year, but we have obviously fished only a fraction of the water that we could have reached.

The inadequacy of the method lies in the fact that we are both looking downwind and cannot observe what the other is doing. We are so much concentrating on our own fishing that we are each unaware, except when we deliberately think about it, of the other's actions. Since I cannot see him cast I must cast straight in front of me – if I cast slightly to one side my line will strike his before or behind the boat if he happens to be casting at the same time ... and, if this happened repeatedly it could try the best friendships. For obvious reasons too, my companion must cast over his left shoulder to avoid striking me from time to time.

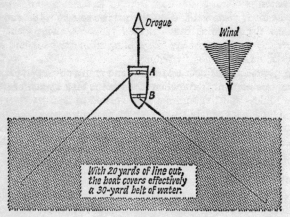

With 20 yards of line out, the boat covers effectively a 30-yard belt of water.

Diagram 14.3

For some reason not clear to me the method shown in diagram 14.3 is seldom seen but it has many advantages. When angler B casts he is in full sight of Angler A who should cast when B is fishing. Both anglers cast over their right shoulders without danger to the other. Finally and most importantly much more water is covered and each angler fishes to different fish.

The ultimate development of this technique is described by Dick Shrive in Chapter 15 and further illustrated in the addendum to that chapter.

Bank v boat

Returns by the Mid-Northants Trout Fishers' Association show that fish caught from the bank are heavier; but the expectation of sport is better from a boat. Over a season the catch per boat-rod-day is up to $2\frac{1}{2}$ times as good, but there are periods in each year when boat and bank anglers fare equally well. This was true, too, in September 1967, at Grafham when brown trout fed hard inshore between Hill Farm and Marlow Park and many bank anglers fared better than the boats. But with greater availability of boats, and far more anglers skilled in bank tactics fishing from boats and using those same effective methods to cover far more fish the balance has swung markedly in favour of the boats.

Diagnostic fishing on a northern reservoir in 1968 showed that fly fishing from boats yielded twice as many trout per angler/day as worm fishing or spinning from the bank and four times as many as bank fly-fishing.

At Grafham, the boat and bank returns are not separated but there were certainly days when fifty anglers on a stretch of shore were fishless and I should not be surprised to find that over the season boat rods caught six or even eight trout to every one from the bank. The predominance of rainbows which cruise open-water in shoals is partly the reason for this, and the lack of marginal weed-bed cover is the aggravating factor.

Bank and boat

On small waters where bank rods may be, rightly, restricted in numbers, a boat angler may not fish from the shore. This does not alter the fact that you will make your best bag by fishing inshore or afloat as conditions warrant through the day. I have frequently used a boat merely as a means of transport. Even where there is a road round the water it is usually quicker to dump the assembled gear in a boat and row to the other side.

Mathematically, the bank:boat success ratio must vary closely as the ratio of the perimeter of the water multiplied by 40 yards, to the area in square yards of the whole lake. Sure there are many influencing factors such as bank disturbance, lack of or excess of marginal weeds, competence of anglers and so on, but if the water is shallow and fish feed over most of its area, and most of that area cannot be reached from the bank, then the far-ranging skilled boat angler must win the day.

Clothing, equipment and companions

Clothing that will meet the exacting requirements of boat fishing will certainly prove correct for bank fishing.

Fishing from a boat, you are exposed to the full effects of wind and driving rain, and full storm-clothing is a necessity. I recommend 'Maxume' lightweight plastic-cotton sou'wester and jacket, and overtrousers too, for when seated your thighs are exposed. A very satisfactory alternative, though more expensive, is the Vinyl-proofed nylon parka and trousers which have been developed for polar exploration, though I found the welded seams of the trousers began to part midway through their second season, the defect becoming apparent when one inch of rain fell from 3 PM to 9 PM one day at Packington! Obviously when bank fishing in thigh waders you can dispense with waterproof overtrousers provided your jacket is long enough to come halfway down the thighs. Ultra lightweight weather clothing clearly has a great advantage in midsummer.

Avoid like the plague hooks, buttons, flaps and buckles that can catch the line. Zip fronts at all times!

Boat seats are horribly uncomfortable after a few hours, so if your enjoyment is not to be marred you will need a cushion – preferably of foam rubber *with a waterproof cover*. Not that I object to the Kapok-filled floatation cushions provided by many water authorities in lieu of lifebelts. I only insist on having two of them and that they be *dry*!

Where boat seats are fitted at the usual awkward level – and

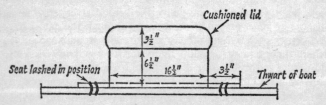

Diagram 14.4   Seat box on boat seat to increase height of eye and provide leg comfort

this means, at the moment, everywhere you are likely to fish – I take along my seat box.

This seat which is lashed by a length of parachute cord to the boat seat, holds all my tackle, and the removable lid has a Vinyl leather-cloth cover over a good filling of foam plastic. I still like to add a Kapok cushion nonetheless.

The bottom of the boat is a sounding board for every movement of tackle, oars, weights and so on, but above all for the angler's feet. Dunlop Caraboots are light and waterproof and they do reduce the noise. Rope-soled shoes are every bit as quiet, but they do not keep the water out.

Playing a large or lively fish can be hazardous, particularly when it is being brought to the net . . . on the upwind side of a drifting boat. It is unfair to expect your companion to perform the task regularly but it is wise, with a real good 'un, to lift the drogue or anchor to eliminate at least those hazards over which you have control. It is comforting to know when a fish swims towards you and under the boat that you can with safety swing your rod round the end of the boat (either end achieves the same result) and without trying to hold him away from the drogue.

In a boat the largest net will not inconvenience you, so let it be a big one, 24 in diameter with a deep net, and on a stout cane handle at least 4 ft long.

'We're all in the same boat,' is an expression which will assume horrible significance if you choose your boat companion unwisely. Inane chatter; murderous casting; throwing at fish which are in 'your' water; inability or unwillingness (plain laziness) to row; fish-scaring clumsiness; every moronic manifestation is with you for the day, and however justified, you really must not throw him overboard and hold him under – not in a water supply reservoir anyway. Neither can you get out and walk away from him. If you have a companion whose company in a boat is a joy of understanding, good humour, stimulating conversation, you have it all. Work hard at that friendship; it is priceless.

Seeing and hearing

In all but the heaviest rain I dislike a parka hood over my head because it reduces my ability to hear a rise. My usual head cover, rain or shine, is a Grenfell waterproof hat with a peak fore and aft to keep the sun and rain off my neck and face. Dazzle and sunburn can be a serious problem when boat fishing, particularly on an angling holiday when you may get the same intensive double dose of ultra-violet day after day from sky and water.

Be practical about it. You may not look very pretty with a handkerchief sandwiched between hat and scalp and arranged to hang down over neck and both cheeks, and your photo certainly won't appear in *Field* or *Country Life*, but you'd look and feel much sillier with second-degree burns that kept you off the water after a day or two's exposure.

For near vision, tying on a fly and so on, I use corrective lenses fitted in the bottom portion of the otherwise empty frames of standard spectacles. These leave me with no light loss for seeing at a distance and provide a safe means of attachment for my clip-on Polaroids. Except in the dullest of conditions and at dusk I wear my Polaroids all day and every day. I cannot recall ever suffering any form of eyestrain, no matter how brilliant the day or whether I cast into the sun.

Physical condition

Some kind of training before opening day is a great help. The muscles of one's forearm are not in condition after six months' close season, and I like to get in at least two hours' hard casting practice on a couple of occasions just before the season begins.

I find that excessive foot perspiration, which in April often results in cold feet when wading, can be prevented by dusting the feet with boracic powder when dressing. Cutting down perspiration is also good for the lining of your waders. Again, be sure that waders are big enough for you comfortably to wear an extra-thick pair of socks. Tight waders mean bad circulation and cold feet.

As to food, my standard requirements are a plastic food container holding a sharp knife, bread rolls, butter, cold sausages, hard-boiled eggs, cold chicken, cheese, tomatoes and cucumber. Such fresh food is more appetizing than sandwiches and is easier to prepare. Fruit is always welcome, and chocolate too, although the latter does tend to make one thirsty.

In winter time a flask of soup or cocoa is my choice, but in summer time I prefer hot tea or black coffee. Fizzy fruit drinks never seem to quench my thirst, and beer makes me feel drowsy on a hot afternoon so I leave them both alone when fishing. We all have to find out what suits us best.

A recent and very useful acquisition is an army-surplus kettle with a spirit burner. It cost me 50p. A kettle full of lake water (why not if you're going to boil it!) brews up nicely in ten minutes, either ashore or in the bottom of the boat, and the tea bags go into the kettle a few minutes before the milk and sugar. There is no question that fresh tea beats the flask every time.

Physical well-being is important to angling success, but so too is our mental approach.

Occasionally we go fishing because we are worried and seek relaxation and undoubtedly we come home better for our day by the water. But such a mental state is not a desirable preliminary to a good day's sport. To achieve success in any field of activity one's whole effort must be directed with complete singleness of purpose. Unfortunately, this modern world being what it is, complete freedom from worry seldom manifests itself – the angler usually has other things on his mind when he sets out. Nevertheless, it is surprising how much a wife can contribute to her husband's enjoyment by sending him out with a smile and a kiss after a good breakfast.

Much can be done to avoid annoyance accruing during actual fishing. Leader strength should be checked the night before, and rod-rings can be inspected and cleaned at the same time. Ferrules, too, are best greased with tallow before setting out. During fishing, it helps to prevent future annoyance if you clear the hook-eye of monofil before putting it back in the box. Small delays when fish are moving can try one's temper sorely, and at the very time when completely calm action is wanted something happens to make us incapable of it.

There are hundreds of things which intelligent anticipation can do to make your fishing more pleasurable.

A pair of scissors is a necessity when fishing. How easy it is to produce them when they are attached by a 2 ft lanyard to the buttonhole in the lapel and carried in the outer breast pocket! Round-nosed drapers' scissors are the best type. Fastened as I suggest, there is no fumbling for them: you put your left thumb through the loop and pull, and furthermore you cannot lose your scissors.

Captain L. A. Parker rightly suggested good fishing was the

result of taking pains. It applies not only to the fishermen's handling of his tackle but also to his handling of himself.

From slough of despond to joyous triumph

Morale has always seemed to me at its lowest in the evening of a fishless, hot summer's day when the ripple-edge recedes from the shore as a dying wind becomes a dead calm. Tired muscles, tired brain, and the effort of casting in dead air ... it is so easy at this point to wind in the line, and wade ashore – licked!

But the situation is not lost. Bold action is the answer.

On the far shore where uncomfortably strong winds have prevented fishing during the day are trout feeding confidently in water whose surface is now barely rippled. Ten minutes' brisk walk will almost certainly enable you to cover unsuspecting readily taking fish close to the margins.

The gamble pays dividends more often than not and your day can be made and enjoyment increased one hundredfold.

CHAPTER 15

Dick Shrive describes his method of fishing the sunk line

Probably the most successful reservoir angler in Britain today is Dick Shrive. He has caught more than his share of big fish but he is not a specimen hunter. He looks for consistent success and achieves it by eliminating the superfluous, the frills, the esoteric folklore.

Dick catches fish more or less throughout the day and does not rely upon a rise, and particularly the evening rise, for his sport. Every cast covers new fish and throughout his fishing day he thus offers his fly to undisturbed and probably confidently feeding trout. His methods are as remote from Barrie Welham's stalking of an identified fish as is possible.

Dick and I are Northamptonians and among the many Northamptonians who have known for as long as they have fished the Midland Reservoirs that neither chalk stream nor Highland Loch techniques offered more than chance success.

We met as old friends in the summer of 1969 to discuss his techniques ... just him and me and a tape-recorder. This chapter is the outcome of that meeting.

TOM: *Tell me when this all started. When did you discover that deep-lying fish could be caught deep?*

DICK: I should say it started way back when you wrote your first book. It started at Hollowell in 1949–50 when I used to fish with Cyril Cullip.

TOM: *We weren't really aware that you were doing anything different until that season at Ravensthorpe when I think you caught about thirty-eight out of fifty-odd rainbows caught over the season. As we now know they were all taken fishing deep though we were mystified at the time.*

DICK: At a distance you can't tell if anybody's fishing deep, and in the same way we developed and used shooting heads sixteen or seventeen years ago without people really catching on.

TOM: *What were your shooting heads made of in those days?*

DICK: They were made from the old-fashioned silk lines spliced to 30 lb nylon, long before Wet Cel was on the market. Incidentally I think we were the first in Northampton to try Wet Cels.

TOM: *In connection with deep fishing did you tie special flies or did you use traditional patterns?*

DICK: We used to fish special flies with buoyant bodies. The line sank fast and caused the fly to swim after it to the bottom. A lot of fish took the fly on the way down without the angler doing anything.

TOM: *This presumably means you have a deep belly of line between you and the fly. How do you feel the take?*

DICK: We missed a lot of fish this way from an anchored boat, so we developed drifting the boat bow downwind by hanging the drogue over the stern. The boat was then moving sideways to the line so that there was always a belly in it. The belly of the line hooks the fish as in salmon fishing. You get several plucks and providing you don't strike they usually finish-up on.

TOM: *This sounds much the same as trolling with a Devon in an Irish Lough.*

DICK: Yes. They take the fly in much the same way. They pull against the belly of the line which is caused by the boat moving and may have three or four goes before they hook themselves.

TOM: *All of this presupposes that your fly is fishing at the depth at which the fish is feeding. How critical are you on this matter of depth?*

DICK: You determine the taking depth when you start your drift. We usually drift parallel to the bank and fish fast-sinking heads. The boat is drifting stern to the wind and we are casting near enough across the wind. The drifting boat drags the line round until it hangs astern.

Some days you get all the takes at right angles to the boat. That means they are high in the water. The farther astern you get them the deeper the fish are because the line is slowly sinking as it goes round. I find it best to follow the line round with the rod tip like you do in sea-trout fishing. When we find our takes come right behind the boat, we slow down the boat by putting down another weight or drogue so that the fly fishes longer at the taking depth.

TOM: *Do you change your line if you find the fish high in the water?*

DICK: If the fish take at 90° to the drift or something of that order I change to a sinking tip. Not the ones you buy: ours have up to 5 yards cut from proper sinking lines spliced into 6, 7 or 8 yards of floating line. As soon as you have caught two or three fish you have solved the problem and you change your line according to the taking depth and use lines with the appropriate length of sinking tip, 2, 3, 4 or 5 yards, so that the fly is fished effectively all the way round.

TOM: *Do you attach any importance at all to what the fish are actually feeding on? Let us suppose it is a bright morning in July. We have just arrived at the water; we don't know where the fish are feeding or what they are feeding on. What fly would you start with?*

DICK: I should start with a no 6 single-hooked fly, a 'Missionary' or some white lightish fly. Often I finish up using the same fly all day. And once you have caught two or three on it what point is there in changing?

TOM: *As far as you are concerned, then, a hungry fish is as likely to take one fly as another, and all that is required of you is to present the fly to the fish at the right depth, which you govern mainly by the weight of the head that you use and the speed at which you recover line and drift the boat.*

What happens when it is a flat-calm day?

DICK: In flat calms I usually sit between the two seats on a plank that you may have noticed. I sit in a position where I can cast out and give an occasional pull on one oar. It is surprising how far this will take you, 30 or 40 yards, and that little bit of movement makes all the difference. But usually if it is calm we fish just a sinking-tip line, not a full-length fast-sinking head. This means we have most of the line on the surface and can feel the take quite easily.

TOM: *You have said that the depth at which you present your fly must be the depth at which the fish is feeding or thereabouts. At what depths do you in fact find your best sport?*

DICK: Early in the season, and at Grafham that means from May until the end of June, I never like to fish in water much more than about 10 or 11 ft deep. During the summer months

I prefer depths up to 15 ft and in the backend I look for water up to 8 ft deep.

TOM: *In mid-summer when the water is stratified and you have got a cold layer around 30 ft down, do you try to get a fly down there to fish?*

DICK: No.

TOM: *Do you fish out in the middle?*

DICK: It is very unusual for us to fish across the middle except when there is a good evening rise, though occasionally we might be tempted if there is a rise of rainbow trout way out during the daytime. No, we catch our fish at the sides about 10 or 11 ft deep. I usually stick my rod down to feel for the bottom . . . I expect you have seen me do it.

At Grafham our favourite drifts are between the sludge pits and the dam, and on the north shore from Hill Farm westward to the wood. If the wind is north/south we fish between Mander Park and Savages Creek. These give us all the fishing we want.

TOM: *Do you ever set out to catch rising fish?*

DICK: If I fish the rise we fish only to rising fish. We never bother to cast unless there is a fish to throw at.

It is no good waiting until the fish come to you. We 'tiddle' the boat along with one oar and keep it moving fast. We meet with far more rising fish that way than we would drifting broadside to the wind. And what's more with the bow downwind we are casting both sides.

When Cyril Cullip and I fished together, we reckoned we were covering 90 yards of water, 45 yards each side. That is much better than casting straight downwind from a boat drifting broadside. We worked it out when I first started lake fishing that by casting 30 yards downwind from the boat as it drifts broadside, you only fish the distance the boat has drifted, that is about 2 yards of water. The next cast mostly covers exactly the same water and the same fish. And what is more, you are closing on your fly all the time and really are not feeling your fly or the taking fish.

I don't cast 45 yards now like I did when I was a youngster. But with the boat bow downwind I cover, by casting across wind, a new 35 yards of water every time I cast. In other words, I fish that bit of water and finish with it. I don't cast twice at the same fish.

TOM: *Where rainbows are concerned, I have a theory that once a rainbow has seen a fly and refused it not only has he finished with it but his pals near by remain uninterested too.*

DICK: Well that's as maybe. There might be something in it but I won't commit myself. I usually give them one chance. If he wants it he has it first time! He gets no second chances. If he doesn't take it I look for a new customer. If a trout wants the fly and you cast 5 or 6 yards short he will turn and rush at it.

TOM: *Well, this hasn't been my experience with surface-feeding rainbows. Often when they have been dimpling right on the top with back fins out of water the fly has got to be ahead of them and remain virtually in the surface. If it sinks 6 in they often just are not interested.*

DICK: We aren't really fishing by the same method. In flat calms if I find they refuse small flies, say 10s, I usually go back to size 6, and, this will surprise you, I use a leaded fly, and cast it so it goes in with a pop and makes a big round circle and ripples. The rainbows may be 5 yards away but you will see the back fin turn and go down. You give your fly a pull and immediately you get a pull back from the fish.

TOM: *Well, you will be very interested to read what Barrie Welham has said to me on this. He does precisely the same thing with much smaller nymphs and designs them so that they go in decisively and definitely and then they hang an inch below the surface suspended by the grease he has on his leader.*

DICK: I do not bother with the grease on the leader. It is the 'pop' that does the trick and you can count five and pull, and they are on, or no longer interested.

TOM: *Well this is so often the case with rainbows isn't it? 'Pop' or no pop. You make your cast and if you don't have a pull on the first or the second draw of the line you are unlikely to get a fish that cast.*

Now one thing we must emphasize is that we are talking about rainbows. The thing which somehow has not been emphasized sufficiently by the writers is that when you are fishing for rainbows you are fishing to a different species with behaviour very different from brownies, and that completely different techniques seem to apply.

DICK: It's a different technique all the time.

TOM: *I can recall using a sunken silk line from the dam at Ravens-*

thorpe on a brilliantly hot July day some fifteen years ago. I had tied a beetle-type lure that I had read of in one of the journals. It consisted of a bunch of peacock feathers tied in at the hook bend and carried forward to the head so they looked like a sort of umbrella of peacock herl round the hook shank. I soaked an old silk line, let it sink right down and after about three draws I was into a brown trout of about 2¾ lb. I never did it again as far as I can recall for the next ten years.

Obviously it was effective but I think I am one of Barrie Welham's active anglers. I like to be on the go and this business of waiting a minute and a half while a silk line went down 20 ft was a bore. 'Wet Cels' have changed all that.

Tell me, do you ever use a shot or anything like that on a leader to get it down?

DICK: I sometimes put on a shot or use a leaded nymph but I am not keen on leaded nymphs because they get mixed up with your ordinary flies and you don't know what you've got on or how the fly is fishing. It is much easier to pinch on a dust shot or to pinch a larger shot on the line.

TOM: We have talked about rainbow trout and their decisive acceptance or rejection of a fly but as we both of us know from long long years of fishing at Hollowell, brown trout can be fished for for half an hour before they will take.

You can take one point from the bank and cast over and over again and provided you are on a known feeding ground you can pick up fish after fish. You will remember Dusty (Colonel) Miller's 'hot spot' at Hollowell.

Is there anything of this deep-fishing technique of yours which is particularly valuable when it comes to brown-trout fishing? Or is it equally effective for both types of fish?

DICK: You catch a lot of brown trout at Grafham in May by fishing deep, but again 10 ft to 11 ft is plenty deep enough. As the water deepens the pulls get less and less though occasionally you will catch brown trout out in the middle. On some days you may catch 50 per cent brown trout 50 per cent rainbows, and the take seems to come at about the same place as it would be with the rainbow. In the daytime brown trout seem to take a fly fished really deep. The next favoured moment is as the fly comes up from the bottom as you lift to recast.

TOM: Well, I have had a lot of rainbows do this too, particularly *when I am bottom crawling with a black lure, fishing it very slow and very deep. As I lift to recast, or as I roll the sunk line on to the top before I throw back, comes a snatch, or a great swirl just where the fly came out of the water.*

Well, we've talked a lot about boat fishing: what about bank fishing? Do you do a lot of it?

DICK: I do a lot of bank fishing in the week.

TOM: *Why the week?*

DICK: My bank-fishing techniques are much the same as my boat fishing. I don't like to be hemmed in by other anglers near by: I want a lot of room – at least 100 yards – to operate.

Basically my methods are much the same as for boat fishing. I always fish with a side wind, never a following wind and I don't mind whether it blows from the left or the right. I cast whilst moving slowly back. Your fly goes out across wind and by the time you have retrieved it you have 'otched' back 5 yards, which gives you a new bit of water. Always a new bit; never fish to the same bit twice.

When you are moving upwind you fish reasonably shallow because the wind catching the line blows it round fast and this, combined with your movement, keeps the fly reasonably near the surface.

When you have reached the end of your stretch of bank you reverse the procedure and fish moving downwind. Now you and the wind are moving in the same direction, keeping the line fairly straight. This lets the fly fish deep.

You find that on some days you catch your fish whilst moving upwind and others whilst moving downwind depending whether they are feeding shallow or deep.

TOM: *You seem to favour the idea of tightening into a fish against the belly in the line. This must surely have its effect too on the security of the hook hold.*

DICK: Yes, it does, because you are never pulling straight into the fish, you are always pulling into a bent line. The fish can pluck gently without being hooked or without pricking himself. But when he seizes it to turn away the weight of the line will put the barb in properly.

TOM: *We have not discussed so far your ideas on rods, reels and leaders. What type of rod do you favour?*

DICK: Fibreglass, 10 ft–10 ft 4 in, I make my own rods with fairly stiff butts and plenty of tip action. My lines, as I've said, are made from short lengths to achieve varied sinking rates.

TOM: *What about shooting lines? I think most people use monofil shooting lines which are much too light and which kink and snarl and so on. Again if a wet monofil shooting line dries on the reel it assumes coils when next you strip it off. How do you cope with this?*

DICK: Well, I used every time I came home, to wind my line on a big line winder so that it dried straight. But it was too much trouble and I cut it out. I now find it better to use a shooting line twice and then cut 20 yards off and resplice to the line. Nylon is cheap enough and I have a nice new shooting line every weekend.

TOM: *Are you using the nail knot to tie your nylon leader to the line?*

DICK: No, I use a knot of my own. I whip on a loop no thicker than the line itself so you can't feel it come through the top ring. It takes about ten minutes to do and it is quite easy. The important thing is to remove the plastic dressing by dipping the line end in cellulose thinners so as to soften it and make your splices and loops onto the braided core of the line.

TOM: *Because of the stretch of ordinary monofilament, do you think you have a better hooking percentage if you were to use say 30 lb 'Stren' which does not stretch anywhere nearly so much.*

DICK: I always use Platil of 30 or 35 lb BS.

TOM: *Some people use a single fly, others use a dropper. I have for years preferred a single fly and have found that when I do fish a dropper I miss far more fish. I think somehow or other the fish that come up at a dropper don't get hold of it somehow. How do you approach this matter?*

DICK: I always hold that if the fish are taking, one fly is enough because you only want to catch one at once. If they are not taking, two flies do not bring them onto the feed and you will spend time untangling the dropper. I always fish with a single fly.

TOM: *Invariably?*

DICK: Always. I fish with a single fly.

TOM: *Going back to this boat technique of yours there must be occasions when you fish from an anchored boat. How do you set about it?*

DICK: The technique when fishing from an anchored boat is the same as from a drifting boat. We always anchor by the bow so that the stern of the boat lies down the wind. The chap at the bow has the wind on his right shoulder and it's a bit awkward but you are not fighting for the same fish. You each have your own side of the boat to fish to. The only time that it does not work of course is when you have a left-hander in the boat!

TOM: *Well, he can fish on the left side of the boat.*

DICK: Yes, but that means we are both fishing the same side, which is not good; we never fish the same side. I always think that if both anglers fish the water on the same side of the boat the other side of the boat is wasted!

TOM: *Going back to this hooking business, I think we are both agreed that there is a tendency, particularly with lures, to get a lot of plucks or even to hook fish and lose them during playing. Somehow the hooks are not home. Do you favour a single hook, double hooks, or trebles?*

DICK: I favour the single hook, every time. Over the years, I have come to believe they hook better. In tandem hooks the hooks, two no 10s, are too small. If you hook a fish of 3 or 4 lb on the tail hook of the tandem you tend to pull out, but if you are using, say a number 8 or 6 single, once it is 'in' they don't very often get rid of it.

TOM: *Do you favour the upwind shore when boat fishing and if so, why?*

DICK: A lot depends on the time of the year. At this time of year (August) I like the downwind shore because the water is warm and I think the fish like it well stirred up.

TOM: *What about a clay bottom as you have at Grafham where you get clay in suspension on the downwind shore?*

DICK: I don't think the mud makes the slightest bit of difference. I would fish in the thickest mud you would like to find and still catch fish. The fish can still see the fly if the water is black as your hat. We often anchor the boat in the roughest water we can find and where the mud is well stirred up and catch fish galore.

TOM: *Close to the margin or in your 10–11 ft of water?*

DICK: Close to the margin, anything from 10 ft into the shallows.

TOM: *One last point on tackle handling. I have watched you fishing on many occasions and have seen you lift off and back and immediately cast out a very long line, how do you achieve this?*

DICK: This is done with the 10 ft 4 in rod. Leaving just enough line beneath the water to flex the top of the rod I lift out and throw back. The line moves fast enough to flex the rod and with the single forward throw I shoot up to 30 yards.

Addendum

Dick and I shared a boat at Grafham a few weeks before the close of the 1969 season.

A series of brilliant September days had been followed by unseasonably hard night frosts and we fished in a cold westerly wind on a day that befitted November.

Until mid-September, Dick had had limit bags (eight fish) on every outing, but with the change in the weather even he had found fish harder to catch. Our day together was to be no different.

We started the day in Dick's usual manner and the fish being right off the feed we saw no reason to change. Diagram 15.1 shows the general idea. A sinking head was thrown at right angles to the boat and line recovery and boat drift kept the fly moving. Provided the rate of drift remained slow the line continued to sink as it trailed round and the position relative to the boat where the takes occurred were indicative of the depth at which fish were feeding. A fish caught at 'A' just after the entry of the fly would probably be a surface feeder while those taken when the fly was almost astern at 'B', would almost certainly be bottom feeders.

Our fish were taken well behind the boat and we carried on fishing with sinking lines. Had they been taken at 'A' we would have changed to slow sinkers or even sink-tip lines so that the fly fished all the way round at the taking depth.

We fished with our rods pointed down the line, and, just as in sunk-line fishing for sea trout in a deep pool, the tentative takes of the fish were clearly felt.

The light exploratory nips were repeated several times but provided we did absolutely nothing the fish more often than not took hold and turned against the drag of the line to hook themselves.

Most fish were hooked well inside the mouth or in the scissors; in no case did we suffer the light holds at the front of the jaw so common when 'stripping' a lure.

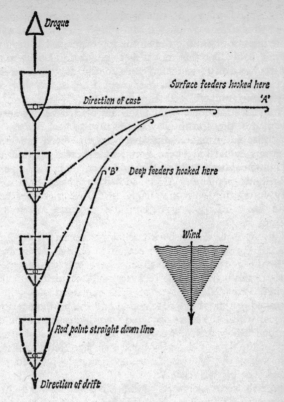

Diagram 15.1

All in all it was clear Dick's method killed fish rather than scaring them. Certainly it appeared to me kinder to the fishery than those teams of anglers who take fewer fish but who drift across the water all day stripping frenetically and hooking four or six times as many fish as they catch.

Dick's boat handling was like his fishing; practised and expert. He trimmed his boat to drift parallel to the shore even in a slightly offshore or onshore wind. We drifted, still fishing, through a huddle of other boats, and as surely, kept the whole length of a calm lane within casting reach all by clamping the rudder so as to hold the boat's head in the same position relative to the wind.

During our day out, we saw only three or four rises and those in the evening. Most boats had very few fish indeed, and never did we see a fish caught. We ended the day with three fish apiece, all around 2 lb. The best bag I heard of was six *from the bank* . . . by another Northamptonian!

Probably – in other company – I would have changed my style several times in the day in an effort to beat the fish. It is likely that the results would have been no better, and judging by others, could have been very much worse. When fish are feeding sporadically . . . only proven tactics can really pay off.

CHAPTER 16

Grafham: a new reservoir with new conditions and new problems

Raw figures can make exciting reading; so here they are, unadorned.

Area
1,600 acres

Stocking

		Brown trout		Rainbow trout	
Spring	1965	28,000	5–7 in	6,000	7–10 in
Spring	1966	15,000	5–7 in	9,000	8–10 in
		10,000	5–6 in		
Autumn	1966	12,500	8–10 in	54,000	8–10 in
Spring	1968	4,000	8–10 in		
		7,000	10–12 in	30,000	10–12 in
Autumn	1968	7,500	10–12 in	5,000	12–14 in
Spring	1969	3,000	12–14 in	5,000	10–12 in
Schedules for	May	5,000	12–13 in		
summer 1969	June	5,000	12–13 in		
	July	5,000	12–13 in		

Catch 1966

Details by month not published

1 July to 30 September	4,211 brown trout taken
	5,956 rainbow trout taken

Of the 10,167 fish taken	2,383 were between 1 and 2 lb
	4,102 „ „ 2 and 3 lb
	2,202 „ „ 3 and 4 lb
	1,079 „ „ 4 and 5 lb
	333 „ „ 5 and 6 lb
	53 „ „ 6 and 7 lb
	15 „ „ 7 and 8 lb

Catch 1967

15 April to 30 September

	April	May	June	July	Aug.	Sept.	Total
Brown	1,605	1,417	1,038	815	1,485	2,482	8,842
Rainbow	3,941	4,388	4,866	4,294	2,925	3,773	23,187
Total	5,546	5,805	5,904	5,109	4,410	6,255	32,029
Fish/rod/ day (boats and bank)	1·5	1·3	1·65	1·6	1·25	1·46	
Browns, per cent of total	29	24	17	16	34	40	28
Rainbows, per cent of total	71	76	83	84	66	60	72

23,187 rainbow trout taken at an average weight of 1 lb 13 oz

total weight of 43,651 lb

8,842 brown trout taken at an average weight of 2 lb 6 oz

total weight of 21,000 lb

Three rainbows were caught for every brown.

Total weight of crop 64,651 lb

Assume av. wt. each fish 5 oz when stocked, and subtract   10,009 lb
_____

Live weight gain of crop   54,642 lb

Total weight gain per acre: 34 lb

The total weight of trout taken in 1967 was approximately 28½ tons.

22,861 day-permits and 33 season-permits were issued.

Published returns do not distinguish between fish taken by boat anglers as opposed to bank anglers.

Catch 1968

Summarized from the Great Ouse Water Authority's published statement.

20,120 rainbow trout taken at an average weight of 1 lb 12 oz

10,240 brown trout taken at an average weight of 2 lb 6 oz

Two rainbows were caught for every brown trout.

20,795 day-permits and 71 bank-permits were issued.

Cautionary note: Most recorded weights are estimated rather than actual. My rainbow average weight in 1968 was 1 lb 5½ oz.

If we look only at the years' totals and average weights, 1967 and 1968 provided equally good sport. But it so happened that 13¼ thousand fish, 42 per cent of 1968's 31,000 fish, were taken in May, and the latter months of the season were very thin indeed, particularly for the bank anglers. How much the very wet summer and cold early autumn had to do with the reverse it is still too early to say.

Probably the most important deductions and inferences that may reasonably be drawn from 1967 monthly figures are the importance of rainbow trout as sport providers in June and July when the browns are playing hard to get, and conversely, the importance of the brown trout as a sport provider in August and September. We have long experienced on other waters the phenomenon of hard feeding by browns as milt and ova develop before the spawning season, and it is fair conjecture that Grafham rainbows (mainly a late-spawning type) commenced their prespawning feeding in October and November. It is interesting too, to note that whereas in 1967 the ratio of rainbows to browns was 3:1, in 1968, as was predicted, the ratio became 2:1. Probably in 1969 it will become 3:2 or even 1:1 if we ignore the newly stocked rainbows that will be a feature of midsummer catches.

What the figures cannot show is that Grafham browns are in tip-top battling condition in April, yet in 1968 and 1969 the season did not open until 1 May. Nor does it make any sense at all that the closure on 30 September is a fortnight earlier than Blagdon. Grafham's five-month season, is I think, the shortest of any of the major reservoirs.* Paradoxically, it is also the only reservoir which has been planned as a recreational centre. I feel it is high time that we began to think in terms of stocking some of our reservoirs with rainbows only and extending our fly-fishing season through to November or even December, for the statutory season for trout applies only to brown trout. A wholly rainbow fishery could be managed to suit fish and fishermen merely by amendment of the River Boards' By-laws.

I first fished Grafham in the last week of July 1966, when I took the family over and fished for a few hours in the afternoon. My eldest son, in brilliant sunshine, had a shapely brown of 2½ lb on a B & P Spider, I was blank.

The banks were crowded to an extent I had never seen before and the uproar was beyond comprehension. We walked about a mile from where the car was parked to find a spot where we

* In 1969 fishing continued through to 14 October.

could get into the water and then had to fish in a station that had no feature to commend it.

Everywhere, so far as we could see, the same large lures were being recovered at the same alarming speed.

We returned to the car about 5 PM and motored round to one of the official parks where stood several hundred cars with probably 1,500 anglers and day-trippers near by. Ice-cream vans and hot-dog stands were doing a roaring trade. The environment resembled Hollowell in 1950 about as much as Blackpool resembles Ballycotton.

These were conditions that earlier editions of *Still Water Fly-Fishing* had not catered for. Nonetheless a Welsh angler fishing near a small promontory not 50 yards from the car park and with lovers rotating and dogs and children running under his back-cast, took a rainbow of 6 lb while I watched, and he had five others from 2 lb upward in the back of his 5 cwt van. All were taken on a tandem-hook and wormfly about 1½ in long, fished slowly and probably touching the bottom.

On the following Saturday I fished seriously on the west bank of Savages Creek in a small bay that Mike and I, with excellent reason, later christened 'Heartbreak Bay'.

As I walked the mile and a half of bank to reach my spot, I noticed a number of good fish apparently caught in the first half-hour's fishing. Stripping-through with a big lure was virtually the only technique in use.

Later I came to appreciate that many anglers were fishing their first reservoir and were using the techniques publicized in the angling press, often enough written by very good anglers who at that time lacked a deep knowledge of this specialized subject and who had failed to appreciate that their early successes were attributable not so much to lures and high-speed fishing as the enormous stock of big, very young fish with virtually no experience of man. Fish that in the first few days were too stupid to go and feed out in deeper water.

At about 2 PM several fish began to show sporadically out in my chosen bay. The water was calm and the sun shone brilliantly. I tied on a B & P Spider and greased all but the last 3 ft of the leader. Ten minutes later a rainbow of 3 lb 7 oz took the slowly fished fly and was played out and netted.

Another thirty minutes with the same fly brought no new offer but the fish still showed and I changed to a size 4 nymph with a white wool body and a clipped ginger hackle. Its only virtue was its fat, translucent maggot-like body, and three more rainbow came in quick succession. All were over 2 lb, fat as butter and fighting mad. This was the nymph that has since been christened 'The Gentile'.

The evening produced two more on the B & P Spider, the biggest 5 lb 9 oz. All were rainbows and all took a slowly fished small fly or nymph.

A week later Mike had five and I had four in the same spot. We then had five blank days in succession!

Truth was that very few anglers were getting fish by any method in that part of the water and we ought to have fished elsewhere. But our earlier success had us rooted.

Now, it so happened that we experienced moderate to strong along-shore and on-shore winds during our period of blanks and for much of the time the water held a suspended cloud of yellow clay. We have since noticed that whilst you occasionally take browns in the coloured water on the lee shore, rainbows are either missing entirely from turbid areas, or they are off their feed.

Then on 3 September we each had a fish first thing in the morning—9.15 AM (until 1968 the rules precluded fishing before 9 AM) and a further fish apiece at dusk. All four were taken fishing over old hedgerows, as were almost all the other fish we got before the season ended.

Those old hedgerows were grazing grounds for snail, and cover and nesting haunts for stickleback. Careful, quiet casting before the wading hordes drove the fish out, almost invariably produced fish, and we have since had the same success up to 150 yards from the shore fishing the line of a hedge from a boat. Part of my 1968–9 close-season activity was devoted to plotting on the published chart of Grafham all the old woods and hedges shown on the ordnance map of the area before it was flooded, as a further aid to fish-finding when using a boat.

From mid-August to the end of the season we rarely saw anything approaching an evening rise within casting distance and it was clear that clumsy angling and wading had brought about a complete change of feeding behaviour. Man was now known and feared.

Grafham, we were by now aware, was anything but an easy water. The marginal waters lacked weed-bed cover, and the wading angler and his tackle splash and flash were naked to the trout's keen vision. The lake bed was covered in blanket weed in which lived an abundance of snail and wriggling animalculae ... An artificial fly had competition aplenty!

Hour after hour anglers tramped the banks neither knowing nor apparently caring that the trout's senses were too keen to brook the presence of berserk waders, their nightmare lures and the line-wake which does so much to reduce the effectiveness of stripping through.

Two other matters began to impinge upon our thoughts. At Grafham we were catching three times as many rainbows as browns, and yet our methods were basically those for brown trout. Again, Grafham was deep enough to stratify whereas the other lakes we fished were so shallow that a persistent blow of wind would start the whole body of water circulating so that from surface down to the mud there was no depth of water markedly more comfortable to a fish than another.

First let us take the matter of species.

The rainbow trout is a very different animal from a brownie. We knew he grew fast, and that some strains had a tendency to migrate. What we did not know, and could not know until we fished a water well stocked with wild-grown fish, was that rainbow trout are shoaling fish that hunt rather like a shoal of mackerel or sea bass and with very similar voracity. They are with you for moments or minutes and soon move on.

While they are with you and feeding confidently they will strike at the fly – any fly of almost any size. When suspicious their behaviour is quite different – they follow the fly without taking, 'boiling' as they turn away. If they do seize the fly their heads remain towards the angler. It is as though they used their mouths as we would use our hands. Their seizure of the lure is tentative, they probe and savour without turning. If you do not tighten they will drop the lure and take it again.

Usually, of course, you tighten the moment you feel or see anything that might be fish and inevitably your hookhold is miserably insecure right in front of the jaws. Indeed, if you are stripping-in line you hit the fish quite involuntarily as you haul, and the meat-hooked monstrosity of a lure you are towing hasn't a snowball's chance in Hades of getting a secure hold.

As the 1966 season wore on, short-rising became an increasing facet of rainbow reaction to lures but it was most noticeable that nymphs or deceivers fished slow and deep were taken slowly and firmly, the hook securing a hold in the scissors or back of the mouth. They took a double B & P Spider fished slowly at the bottom in the same way.

In 1967 when Mike Brady and I fished almost exclusively from a boat, the familiar pattern of chasing, boiling, short rising and plucking was again evident with rainbows from the start of the season. It is now clear to me that a major factor in rainbow behaviour is curiosity – he is much more likely than a brown trout to 'come and have a look', but he only takes solidly when unafraid and when the lure looks and behaves like food. In this respect he is just like a brown trout.

But by whatever method you fish you lose a much higher percentage of rainbows than you do browns. I have come to the conclusion that rainbows are much like sea trout: they grow so fast that they are still soft-boned and tender-skinned even though they weigh 4 lb and more. As with sea trout a hard fight frequently tears out the hook. (See also the footnote to Chapter 17, page 217.)

When I am fishing big flies, size 8 and bigger, I have considerably reduced my losses by striking a second time as soon as the first rush is over, thus getting the hook deep into gristle or bone.

Now to deal with the effects of Grafham's depth. In the summer of 1966, the water dropped scarcely at all, and in 1967 and 1968, it dropped only 2 ft. There remained then, a very substantial body of water between 30 and 63 ft deep. A thermocline was thus well established, with shallow hypolymnion below it, typical of the type of eutrophy depicted in diagram 20.5 (page 258).

On a hot July day, varied water temperature and oxygen content within the thermocline's 15 ft stratum provide for both brown and rainbow trout conditions of infinitely greater comfort than the surface water's near-70°F. Vertical movement of only a few feet enables a fish to find a water temperature that will match blood temperature. Some fish may well remain there the whole season provided the food supply is adequate, only moving to the surface waters when, with the onset of dusk, so many plankton creatures migrate towards the surface.

Contrast this comfort with the fact of weedless margins, heavy bank traffic, frenzied stripping of lures, the rainbow's shoaling and wandering tendencies, and we have adequately explained the reasons for the Grafham bank anglers' poor catches in 1967 and 1968.

It is all so logical that we should have predicted it. Just as we can now predict that bank sport will improve as the brown trout get larger and more numerous, and permanent weed beds become established in the margins.

The brown trout, like so many wild animals, is a 'territorial' creature: he has a beat and maintains it against others of his kind. He is less inclined than the rainbow to wander off to a distant thermocline. He comes, by frequent sightings, to know man as an enemy and to recognize line, leader and lure as part of that enemy. But he remains on his territory and is virtually uncatchable until darkness or the murk of a wave-beaten lee shore obscures the angler whose fly is near and so temptingly foodlike. Or until the lone angler, knowing his presence, stalks him and casts just once to the right place at the right time, with the right kind of fly.

Fishing at great distance

It was inevitable that bank disturbance and an increasing scarcity of fish inshore would lead to renewed emphasis on long casting. Everyone set out to fish his fly beyond the disturbance caused by his neighbours' fishing as little as 15 yards to either side.

Casting distances of 40 yards are fairly common at Grafham today, and what visiting anglers have learned at Grafham they are taking back to their home waters.

Now, if this distance emphasis had been accompanied by quieter entry to the water *and very much quieter wading ashore;* if anglers had worn inconspicuous clothing; if they had walked the banks well back from the water; and if, above all, anglers after casting their impressive distances had fished small flies slowly, many more fish would have remained in the margins and would have been caught.

High-speed line recovery meant of course that most anglers were fishing their lures high in the water when fishing at depth would have been more productive. Very few anglers gave a sporting chance to leaded nymphs fished on long leaders. I came to regret that I designed the Jersey Herd ... and have little doubt that the abuse of his Polystickle has at times occasioned similar regrets with Dick Walker.

Getting down to the fish

The importance of the thermocline has long been known to American anglers who troll their big lakes using Monel (metal) lines adjusted to a length which would ensure the bait was in the thermocline. They know, too, that to fish a few feet above the thermocline means smaller catches – for a comfortable fish has no inclination to forsake his comfort, or the food species which shares the thermocline with him. Our problem is to get down there with fly tackle.

Because fishing from the dam is illegal there is regrettably no part of Grafham's shore from which you can cast to water 35 ft deep. Of necessity, therefore, thermocline fishing is a boat operation. By the end of 1967 the techniques were well developed and are described in Chapters 15 and 17, nonetheless only from a moored boat is it possible to fish a fly in the thermocline with conventional tackle.

What can be done for the bank angler?

Few would dispute that the bank anglers' lot in 1967 or 1968 was far from a happy one. In September of both years permit sales to bank anglers were low although the brown trout fed hard inshore. The rainbow trout take at the backend was well down on earlier months for biological reasons and the boats, too, often brought in very poor bags.

Considerable improvement should result from the heavy stocking with brown trout which was begun in Spring 1967, and continued in 1968 and 1969, but Grafham can never wholly rely upon brown trout, for there is a population of coarse fish that will only be controlled by predation by the more vigorous and heavily-feeding rainbow trout.

Pike are present at Grafham, but they eat trout when they catch them as readily as they eat coarse fish and could in time destroy Grafham as a trout water as surely as they did Hollowell.*

Considerable improvement would attend the planting of the margins with non-choking weeds such as *Potamogeton lucens* which allow trout to swim through as well as around, and provide ideal cover for food creatures too.

But this is only touching on the problem. Very large lakes

* When at the backend of the 1969 season we were catching up to a dozen 8 in to 9 in pike in a day's fly fishing, Dick Shrive told me he had had four browns all with small pike in their stomachs.

such as Grafham present fishery management problems upon a vast scale. We had best learn to solve them for there are a number of other big reservoirs under construction or in the planning stages. These sporting amenities are now acknowledged to be of national importance as recreation centres and their value must not be allowed to decline merely because water engineers, the traditional custodians of reservoirs, have no training in fish farming and even less experience of the leisure industry.

Fishery management as a positive science is almost completely lacking in Britain. It has always been so, but has become a blindingly obvious need at Grafham because the fishery has probably begun to decline earlier than is the case at most waters and that decline is being felt by far more anglers.

In 1968 I gave considerable thought to the problem and the chapter 'Fishery management and advisory associations' includes a synthesis of two of my articles published in *Angling* magazine, whose editor, Brian Harris, shared my concern.

CHAPTER 17

Boat fishing at Grafham

Of all the Midland reservoirs, Grafham is that where boat
angling enjoys its greatest success. What more natural therefore
than to use Grafham as the background to this account of boat-
fishing tactics!

Spring

Sunday 5 May is a day worth writing about. By no means was it
one of those days of slaughter when one wastes time trying
unlikely methods in an effort to avoid a limit before lunch. It
was a day when we fished hard from 10 AM and took our last
fish only minutes before closing time.

Now when we opened the previous season, 1967, we had pulled
the boat down to Valley Creek and taken three or four fish
apiece in a matter of forty minutes. All of them were brown
trout between 2 and 3 lb taken stripping through with a tandem-
dressed Black Knight in my case, whilst Mike fished his usual
Black Pennell. We had to move from the creek to avoid a limit
by 11 AM ... and of course we then had to struggle in the early
evening to get the limit!

So what more obvious in 1968 than to start again in Valley
Creek. The day was cool, without being cold, and the south-west
wind reached force 7 in the afternoon.

Lures, nymphs and small flashers were equally ineffective
fished for the first hour well sunk using a DT floater with a
4½-yard length of no 5 fast-sinking level line spliced to its end.
Nor had marked variation in the speed of recovery made any
apparent difference. I say 'apparent' because it is impossible to
tell what interest a medium-deep-fished fly arouses unless something actually plucks at it. You see nothing of those fish that
examine the offering and turn aside without actually taking.

The only success of the morning was a fat rainbow of 1¼ lb,
which took a brown nymph fished close to the surface. It

sometimes happens when fish are dour that they can be teased into taking at the surface by fishing in an adaptation of classical loch-fishing style working the dropper so it trips along the surface. As in loch fishing the rod is held well up and the line lies in a great bow from rod tip to water. Recovery is in quick short pulls to give the fly brisk action.

Now a fish that is teased into taking can seldom be a genuinely feeding fish; it is, I believe, teased fish that we so often prick and lose. Fishing with the rod point high gives us, paradoxically, a better chance of hooking shy fish well for that belly of line makes it impossible to hit them too early. They have turned down with the fly before we tighten and the hookhold usually is secure.

From 11 AM to 3 PM we took no more fish, and acting on the old maxim that if they're not feeding at the surface they must be feeding deep (we proved that not always to be true on the following Sunday) we put up deep-sinking shooting heads and drifted size 6 Brown and Green Nymphs from the upwind side of the boat. Mike's size 9 level head was spliced to a monofil shooting line, my size 10 level sinker was spliced to no 5 level floater. The nymphs, with some 35 to 40 yards of line and leader out, were probably 15 to 20 ft beneath the surface despite a high rate of drift in the strong wind. We found it necessary to clear the hooks of blanket weed from time to time.

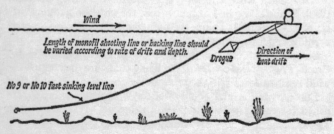

Diagram 17.1   Fishing deep upwind of a boat

We drifted from the south side of Savages Creek across its mouth so as to continue parallel to and 100 yards from the far shore.

Three brown trout from 2½/3 lb in tip-top condition came in the first half hour, and then after changing to a Jersey Herd, came a take from a very heavy fish which broke away after a few seconds ... leaving a hook shank and dressing but no point, barb or bend. This was the last of a stock of Jersey Herds tied many years ago on long-shank fine-wire hooks. The remainder of these hooks have been thrown away lest I commit similar folly at some future date!

It was noticeable that the three brownies and the unknown escaper were all hooked within 50 yards of each other. Those caught had been feeding heavily and their mouths were full of a wriggling transparent worm-like creature up to $1\frac{1}{4}$ in long and with what appeared to be a sucking mouth at one end.

Over the next hour came several rainbows from 1 lb to $1\frac{1}{2}$ lb from the area half-way across Savages Creek but the brown trout were no longer to be found.*

At about 5 PM the strong wind began to abate and at about 6 PM we made for fairly calm water off the bank running north to south in Lymage Bay.

Already a number of fish were showing at the ripple edge but they were cruising fast and disinclined to take, even when covered.

They appeared to be taking a surface fly, probably a small midge, and the rise form was that ominously quiet upthrusting head and dorsal fin followed by an equally disturbance-free tail-wagging disappearance.

There are two basic gambits: to fish a Butcher, Pennell, or Invicta fairly fast through the area of activity and hope to provoke a take, or to grease the leader and fish a nymph of some kind just beneath the surface film and so slowly that there is no apparent line wake. We tried both methods.

Between 7 PM and near-darkness the fast-fished flasher provided perhaps three dozen follows, quick snatches and savage takes that must have driven home any meat hook let alone size 6 short-point Sproats. But, somehow the hooks weren't home and where, briefly, the fish was actually felt struggling, the hookhold was lost in that same instant.

Around 7 PM a rainbow about $1\frac{1}{2}$ lb was taken in exactly the manner of the first of the day: rod point high and a nymph worked in quick short pulls just beneath the surface. The 'answer' having been found, failed to work again. The fast-

* April 1970. Newly published Rules for Grafham appear to render this method illegal there.

fishing flasher, on the other hand, received plenty of offers though no takes.

By 8 PM a few fish were to be seen moving shoulders out of water, mopping up everything. The last few inches of the leader were greased and a size 14 well-chewed Green and Yellow Nymph was tied on. Line recovery was by slow figure-of-eight winding, rod-point again well up, say, at half-past ten.

The surface-fished nymph was immediately attractive and over the next thirty minutes it was followed, sometimes for several yards, on perhaps half a dozen occasions. Whether any of these fish actually mouthed the fly is impossible to say, but I feel it likely that several did. Had I been stripping through, several would doubtless have been pricked.

And then came a boil, no follow or indication of a fish near by but a healthy taking rise. The fish, a very plump one-and-a-half pounder, was hooked in the scissors.

Again, the 'answer' produced no more fish, not even follows, and in fast-failing light, on went a Fuzzy-Buzzy.

It was of immediate interest to several fish and the pattern of follows was repeated. With only minutes to go the slowly figure-of-eight-recovered 'haystack', gently furrowing its way across the water, was decisively taken. The belly of line from high rod point to water gave the fish ample time to turn down and the hook was well home. This was a picture of a rainbow of just over 3 lb. A fitting close to the day.

If any day's fishing proved it true that in wet fly fishing it is the fish that determines whether the hook is home or not, this one did. There were nine takes to one rod and nine times the hook was home, eight fish coming to the net. Only in surface fishing had the angler done anything to help and that was in a sense negative action . . . he avoided tightening sufficiently long to let the fish turn. On one of these occasions he achieved this by happening to be looking elsewhere when the take came!

Summer

3 June 1968 was a day that made nonsense of so much of the accepted lore of lake fishing. The wind was north-west backing to north-east. The sky was dull and misty . . . that 'milky' light I wrote of earlier. Later we had cloud and a little rain and in the evening the sky cleared and the light wind died completely to leave the water an unbroken calm.

Fishing at the surface, midwater and near bottom proved fruitless until 3 PM. Not a sign of a fish.

By this time we had moored the boat by the catwalk between the dam and the valve tower where several rainbows rose sporadically. I was vaguely interested to note that each time I changed the fly a fish nipped it and like lightning dropped it. After about twenty minutes of this nonsense I put up a sinking head and a tandem B&P lure and allowed the line and fly to go to the bottom. Line recovery was three sharp hauls then a prolonged pause. At the second cast there was a quiet slow drag and then the fly was dropped. Two casts later the same slow drag and the fish was on. A very strong rainbow that fought all the way and went 2½ lb when weighed. And then, again, nothing.

Around 4.15 PM we anchored 40 yards off the south side of Savages Creek where a few risers showed. The water was around 8 ft deep, clear, and calm. A double-taper line and greased leader was indicated, and a smallish nymph. From 4.30 to 6 PM I rose fifteen fish, none of which apparently touched any of the half dozen flies and nymphs that I tried. Nor was a dry fly any better.

A further hour off the north shore to the west of Hill Farm proved just as hopeless.

Around 8 PM we noticed a number of fish rising several hundred yards out and we started the motor and moved towards them.

Although we moved at low revs for the last 150 yards and cut the engine 70 yards from the fish so as to make our approach in silence the fish had ceased to rise by the time we were within casting distance. They then showed again 70 yards away.

This is the usual pattern of behaviour when you move a boat towards fish in calm . . . and the only answer I know is quietly to work out line and fish until they start to rise again within range. Which they did on this occasion. By 9.30 PM I had had six rises and six fish, all on a size 14 Cinnamon and Gold and a Corixa.

All of the fish were rainbows, as were those risen and missed in the afternoon, so far as I could tell. Short rising and the general cussedness that so many of us encounter at Grafham seems peculiarly a feature of fishing to rainbow trout: browns seem to rise and take with determination or not to rise at all.

30 July 1967 was markedly a different day. The wind blew force 5 to 6 from the south-west. It was dry and dull until 4 PM,

when the sun shone brilliantly. We fished a succession of drifts towards the north shore, west of Hill Farm, starting near Savages Creek and moving east until finally we were drifting into the sunken road near the farm.

Big flies which had seemed obviously right in very rough water were quite useless and around midday we suddenly became aware, looking along the troughs of the waves, of the odd dorsal fin breaking the water. The fish were right on top. In fact, we then began to notice that we drifted over the occasional fish without it showing any sign of seeing us. It was almost as though they were fast asleep.

Around 2 PM using the Cinnamon and Gold size 12 at dropper and tail we began taking fish at almost every drift, rainbows from about 150 to 100 yards from shore and then browns as we drifted and fished right into the wave-beaten and coloured margins. Easily our best drifts were those over the sunken hedgerows. This became one of those days when you could fill the boat and we left the water in the late afternoon.

But the 'limit' days teach you very little that is new, for, on such days, the probability is that whatever style you fish well will be successful. 29 June 1968 was a very different day. The wind was south-west through the day backing to south in the evening. We fished near the surface most of the day, sometimes drifting and sometimes at anchor. My first fish came at noon, and though I continued fishing to the same shoal, not another offer until I changed the fly when I immediately missed a fish.

Fishing to another shoal in a calm lane around 5.30 PM I missed a fish, and then had persistent refusals followed by a solid take as soon as I changed the fly. I again changed the fly and immediately had another. In the evening rise, changing the fly again produced immediate offers and two more fish were killed before we went ashore.

The implication is clear: there appears strong evidence justifying research into the possibility of inter-communication between rainbow trout in a shoal. Perhaps brown trout also communicate but we have less chance of finding out because they tend to shoal to a lesser extent than rainbows and the most obvious occasion is the silverhorns rise! And as soon as we think about the chasing and missing and pricking that then goes on, we begin perhaps to wonder whether the one fly is detected early for what it is and rejected thereafter by every fish that has got the signal.

But where rainbows are concerned my questioning amounts sufficiently near to belief as to encourage me to change my fly every time I rise a fish and fail to kill it. In fact I dislike missing or pricking a rainbow almost as much as I disliked hooking and losing a roach years ago because the whole shoal often went off the feed for a short while or even moved out of the swim.*

The backend

In 1967 when the brown trout moved into the shallows in enormous numbers, and when the rainbow trout were on several days almost entirely absent from the bag, fishing from a boat was at times effective only in the last few yards of a drift with the flies dropping 25 yards and less from the downwind shore ... and there were few places free of bank anglers where one could drift that close.

Away from the banks the fish were markedly localized, takes coming fast over perhaps 60 yards of a drift and nothing for hundreds of yards either side of that spot. We made it a practice to lift the drogue and go back over good ground again and again rather than waste time over seemingly empty water.

Our most effective flies were Black Pennell, Claret and Mallard, and Brown and Green Nymph dressed large on hooks sizes 5 and 6. It was noticeable most of the month that takes came far more freely to Mike's rod despite matching of patterns and speed of recovery, and we finally established that his worn weight-forward 'floating' line, with its last 5 yards sinking instantly, meant that his flies were fishing perhaps 4 or 5 ft down whilst mine were near the surface.

It was not the case that his elimination of line-wake near the fly was improving his sport since at one time I was fishing a 20 ft leader to check just that point. Not until I spliced $4\frac{1}{2}$ yards of no 5 rapid sinker to the end of my floating line did I begin to hold my own ... too late to achieve much benefit.

Looking back, it still seems incredible that hard-feeding fish in mid-lake over 30 to 40 ft of water would come to a fly 5 ft down, and ignore one at 2 ft. But it happened during daytime feeding too consistently over too many weeks to be attributed to happenstance.

And what of the evening rises? What of those shoals of rainbows feeding only feet away from the concrete slope of the

* See footnote page 217

dam? At first, I took them to be shoals of coarse fish. Their behaviour was identical with that of a rudd shoal in a warm dusk at Ravensthorpe; dozens of nebs slowly furrowing the surface. Usually they took or plucked the first time you covered them and from then on ignored your fly. Once, in five minutes close to darkness, I struck at dimples inches from the dam and landed a brace of rainbows at 2 lb 4 oz each.

My fly was a size 14, almost unrecognizable, olive nymph.

One of the most intriguing aspects of fishing the evening rise during 1967 and 1968 was my experience that casting to the rise or ahead of the rise was unproductive. It was as though the fish refused 'food' *that they saw to come from aloft*. They seemed so often to take only that fly or nymph that they happened upon as they swam, one that was below the surface and which seemingly had never been elsewhere.

Again this happened to me too often to be chance.

So far I have found only one common factor: a large number of the rainbows taken in the height of the dusk rises have been feeding on zooplankton, mainly water fleas, their stomach contents being a grey jelly-like slime with black 'pinheads' in it. Often there have been a dozen *live* creatures only $\frac{1}{8}$ in long in their mouths when brought to the net. And once again I am back to the old question: are the fish that show at the surface actually feeding on flies? ... or is it that they take a surface midge in mistake, so to speak, for the daphnia and other little duddybugs, that they are ingesting in quantity only inches from the surface?

Most of us who have sailed warm seas are familiar with the 'flashing lights' of surface organisms disturbed in darkness by the passage of the hull, and the brilliant glow of the wake from the screws. Clearly at night, the sea's surface must be thick as soup with micro-organisms.

Macan and Worthington writing about Windermere on pp 99 and 100 of *Life in Lakes and Rivers* (Collins, 1951) tell us: 'At midday the animals are in greatest abundance at some distance from the surface, and in the upper layers of the lake they are few. As the day draws on there is an upward migration, and round about midnight it is the surface layers of the lake which are most thickly populated.'

The upward and downward migration is believed to be a reaction to light.

I have mentioned elsewhere how seldom surface food forms were found in brown trout caught in the height of a rise, and conjectured that most of the fish we actually catch are probably not those seen feeding at the surface. I suggest the evening 'rise' in lakes might be a form of sub-surface feeding having little to do with the flies actually seen at the surface. Particularly is this possible in the case of rainbow trout which have been recognized for forty years in USA to be plankton feeders.

Which brings us to the crunch question.

I know well that trout can see a water flea or similar-sized 'bug' and I have seen trout check their advance and snap up something, to me invisible, but probably of water-flea dimensions. But can a fish of 2 to 4 lb get enough of such tiny creatures to grow fat by taking only one here and there – as a deliberate bite and swallow so to speak. Or is it possible that a shoal of rainbows having come upon a concentration of zooplankton swim through it, mouths open, sieving the meat from the gravy like a blue whale eating krill?

Rainbows obviously do not have the advantage of whalebone, but I suggest the general structure of mouth, teeth, gillrakers, and throat are sufficiently similar to make the possibility worthy of further investigation. If, in fact, rainbows do at times feed without closing their mouths, hooking them would then be more a matter of chance than skill.

It is easy enough to decide what to do when fish can be seen rising. But the afternoon periods can be deadly dull when boat fishing. The standard gambits are three, and all of them adopted with persistence are successful.

The first demands local knowledge or keen observation or emulation of other anglers known to have the essential knowledge. The boat is moored in a known 'swim', the anglers fish the buzzer or nymphs slowly and quietly, and in totally unspectacular manner they land a brace every hour or so. It is precisely the same as bank fishing and depends for success on both anglers fishing the same method and achieving concealment and good presentation. It is futile to expect sport if one angler strips through! Stripping a line is essentially a technique for drifting, when each cast is to new fish.

The second method relies on the fact that large numbers of fish feed around 150 yards offshore. The boat is drifted or gently rowed at about this distance from the margin, the anglers throwing a fairly long line and using weight-forward fast-sinkers to fish nymphs or lures deep and at medium speed.

The third method is to look for those offshore calm lanes and drift them until a shoal of feeding rainbow is encountered. Towards the backend of 1968 it became most noticeable that such fish were most easily taken with a dry fly placed a long way ahead of the shoal and in its path. Again, a long line is necessary. Seldom did we rise fish close to the boat.

Somehow, nothing systematic has yet been done with a fourth approach, though I did see one angler in 1967 try the method briefly from the shore near Hill Farm ... to the very great annoyance of several other anglers near by. Heaven knows why they should have objected; the method was and is absolutely legal and I shall certainly use it whenever circumstances are right.

Dapping is what I have in mind. Here we are at Grafham fishing a lake almost on the scale of the Irish loughs – and forgetting everything we take for granted at Corrib. The events that clinched things for me were, first, a morning in July when the water 150 yards from Mander Park shore line was covered with bees ... some dead but many still beating the surface in a forlorn attempt to take off. Up came the trout and the surface was cleared of the swarm in perhaps five minutes. Nothing that we threw at the fish – it was flat calm, by the way – drew so much as a short rise.

But it proved, if proof were needed, that the presence of living and bulky surface food would bring trout up where nothing else would.

Again, one mid-afternoon in early September, hundreds of yards from the shore between Church Hill Cove and Marlow Park, dozens of trout rose freely to the many craneflies drifting and fluttering across the water: the classic rise to the 'Daddy' and we were in no way equipped to deal with it. With little hope, I worked a Fuzzy-Buzzy as a wake-fly and, at last, a fish hit it and all but took my rod with him as he ran 80 yards in a rush that had me convinced I was into Moby Dick's spotted nephew. He was a short very thick cock brown trout of 3 lb 4 oz, hooked in the pectoral fin.

The critical rule at Grafham, so far as dapping is concerned, is that you must use only artificial flies. A 14 ft glassfibre bottom rod, your usual fly reel (or a 4 in 'Flick 'em' for that matter) and 20 yards of Terylene or nylon floss (knotted every eighteen inches) and a 9 ft monofil leader with a Fuzzy-Buzzy or an artificial mayfly or cranefly, or Black Pennell will do admirably as an outfit – the breeze will do the rest. By the way, you will need one of the modern fly oils such as that made by Gudebrod. The fly is dipped in the bottle, shaken, *and allowed to dry for ten minutes*. I carry out this process properly the night before and then top the fly up, so to speak, at odd moments during the fishing. I still know of nothing more effective than amadou for removing water before oiling the fly.

The great advantage of dapping stems from your ability to work your fly onto and over the water just like a natural insect and to present only the fly to the fish, the remainder of the tackle being in the air. A certain skill is needed to keep the fly skating on the surface without its lifting off too far or too often. You aren't going to catch your fish in mid-air.

The 'rise' to a skating fly is often explosive and you will need a great deal of self-control to delay your tighten until the trout has turned down.*

* In May 1970, Mike and I fished the upper Test and lunched overlooking perhaps a dozen rainbow trout from 1½ to 2½ lb in a wide deepish pool below a grille.

We fed a mixture of scraps of bread, Spam, sausage, egg, tomato, cucumber and banana to the cruising fish and found that after inspection and rejection of the first scraps of tomato and cucumber these two foods ceased to be of interest to any fish in the pool.

Bread, Spam, sausage and egg were taken and ingested every time, but except on one occasion the trout rushed at the food scrap, passed it and then took it on the turn. Only once was a particle taken on the approach run so to speak.

Scraps of banana were taken and ejected by several fish and were subsequently eaten by others in the group.

It was evident that rainbows in this group closely inspected and presumably scented foods before seizing them, and when one fish rejected a food (tomato and cucumber), without taking it the others got the message. Of banana the message could well have been 'quite all right if that sort of thing appeals to you'.

I feel the cautious inspection before acceptance of Spam, sausage, egg, etc, all of which smell like food, has important lessons for us in 'fly' fishing. Maybe the next step is 'scented' lures.

Another visit to the Test, this time near Romsey, afforded an opportunity to fish the Mayfly to rainbows which again patrolled in groups over well-defined beats. Either the fly was taken as soon as correctly presented or it was rejected by one fish and remained thereafter of interest to none. If however you put on another fly the fish were immediately interested again, and they would accept the first fly quite happily if you rested them for ten minutes or so and then tried it again.

I feel this intercommunication, if such it proves to be, is akin to the instantaneous shying away from a predator that we see in underwater films, of tropical fishes. We see the same reaction to danger by birds in flight, every individual wheeling in an instant to the same new course.

I now believe that putting the same fly more than three times to the same group of rainbows is to waste time. Changing the fly and trying them again seems the obvious solution.

By contrast, it was noticeable that a brown trout could become increasingly interested the more frequently a fly passed over him. I got a really handsome 2½ lb wild brownie at perhaps the thirtieth cast.

A most interesting facet of rising to the Mayfly was the number of times the artificial was taken in preference to a natural only inches away. Again it was noticed that fish frequently dropped back several yards before taking an artificial but that the take inevitably followed the dropping-back process despite the prolonged opportunity that such fish had to detect the falsity of the fly.

On the Test as elsewhere rejection or acceptance seems related to things other than the 'make' of the fly. By the way, on dozens of occasions a struggling natural was missed by a rising trout and subsequently struggled into the air to make its first flight to safety.

Part Three

CHAPTER 18

Fishery management and advisory associations

Many keen trout fishermen remain for years unaware that their drinking water comes from reservoirs which hold trout. Friends in Northampton often asked where I caught my trout and were almost disbelieving when I told them they were caught locally.

Obviously, this ignorance has much to do with the fact that water-supply reservoirs and their environs are frequently closed to the general public. The picnic party and the coach seldom find their way to the waters. Often, too, they are set in secluded country several miles from the nearest highway.

Sometimes you will find that the water is leased to a club or a syndicate but usually you will find that any fishing is by permit, varying in price from 50p to £1.50 per day; often the ratepayer receives especially favourable treatment.

There are some reservoirs which are completely closed to

anglers, or which are fished only by privileged friends of the board or its officers. Here the only remedy is to awaken the authority's social conscience and link your plea to the possibility of increasing its revenue whilst improving the local sporting amenity. Generally speaking, the root cause of reservoir closure is ignorance, albeit well-meaning ignorance, on the part of those in authority. Macan and Worthington state that closure is quite illogical for standing waters inhibit the growth of harmful bacteria, while the general practice of chlorinating the water during treatment entirely disposes of risk.

The prohibition of angling by water authorities is seen at its most absurd when we consider the unlikelihood of man-borne infection and the far greater possibility of bird-borne infection. Ducks, geese, gulls and swans, it must be remembered, are frequent visitors to both sewage works and reservoirs and they are not particular as to which they visit first. It is to be hoped that those authorities who dislike fishermen on their reservoirs introduce, and enforce, a rule to cover the bird menace.

Neither is the attitude to infection always consistent between man and man. It is not so long ago that several Devonshire reservoirs were open only to season-ticket holders who presented a clean bill of health. Presumably, a bill-of-health from a would-be day-ticket holder could not be relied upon. At any rate, he was not given an opportunity of providing one.

Water authorities and the angler

Few water authorities are interested in their waters as fisheries: an alarming fact when we consider the rapidly increasing array of anglers and the ever-growing shortage of good fishing water.

With one or two notable exceptions such as the Bristol Waterworks Company, there are no keen anglers on most water boards and the attitude of members is not one of antipathy so much as apathy. When the general run of members are quite wrongly convinced that even slight contamination means water-borne epidemic and they are uninterested in angling anyway, it is so easy for them to be panicked into stopping fishing altogether or to limit the possibility of contamination by leasing the water to a small club.

If a water authority owning the riparian rights on its reservoirs permits any fishing at all the right to enjoy the amenity belongs to the whole of the ratepaying public, just as they enjoy the right to play their football or cricket matches on pitches owned by the authority, subject to the observance of reasonable rules and by-laws.

Advisory associations

Although I wrote the above words in 1952, most of the passage is still applicable to anglers, their reservoirs and water authorities over most of Britain.

We in Northampton were faced at that time with deteriorating sport in our reservoirs but we made no determined attempt to set matters aright. A few public-spirited individuals wrote letters to the water board requesting stocking, weed-cutting and so on but these, quite understandably, had little effect: public bodies must always cater for the wishes of the majority and it must be manifest that spokesmen do in fact, represent that majority. In December 1951, therefore, the late Colonel S. W. Miller MC, Mr C. C. 'Jim' Robinson and I decided that we would try to form a representative organization.

We advertised in the local press our intention to hold an inaugural meeting, and on 10 January 1952 more than one hundred local fly-fishers met in a Northampton hotel, decided that an association should be formed, and appointed a committee to thrash out rules. The first general meeting took place a month later; rules were adopted, and a committee proper appointed.

Although prior to 1952 there had been widespread dissatisfaction with the reservoir fisheries, both meetings were notable for the highly responsible attitude of local anglers. Everyone was cognisant of the fact that the fishing we enjoyed was a privilege, and that the association, far from seeking to impose its will, must support the water board in ensuring clean water supplies. We were also aware of the need to allay understandable public suspicion that we were seeking to transfer to a club, fishing privileges which previously had been enjoyed by all ratepayers.

Everything that we did was communicated to the water engineer and to the chairman of the water board by official letters. We also invited officers and members of the board to come to our meetings and we gave every facility to the local press.

Since so many people look upon the press as willing to throw aside all decencies to create a sensation, I would like to state that we were never caused any embarrassment, nor was there any breach of confidence though, at times, there was a 'background' known to the press which might have made screaming headlines had it been published.

If you are forming an association I am convinced that you cannot prosper without good local and angling press relations ... particularly when the local press has some effect on local voters, and therefore has the eye of councillors, many of whom will sit on the water board.

A word of caution ... Although you may feel that you have a genuine grievance against the water engineer, or even the board, to publish your criticisms can only do harm. Ultimately, you rely upon the good will of local representatives and officials and they are unlikely to respond well to pressure tactics. You will require persistence, determination and good humour; righteous anger (pique?) and public squabbling will get you nowhere, though at times your anger will certainly be justified!

We looked upon our association as a ratepayers' association and this turned out a most effective policy. One of our rules stated that the association would never seek for itself privileges which were not equally available to ratepayers who were non-members. Amendment of this rule required a 7/8 majority, and it was, therefore, virtually unalterable. It was our intention from the first to avoid patronage by one political party or another, and our ratepayer status was always accepted by both major political parties represented on the board. As a result we never suffered any difficulties through changes of political power.

We were greatly helped in the early days by a local alderman. On his advice we ignored our major problems and sought the granting of an apparently trivial concession: we asked the water board to extend the hours of fishing to one hour after sunset throughout the season. This was granted subject to the association weighing in the fish and enforcing closing time (the avoidance of increased overtime pay was the probable aim of the board). We accepted the responsibility and members and non-members played their parts magnificently. Only twice was it necessary to take any disciplinary measures and in both cases the committee's decisions were accepted by the defaulters. The association proved it could shoulder responsibility.

In October 1952, Colonel Miller and I as chairman and secretary were received by the Works Committee of the Mid-Northamptonshire Water Board, when we presented stocking proposals (which had been checked as to their practicability by Doctor T. T. Macan). We were astonished that laymen on the board so readily grasped such technicalities as we had included in our statements and we were very glad indeed that we had prepared our material with great care. It is a point always worth bearing in mind that good administrators are quickly able to differentiate between probabilities and improbabilities, even when the technicalities of the subject are beyond them.

On 11 December, with the help of the water board workmen, we distributed about £200-worth of fish around the margins of our reservoirs and the stocking has been on an adequate and yearly basis since that time.

Concessions gained subsequently include the granting of Sunday fishing, provision of more boats, reductions in the cost of boat permits, increases in the permitted number of bank rods, extension of the fishing season, and Easter fishing when Easter falls before 1 April opening date. The netting of coarse fish at Ravensthorpe Reservoir has been regularly carried out as a result of negotiations with the Nene River Authority and on several occasions we negotiated trout in exchange for the coarse fish netted.

The method by which the Mid-Northants Trout Fishers' Association was set up remains the foolproof approach that it was in 1952 because local government, the democratic process, and the appointment of water boards remains virtually unaltered.

That we had worked to good effect in quite another direction became apparent only when in 1968 I read that most important of all officially presented 'papers', *The Recreational Use of Waterworks*.

The paper was read to the Conference of the British Water Works Association on 19 April 1967, by Walter Winterbottom (Director of the Sports Council) and Leonard G. Brown, Engineer and Manager of the Mid-Northamptonshire Water Board, the same Leonard Brown whose help we sought in 1952.

Both gentlemen made it clear to an audience representing almost every water undertaking in Britain that whilst the supply of healthful water is their first priority, this aim is fully compatible with recreational use of their reservoirs.

May I quote Leonard Brown:

'It seems obvious that if any of you have reservoirs surrounded by thick hedges or high fences from which everyone is excluded, you are really living in the past and you will shortly have to open your gates for the benefit of the people who, after all, are providing the money, or their forefathers did, to help those works.'

Again, he says: 'Storage filtration and sterilization will render any water safe from the usual organic pollutions, but it is desirable to reduce those pollutions as far as possible. If you are to have a recreational use, the first contribution to reducing this pollution is by the formation of a club to control whatever sport you are thinking of. A club can impose discipline on its members, and that is the great thing.'

Northampton's place in reservoir angling is much older than that of Bristol for Leonard Brown's water undertaking or, more correctly, the organization from which it grew allowed trout fishing in its Ravensthorpe Reservoir as long ago as March 1893 and 'Red Spinner' writing in *The Field* of 9 November 1895 reported that 209 fish averaging 3 lb 5½ oz were caught in 258 man-days' fishing. (I like this 75-years-old reference to 'Productivity' – there are few ideas that are really new.)

In 1896, the Reverend Charles Brooke's eight-fish limit in one day weighed 38 lb 12 oz.

Short of a series of damn-fool actions by anglers on reservoirs it is safe to predict that although many reservoirs are still closed to anglers, all or nearly all will have been opened by 1975. Where authorities prove stubborn, the right method of tackling the job is the setting up of an association by the method used so successfully at Northampton.

First make sure the board owns the riparian rights – I know of several cases where the board could not allow the public to fish, however much it wanted to – and then get the help of the local and the angling press. Other ratepayers will object to financing your fishing, so your attempts to get local reservoirs opened must contain acceptable budgetary proposals. Try to get an accountant onto your committee. Keepering, boat purchase and maintenence, provision of toilets and shelter, issuing of permits and so on are charges which someone must meet and they are likely far to exceed the cost of trout for stocking. Nor is it sensible to expect fifty anglers a day at £1 a permit if the average catch per rod/day is likely to be one fish averaging 10 oz.

Budgets must relate to what the water will produce under

average management, availability of other fishing in the area and what the local anglers will pay.

In some areas where waters are acid and productivity is low the only financially sound policy may be for the board to lease the rights to a club to carry out the whole fishery management function and to make available an agreed number of day tickets to non-members at prices to be approved by the board.

The need to organize

Anglers are the worst-organized body of British sportsmen by far.

For years I watched, horrified, the feuding that went on between ACA and NFA, and squabbles between major clubs competing for more water. Then, too, there has been for many years almost complete mistrust between game and coarse fishers though this, thank heaven, is fast disappearing as more coarse fishers each year have opportunity to fish for trout as well.

But a new factor has now appeared . . . angling itself is being threatened by two very powerful well-organized bodies, respectively the RSPCA and the bird watchers.

An extremist fringe within the RSPCA managed in 1968 to link angling with several other blood sports and persuade a majority of members to ban them all as cruel. R. L. Marston of *Fishing Gazette* and Wilson Stevens of *The Field* saw this possibility twenty years ago and it was realized even then that as a body, anglers have no joint, authoritative, responsible voice sanely presenting their case to the general public whenever it may be necessary.

The mass media look upon anglers and angling as a kind of joke . . . only recently I watched an advertising film depicting a slap-happy angler overjoyed to bend his rod into what turned out to be only the branch of a tree.

But there is none of this nonsense about the anti-blood sports fraternity, or the naturalists. Their publicity is emotive, biased to the point of fanaticism and presented through press and radio with all the skills that their trained public-relations experts can muster.

When David Attenborough, Peter Scott, James Fisher and others present their admirable TV features, they are recruiting sympathy for naturalists and bird watchers and, by implication, those of us who kill wild creatures in our sport become villains.

Our public image is far from satisfactory and we need to improve it fast.

The biggest threat and the most insidious comes from the bird watchers. Their views are well presented and their requirements are catered for long before the anglers come into the picture.

In many cases where the possibility of opening a reservoir for angling is under consideration, the bird watchers, who have had facilities there for years, are protesting vigorously about the possible disturbance of the birds and more often than not they actually have their members on the water board. In several cases known to me they have succeeded in barring anglers from those western upwind (and protected) shores preferred by bank anglers. The angler learns of it only after it has happened.

This kind of threat can be met only by organization and counter propaganda.

It is high time we remembered that we are the largest body practising any sport in Britain. We also have a very powerful voice, locally and nationally when we go to the polls. It is time we learned to protect ourselves.

Financial aid

A joint circular from the Ministry of Housing and Local Government and the Department of Education and Science on 27 August 1964 (Circular 49/64 MOHLG) established the availability of grants or loans to provide buildings and centres for the use of clubs, societies and organizations having athletic, social or educational objects. Section 10 of the Ministry of Land and Natural Resources Circular No 3/66 also refers to the capital grants available to clubs and organizations to meet costs of recreational facilities, and this circular is specifically about reservoirs as recreational centres.

The key to monetary aid is recognition as a responsible body. Every reservoir fisher needs such an organization.

The politics of angling clubs

Get the right men elected to the committee and give them *carte blanche* to do a job of work.

Perhaps ten out of every hundred members of any association will be prepared to work regularly for the fishery. Between them, the ten will accumulate far more worthwhile knowledge of the water than the other ninety put together. You must remember, however, that the ninety have the voting power to nullify the efforts of the committee, and you must therefore walk the tight-rope between a sound technical policy involving occasional un-popular decisions and the maintenance of good relations with your members. Generally speaking, it pays to avoid deeply technical detail when reporting to general meetings: better by far persuade members to pass omnibus motions to the effect that the management committee take the necessary steps to procure certain ends.

In contrast to the customary yearly election of members of the general purposes committee, I strongly urge that a water man-agement committee should be appointed on a footing which permits continuity of service while avoiding sterility of ideas. The only solution appears to be appointment for, say, five years with compulsory retirement for one or two members each year. In this way there will always be a majority of experienced workers to evaluate the suggestions of newcomers and drastic changes of policy – detrimental to good fishery management as to farming – will be nipped in the bud.

Committee work from time to time is certain to involve un-pleasant decisions and actions. Committee members must, therefore, be loyal to each other and preserve outward unanimity. The alternative is division among the members and a lowering of the status of the association in the eyes of the water board. When you appear before the board your great strength is the one hundred per cent backing of your members.

The vigorous well-being of any association reflects more than anything else the hard work of its secretary. Secretaries become tired and five years of office is quite enough for any man. It is a sound policy to appoint an 'assistant' secretary twelve months before his predecessor retires so that by the time he takes over he has the whole of the organization at his finger-tips.

Delegates to the board

Reservoir advisory associations have a public duty to perform. It is essential therefore that members exercise their votes to appoint competent committees: the more usual method of selec-tion on a basis of popularity is likely to lead to serious adminis-tration problems. Delegates to the water board will need considerable charm, intellectual power and knowledge of fishery work, and you must ensure that there are such men on your committee. Although the water board may receive delegates they will only be guided by them if they are obviously competent.

Reservoir fishery management: the problem

Because we all enjoy more leisure today than at any time in Britain's history and have money with which to enjoy that leisure to the full, the value of shoots and fisheries has soared beyond relief. Road congestion having rendered a weekend trip to the sea sheer purgatory for father, we find families increasingly driving to the inland watering centres like Grafham and Pitsford, and new inland sailing clubs are formed almost every week.

We are reaching the situation that if you didn't have a reservoir there for water supply, you would have to create the lake as a social and recreational necessity. And the economy of such recreational waters can already be justified.

About twenty years ago, I recall demonstrating as part of my thesis *Pond Culture of Food Fishes* that Seale-Hayne Agricultural College's 'Wet Meadow', would be more profitable as a fishery than as grazing. Probably my case was shaky at that time but not so obviously that it could be rejected. Today's leisure and wealth have made sporting fisheries sound business almost everywhere.

Grafham occupies 1,600 acres of land, 22,861 day permits were issued in 1967 to yield at £1 a head, nearly £23,000, whilst boat revenues I compute from the board's returns to be around £12,500.

Gross revenues from fishing only, were of around £35,000.

If originally these 1,600 acres were under mixed farming, it is probable that they never returned as much as £35,000 to the farmers. And, bear in mind that to the fishery revenues we still have to add the returns from sailing and ice-cream/hot-dog concessions.

This reservoir has so high a value as a sporting amenity that we must deplore the probability that, like all first-rate reservoir fisheries, it has in 1968 begun the decline which results from the using up of the store of manure in the land and a rapid build-up of coarse species as a result of the necessary pumping from a coarse-fish-dominated river.

The high nutrient content (around 20 ppm of dissolved salts two years ago is now down to around 15 ppm) and trout growth

228

rate is already slowing, the position probably seriously aggravated by the thriving population of heavy perch, a fish whose diet closely resembles that of the trout.

Let us again state that the first duty of a water undertaking is the maintenance of an adequate and healthful water supply. And then let us ask the question, in view of the economic and social importance of reservoir fisheries, whether the maintenance of a good fishery is not also their duty, warranting the appointment of fishery managers who are also trained in fish farming?

We have already seen that the reservoir is little more than a wet field producing (for maximum fish-crop value in Britain) trout. We have instanced a case where fishery earnings approximate to the farming returns. Now let me ask you what kind of chap we should appoint as farm manager to a 1,600-acre conventional farming unit. Would you not agree that he is likely to be the product of a college or farm institute offering at least a good National Diploma in Agriculture or a BSC (Agriculture), with a further ten years' experience of profitable management of similar land and farm systems? And should we not pay him a handsome salary!

Now examine the fishery management of any water in the country and almost without exception you will find that it is QBE (Qualified By Experience). Much worse, it can be a position given to a socially acceptable semi-retired military gentleman who can kill his share of fish but knows as little about population counts as he does about parasitic infestation.

The honest 'practical' head bailiff has done and still does a very good job on a great many waters but with every recognition of his worth he lacks knowledge of the sciences which could help him to produce the more consistent and improved results that our leisured society needs and is prepared to pay for. Usually he ends up as a kind of junior administrator – issuing permits – supervising boat cleaning – checking the returns and accounting for the money.

But let me return to this matter of declining productivity of new reservoirs. By and large, water engineers like a water to have low nutrient content because this simplifies filtration, reduces plant outlay and processing cost and results in cheap water. Those authorities with mountain water of between 1 and 2 degrees of hardness are envied by those in the Midlands with highly productive water requiring much more treatment.

Both, however, produce palatable, healthful water.

Industry frequently prefers or even demands 'soft' water supplies and almost as frequently reduces the productivity of the rivers into which it passes its effluents. But the wishes of industrialists are not paramount, nor can they truthfully state that 'soft' waters are essential when their raw materials and processes today are markedly different from those processed a century ago, and when competitors spring up and operate successfully in hard water areas.

In twenty years, I believe we shall largely ignore filtration problems. We shall accept that our reservoirs are fisheries. We shall make them good fisheries by every technique known, including pond fertilization, and as a gifted and rich nation we shall buy more plant and more chemicals to treat the water before it goes into the distribution system. Probably too, the fishery manager will be a chief officer working with the engineer, and certainly he will have his own department run to its separately formulated policy.

Management as a positive function

But none of these things can come about until the general angling public wakes up to the fact that management must be the same positive function in fisheries that it is in industry.

The word 'manager' starts with the syllable 'man' . . . and if you wish to know the quality of a manager, you must look first into the man himself, his mind, his experience, his age and health, his attitude and the attitude of others to him, his courage, his honesty, his ability.

Fishery management is no different from other pursuits; only when the man is right can the management function be right. Only when you have met good management are you able to discern clearly its lack elsewhere. It is often said that fit people make very bad patients and of course it must be so . . . they know and fear sickness and the loss of their customary power which they then experience. Ailing people resemble ailing businesses and ailing fisheries: they often make little progress because they know of no other state of existence.

I suggest 90 per cent of our fisheries are mediocre because 90 per cent (at least) of so-called fishery managers have no real idea what can be achieved, far less how it can be achieved.

I have met one outstanding example of fishery management and we can do no better than examine the man responsible.

Alex Behrendt is owner and fishery manager *par excellence* of Two Lakes at Crampmoor, near Romsey. Alex was born in the Ukraine of a Polish mother and German father. From 1914 to 1920 he lived in Turkestan and then moved back to Silesia. Clay extraction for his father's brickworks left eighty acres of water in the form of five ponds which, from age seventeen to nineteen, he ran as a carp, trout and tench farm. Ducks also featured in the economy.

In 1929 he spent a year in Norway – oyster farming, and then in 1930 began eight years of wandering through middle-Europe and Asia, ending in a return to manage profitably the parental fish farm in 1938 until his call-up.

Alex's pre-war background may be summed up as a diversity of experience of European fish farming stemming from an abiding interest in natural history and a determination not to work with machines. Working with fish was accompanied by a deep study of fishery management as practised in Germany, Russia and other states where fish are farm produce. Above all he knew that fish farmers were much wealthier than graziers or those who grew arable crops.

Let us get this fact established. In areas remote from the sea, a well-managed fish-pond produces more revenue from sale of fish than from any other crop of similar labour content; and this has so far been true of Grafham.

In 1946, Alex was brought to England as a surrendered enemy. He was imprisoned at Romsey. By the time of his release in 1948, his father in East Germany was dead, the family business had been compulsorily acquired by the State and he had met his very charming and capable English wife.

He decided, to his and our advantage, to stay in England and farm fish.

At first, he thought to grow carp but soon realized that their commercial value in England made this a precarious prospect ... though there is, of course, a substantial sale of mainly imported carp to our Jewish community. Trout it had to be and his wife was quick to point out that a trout crop was more remunerative as a provider of sport than dead on a fishmonger's slab.

231

'Two Lakes' was acquired in 1948. And what courage it must have taken to begin at all!

The report prepared for Alex by one of our leading experts told him that his water had a pH of 6·4; nitrates were nil; hardness as calcium carbonate: 100 ppm (not good, but many waters have less). The report ended with the words: 'It is not really the type of water for letting as a trout fishery.'

Alex and that expert have since become firm friends and the expert is the first to admit that his report assumed the usual state of competence, that is, incompetence on the part of the would-be fishery manager.

How was he to know that his client had the European's willingness to work hard for long hours? How was he to realize that this client, and his wife, would shovel mud, excavate new ponds, build dams, make rearing ponds, and themselves carry out all the labours necessary, summer and winter? Above all, how was he to know that his client had a training and experience quite unknown in this country which enabled him to treat as commonplace apparently insurmountable fishery problems?

Nor was this a heavily financed project: expansion had to be carried out gradually out of income. A daunting procedure with the inbuilt advantage that there was time to learn the differing management requirements of each pond.

In 1948, Two Lakes was truly two lakes, the one four acres and the other, one acre. Excavation enlarged the fishery in 1951 and Spring and Border Lakes were added in 1956. Chalky Pool was added in 1958–9 and Home Pool in 1961.

There are now thirteen acres of lakes, offering widely different fishing problems and providing more good trout fishing for more people than any other similar area of water anywhere in Britain.

Nor as Brian Harris made clear in his Editorial in *Angling*, September 1968, is this like fishing in a goldfish pond. The fish are hard to catch, and the big ones very hard to catch. Nor are the big ones few and far between for on my first visit I was broken twice in the day, something which I have not experienced in reservoir fishing for over ten years. As to the quality of the fish – Barrie Welham's 6 lb 9 oz brown trout taken on dry fly on 26 August and a more recent fish of 9 lb 7 oz is ample evidence that big Two Lakes trout are wild-fed fish by the time you catch them even if, like Grafham trout, they start life in a stew-pond. Barrie, remember, caught nothing at Two Lakes for the whole of his first season! So much for the 'fishing in a rearing-pond' myth.

Two Lakes trout are well known too for their eating qualities. My best, a 3 lb 6 oz rainbow, was short and very thick and at table at least the equal of big Grafham rainbows.

But the scale of Alex Behrendt's achievement is seen only when we look at the number of rods through the years and the size of the bag.

In 1953	3 rods killed	112 trout averaging	13·4 oz
1954	4	167	15·6 oz
1955	7	278	1 lb 5·3 oz
1956	10	307	2 lb 0·35 oz
1957	14	431	2 lb 2·6 oz
1958	20	617	2 lb 3·6 oz
1959	30	864	2 lb 1·6 oz
1960	30	1208	2 lb 5·8 oz

In 1967, seventy rods each fishing one day in each week, which is the same as saying ten rods per day, killed over 3,000 trout, and by the end of August 1968, with one month still to go, the same number of rods had topped the 1967 return and averaged 2 lb 5 oz per fish.

Alex has reached the stage where his average angler can catch and take away each season an average of forty-three fish weighing 100 lb for his £100 season permit; just under a brace of two-and-a-half pounds per outing. In pounds per acre the return is around 530 lb . . . fantastic, by any scale.

And, let it be emphasized, the fishery has been run so as to provide a comfortable standard of living for the owner and his wife!

The secrets of Alex's fishery management are not for publication (though I understand he will one day publish a text-book) but it is clear that he has solved the problems of providing fish at low cost and stocking at a density which enables them to carry on growing and maintaining excellent condition. He has also achieved an intensity of fishing effort which ensures that fish are caught and killed before old age is followed by natural death.

High in his management priorities is the elimination of poaching which could render fishery records completely meaningless.

His guard-trained Alsatians are the most effective deterrent that I have encountered on any water!

But if Alex's study has been primarily one of trout, their foods and feeding habits, and the science of commercial freshwater fishery management expounded by numerous European authors, he has clearly recognized from the start that you could make a profit only if the customer was happy and wanted to come again next year. If anglers jostle each other to get at the fish, or find in windy weather that it's all upwind casting, there is discord, bags fall and the economy suffers. Two Lakes provides 'stands' for each angler in such a way that nearby anglers are little seen, and their casting cannot cause inconvenience. Two Lakes, incidentally, provides very pretty surroundings.

There are so many stands that it is easy to find solitude; there are, after all, six small lakes between ten anglers. Again, there is comfortable casting no matter from which direction the wind blows. In several cases, banks and jetties have been constructed so that anglers can get sufficiently clear of the trees to throw a long line.

The great lesson for us all at Two Lakes is that good management can create a first-class fishery starting with almost no assets other than a clean water supply, knowledge and courage.

How now shall we assess our reservoir fisheries where we start with clean alkaline water, fertile soil, money and staff, not to mention unlimited though unused opportunity during the construction stages to sculpt margins so as to provide promontories which will make all banks fishable, even in adverse winds?

How too are we to accept the preacceptance by most reservoir staff . . . that the fishing will start well, then tail off after about three years? It has, of course, happened so often that we anglers expect it and regard it as an inevitability in the 'Act of God' category.

We would, if the land were still dry and its production fell back, retrain or sack the farm manager, but because it is a lake and we have little knowledge of what good fishery management can do, we fail to attribute fault where it should lie; namely on inadequate fishery management.

How the Continental farmers are trained

Nor is it readily possible to improve the present sorry state in Britain. Fishery managers in Germany, Poland, Russia or in the

United States, for that matter, receive a formal education in their chosen career which is just not available in Britain.

In Germany, says Alex Behrendt, they first serve a three-year apprenticeship on an approved (progressive and profitable) fish farm and then complete one year at an Institute (like our Farm Institutes). After passing the State-set examination they are classed as improvers and work on a number of farms over the next four or five years following which they take a further examination leading to the qualification 'fishmaster' at around twenty-eight years of age.

I know of no one amongst our many water keepers or fishery managers who can offer such a combination of practical, academic and economic experience of fishery work.

Fishery management, unfortunately, has no professional status, no governing body, no training facilities other than the old and inadequate QBE.

Trouble is, when people say they have twenty years' experience, they really mean six months' experience and nineteen and a half years' application of that six months' learning!

Probably the first step must be the appointment of several competent German 'Fishmasters' to farm institutes where existing fishery workers could receive three-month courses. The gradual expansion of the academic side would follow and culminate in the setting up of a 'Chair' and degree courses at one of the universities which provides training in agriculture. Exeter, Reading and Durham would all be suitable for the purpose.

Side by side with this programme, I hope we shall send some of our own agricultural students to acquire Continental qualifications before returning here to take up management appointments.

Let us hope that within the next ten years reservoir fishery decline will be the thing of the past, that sound, highly specialized management can make it.

Reservoir fisheries need changed administration

It would be futile to appoint a fishmaster and leave the control of his 'farm' (the lake fishery) to the water engineer.

The use of a lake as a recreational centre postulates a completely new approach to water management. Precedent already exists.

Much of London's water supply comes from the River Thames

where it belongs to the Thames Conservators. It becomes the responsibility of the Metropolitan Water Board only when they pump it from the river.

As a recreational amenity the Thames is managed by one body, and when it becomes our water supply another body takes over. Both authorities have been content with the arrangement for a very long time.

How simple it would be if the fishery manager was, with the committee of the sailing club, responsible for the reservoir and its water as a recreational centre, and the water engineer's responsibilities began at the point where the water was drawn off. Obviously the water engineer would also control the filling of the lake.

CHAPTER 19

Where to fish for trout in reservoirs

Probably every directory ever produced was out of date in many details by the time it was published. The information in this chapter has suffered, or will certainly suffer, within a year or two, from the same malaise. Nonetheless, we have to start somewhere and, doubtless, if a club secretary changes or a water board merges with a neighbour, your letter of inquiry will be forwarded to someone else who can help you.

Three hundred and five letters of inquiry were dispatched to water authorities, water companies, water undertakings etc in England and Wales and only ten failed to reply. The information given here is taken from these replies and nothing has been added except information gained by personal experience. What I have tried to do is to list as many reservoirs as I can where trout fishing is known to be available. Omissions and errors I hope I can correct from readers' letters from time to time.

Because many water authorities own reservoirs far from their head offices, all fisheries have been grouped by areas rather than by counties or by addresses of the head offices. It was impossible to find a method of tabulation which would permit information to be offered systematically without enormous waste of space where some authorities could not answer all the questions asked, so I have adopted a continental-guide-book type of code letter for the simple vital statistics of each water. Each board is allocated a section with ruled lines above and below. Its trout reservoirs are listed in turn, each name being in heavy type followed by coded details, always in the same order though not necessarily full details in every case:

NT   Nearest town or village
Cl   Club water
DP   Day permit available
SP   Season Permit available

BP   Boat permit available (in some cases this may be the cost
        of a boat for two anglers)
Ht   Height of reservoir above sea level
Dp   Maximum depth when full

pH   Average level of acidity (figures below 7) or alkalinity
        (figures above 7)
BAv   Average weight of brown trout in 1968
NoB   Number of browns caught in 1968
RAv   Average weight of rainbows caught in 1968
NoR   Number of rainbows caught in 1968

Correspondence: After this word follows an address from which
permits or other information may be obtained. Where a water is
fished by a club the address of the secretary is given where
known. It is also given, when known, even where no permits are
issued because membership vacancies must occur from time to
time. I have also felt it advisable to list waters where the prospect
of membership is remote because leases are offered at tender,
from time to time, and other anglers and associations may wish
to bid when the opportunity occurs.

NORTH-EAST REGION (TEES AND TYNE BASINS)

Durham County Water Board. **Burnhope** NT Wearhead Cl
Correspondence: Brother Lee, Burnhope AC, Westgate, Bishop
Auckland, Co Durham. **Tunstall** NT Wolsingham. **Waskerley**
NT Stanhope. **Smiddy Shaw** NT Stanhope. **Hisehope** NT
Stanhope. All four Cl. Correspondence: J. Sanderson, 3, Low
Westwood, Newcastle-upon-Tyne.

Tees Valley and Cleveland Water Board. **Balderhead** NT
Romaldkirk DP Ht1090 Dp157 pH7. **Blackton** NT Cotherston
DP Ht860 Dp90 pH7·1. **Selset** NT Middleton in Teesdale DP
Ht1037 Dp117 pH7·2. **Grassholme** NT Mickleton DP Ht903
Dp97 pH7·2 BAv (Selset & Grassholme jointly) 9·2 oz NoB
(jointly) 658. **Scaling** NT Guisborough DP Ht607 Dp29
pH7·3 BAv 2 lb 11 oz NoB334. **Lockwood** NT Guisborough
Ht623 Dp43 pH7·2. Correspondence (all the foregoing): Tees
Valley & Cleveland Water Board, Dovecot Street, Stockton.

Tynemouth Water Department. **Fontburn** NT Rothbury Cl Ht611 Dp80 pH6·8 to 7·5. Correspondence: C. Wade, Northumbrian Anglers Federation, 2 Ridge Villas, Bedlington. The association has fifty only season permits on the south-east corner of the reservoir. The remainder of the fishing rights are believed to be privately owned.

Newcastle and Gateshead Water Company. **Whittle Dean** Group of eight NT Newcastle 11 miles DP BP Ht348 to 396 Dp14; 15; 19; 23; 24; 25; 35; 40. pH7·5 to 8·0 BAv 12 oz NoB 659 RAv 1 lb NoR377. Correspondence: The Reservoir Keeper, Whittle Dene Reservoirs, Stamfordham, Northumberland. Tel. Wylam 3210. **Catcleugh, Coltcrag** and **Hallington;** all Cl on leases.

Sunderland and South Shields Water Company. **Derwent** NT Edmundbyers Nr Consett. DP BP SP Ht725 Dp100 pH6·9 to 7·1 BAv 13 oz NoB6541 RAv 15·6 oz NoR5593. Correspondence: Utilities Building, Derwent Reservoirs, Nr Edmundbyers, Consett, Co Durham. Tel Edmundbyers 250.

NORTH-WEST REGION (WESTMORLAND, CUMBERLAND, ISLE OF MAN)

Eden Water Board. **Hayeswater** Cl. Correspondence: E. Wolstenholme, Penrith Angling Association, 21 Victoria Road, Penrith.

Manchester Corporation. **Haweswater.** Correspondence: Haweswater Hotel, Brampton. Nr Penrith.

West Cumberland Water Board. **Crummock Water** Ht323 pH6·5. Correspondence: The National Trust, Broadlands, Borrans Road, Ambleside. **Overwater** Ht627 Dp30 pH6·5. Riparian rights owned by Sir Frank Schon.

Lune Valley Water Board. The clerk writes: 'None of the board's reservoirs is open to trout or other fishing, a decision for which at this time there are cogent reasons . . .'

Lakes & Lune Water Board. **Fisher Tarn** NT Kendal. Correspondence: Fisher Tarn Anglers' Association. The board's other reservoirs are let privately to individuals.

Furness Water Board. The board's reservoirs are leased to various angling associations. The terms of their leases prohibit visitor permits.

South Cumberland Water Board. **Meadley Kinniside** NT Cleator Moor Cl. Correspondence: J. M. Bell, Wath Brow and Ennerdale Angling Association, 33 Weddicar Gardens, Cleator Moor, Cumberland.

Douglas Water Board. **West Baldwin** NT West Baldwin Village DP Ht480 Dp69 pH5·7 RAv about 1 lb. **Clypse** and **Kerrowdho** Reservoirs NT Onchan DP Ht370 and 320 Dp40 and 40 pH7 BAv about 1 lb RAv about 1 lb. Correspondence: Reservoir Keepers' Houses at Baldwin and at Clypse.

Isle of Man Water Board. **Cringle** NT Colby DP Ht565 Dp45 pH6·0. **Ballure** NT Ramsey DP Ht273 Dp41 pH6·0. **Block Eary** NT Sulby DP Ht606 Dp35 pH4·0. **Ballamoar** NT Peel DP Ht260 Dp20. Correspondence: Isle of Man Water Board, 16 Circular Road, Douglas, IOM.

YORKSHIRE, TRENT AND HUMBER

Ryedale Joint Water Board. **Boltby.** Riparian rights owned by Mrs D. F. Place, Gurtof Cottage, Boltby, Thirsk.

Scarborough Borough Council. **Randymere** NT Goathland Ht550 Dp45 pH7·3. Riparian rights owned by Egton Estates Company, Egton Bridge, Nr Whitby.

Northallerton and the Dales Water Board. **Cod Beck** NT Osmotherley, Northallerton DP Ht633 Dp73 NoB665 averaging 10 to 11 inches. Correspondence: Northallerton UDC, 72 High Street, Northallerton.

Claro Water Board. **Lumley Moor** NT Ripon Cl Ht598 Dp32 pH7·1. Correspondence: Ripon Angling Club. **Beaverdyke** (2 Reservoirs) NT Harrogate. Known to have held rainbow and brown trout in 1948. Privately let. Correspondence: Board's Offices, Municipal Offices, Harrogate.

Leeds County Borough Council. **Fewston & Swinsty** Reservoirs NT Fewston DP Ht503 and 449 Dp47 and 53 pH6 BAv 15 oz NoB56. Correspondence: Fewston Reservoir Lodge, Fewston, Birstwith, via Harrogate. No Sunday fishing.

Craven Water Board. **Ponden** NT Haworth Nr Keighley Cl DP BAv $1\frac{1}{2}$ lb. Correspondence: Mrs I. Pickles, Farm Cottage, Scarrtop, Nr Oakworth.

Bradford City Water Undertaking. **Leeming** NT Oxenhope Cl Ht837 Dp57. **Leeshaw** NT Haworth Cl Ht851 Dp55. **Hewenden** NT Cullingworth Cl Ht675 Dp35. **Chelker** NT Addingham Cl Ht721 Dp37. The Riparian rights of **Silsden** (near Keighley) and **Gouthwaite** (Nr Pately Bridge) are not owned by the Corporation. Correspondence: City of Bradford Waterworks Engineer's Office, George Street, Bradford, 1.

Wakefield and District Water Board. **Ryburn** NT Ripponden Cl DP Ht633 Dp95 pH6·8 BAv 10 oz NoB145. Correspondence: Ripponden Fly Fishers.

Huddersfield County Borough Water Undertaking. **Holme Styes** Nr Holmfirth Cl Ht876 Dp63 pH6 to 6·5. Correspondence: R. Burns, 96 Fleminghouse Lane, Waterloo, Huddersfield.

Barnsley County Borough Water Department. **Scout Dike** NT Penistone DP Ht728 Dp40 pH6·6 to 7·2. Correspondence: Borough Treasurer's Office, Town Hall, Barnsley.

Doncaster and District Joint Water Board. **Thrybergh** NT Rotherham DP Ht180 Dp30 BAv 18 oz NoB570 RAv 14 oz NoR 84. Correspondence: Board's Office, Copley House, Waterdale, Doncaster.

Derwent Valley Water Board. **Ladybower** NT Bamford DP SP Ht668 Dp135 pH6·1 BAv and RAv 10 oz No B & R 2309. Correspondence: The Engineer, Derwent Valley Water Board, Bamford, Sheffield. Season-permit holders may at the discretion of the Fishery Warden, fish the Board's stretch of the Derwent below Ladybower Dam.

Sheffield Corporation Waterworks. **Dam Flask** NT Bradfield Nr Sheffield DP Ht505 Dp85 pH9·0 Day tickets from Dam Flask Reservoir ticket office. **Morehall** NT Stocksbridge Ht48 pH8·9. Correspondence: re season tickets: Sheffield Corporation Waterworks, Exchange Street, Sheffield.

North East Lincolnshire Water Board. **Coverham** Reservoir (under construction) NT Louth Ht50 Dp45. Stocking policy undecided.

LANCASHIRE and NORTH CHESHIRE REGION

Preston & District Water Board. **Grimsargh** NT Preston Cl Terms of lease preclude visitors' permits.

North Calder Water Board. **Black Moss** Cl. Correspondence: H. Wiseman, 5 Sunny Mount, Blacko, Nelson. **Walverden** NT Nelson Cl Dp20 BAv 11 oz NoB260. Small reservoir, small club, long waiting list. Correspondence: J. Burke, 34 Berkeley Street, Nelson.

Calder Water Board. **Cant Clough** Cl. Correspondence: R. D. Halsted, Mitre Angling Club, 52 Hillcrest Avenue, Cliviger, Burnley. **Dean** Cl. Correspondence: J. Winnard, Lancs Fly Fishing Assoc., Main Street, Gisburn, Nr Clitheroe. **Lea Green** Cl. Correspondence: J. H. Walton, Burnley Angling Society, 5 Red Lion Street, Burnley, Lancs.

Fylde Water Board. **Parsonage** NT Blackburn Cl DP Ht615 Dp53 pH6·0. Correspondence: J. Morris, Blackburn and District AC 818, Whalley New Road, Blackburn. **Barnacre North** and **Grizedale Lea** NT Garstang Cl DP BP Ht618 Dp22 and 19½ pH5·5 and 6·0. Correspondence: J. H. Boulton, Kirkham and District Fly Fishers' Club, 8 Preston Street, Kirkham, Nr Preston. These three reservoirs opened 1969. **Earnsdale** NT Darwen Cl DP Ht705 Dp60 pH7. Correspondence: D. Isherwood, Darwen AA, 51 Brighton Terrace, Darwen. **Stocks.**

Bolton Corporation Waterworks. **Entwistle** and **Wayoh** NT Bolton SP Ht690 and 573 Dp78 and 82 pH5·1 and 7·3. **Heaton** NT Bolton SP Ht517 Dp33 pH7·2. **Dingle** NT Belmont SP Ht717 Dp31 pH5·0. Correspondence: Bolton Corporation Waterworks, Town Hall, Bolton. **Ogden** NT Haslingden Cl Ht737 Dp50 pH5·4. **Greenfold** NT Rawtenstall Cl Ht968

Dp50 pH6·8. **Newline** NT Bacup Cl Ht902 Dp29 pH7·2.
Cloughbottom NT Lumb (Rossendale) Cl Ht1010 Dp64
pH5·6.

City of Liverpool Water Department, Rivington Group of
reservoirs comprising **Rivington Upper** and **Lower, Angle-
zark, Rake Brook, Roddlesworth Upper** and **Lower,
Yarrow** DP SP. Season permits are available to angling clubs
to cover a group of its members each of whom may fish on one
day. Correspondence: Water Engineer's Office, 55 Dale Street,
Liverpool, 2.

West Pennine Water Board. **Brushes** and **Walker Wood** NT
Stalybridge SP (joint) Ht649 and 588 Dp44 and 61 pH6·0.
Knott Hill NT Ashton-under-Lyne SP Ht589 Dp44 pH6·9.
Correspondence (all three): West Pennine Water Board, 2 Wall-
shaw Place, Oldham. **Lower Reservoir** NT Dukinfield Cl
Ht434 Dp24 pH8·0. Correspondence: Diggle Angling Club.
Hollingworth Lake NT Littleborough Cl Ht562 Dp26. Cor-
respondence: New Hey AS. **Brushes Clough** NT Shaw Cl
Ht924 Dp45. **Ogden** NT New Hey Ht690 Dp38 pH7·0. **Kit-
cliffe** NT Milnrow Ht758 Dp27 pH7·0. **Lower Castleshaw**
NT Delph Ht762 Dp43 pH5·0. **Upper Strinesdale** NT Old-
ham Ht819 Dp38. **Lower Strinesdale** NT Oldham Ht778
Dp56. **Besom Hill** NT Shaw Ht841 Dp33. Day permits avail-
able with some restrictions. All seven waters leased to Oldham
Central Anglers. **Buckley Wood** NT Rochdale Cl Ht563 Dp32.
Correspondence: Rochdale Walton Angling Society. **Hurstead
Nook** NT Wardle Cl Dp10.

Manchester Waterworks Department. **Vale House** and **Bot-
toms** NT Tintwistle DP Ht502 and 492 Dp40 and 54 pH5 to 6.
Cote Lodge NT Glossop DP Ht638 Dp18. Correspondence:
Reservoir Bank Permit Points.

Macclesfield District Water Board. **Ridgegate** NT Langley Cl
Ht763 Dp50 pH7·2. Correspondence: A. H. Arliness, Maccles-
field FFC, School House, Langley. **Bottoms** NT Langley
Cl Ht660 Dp38. Correspondence: C. Sparkes, Prince Albert
AA, c/o Head Post Office, Macclesfield. **Teggsnose** NT Lang-
ley Cl Ht700 Dp41. Correspondence: J. Lawson, Waltonian
AS, 267 Park Lane, Macclesfield.

Leicester Water Department. **Cropston, Swithland, Thornton.** The fishing rights of these three impounding reservoirs are reserved to the original landowners by Acts of Parliament. Trout are known to have been stocked at one of these.

North West Leicestershire Water Board. **Blackbrook** NT Shepshed Cl. Correspondence: Hugh Smith, Two Ways, Toller Road, Leicester.

Rugby Joint Water Board. **Draycote.** Fishing by day or season permit available to all applicants. Ht303 Dp70 pH approx. 7·6. Correspondence: Rugby Joint Water Board, 50 Albert Street, Rugby.

South Warwickshire Water Board. The only reservoir at present fished is let to a club. Correspondence: D. A. Langley, 74 Lime Avenue, Lillington, Leamington Spa.

Empingham NT Market Harborough. A large reservoir under construction. Stocking policy not yet settled. (See Note, p. 251.)

Mid-Northamptonshire Water Board. **Pitsford** NT Pitsford DP BP (2 persons) Ht295 Dp50 pH8·1 to 8·4 BAv 1 lb NoB3400. **Ravensthorpe** NT Guilsborough DP BP Ht348 Dp26·5 pH7·5 to 8·0 BAv 1 lb NoB1600 RAv 1 lb NoR34. Correspondence: Reservoir Banks or to Mid-Northants Water Board, Cliftonville, Northampton. **Thorpe Malsor** (rights privately owned) NT Kettering Cl. Correspondence: British Timken Sports Club, Duston, Northants.

Corby and District Water Company. **Eyebrook** NT Rockingham DP BP Ht227 Dp (average) 17½ pH7·3 BAv 1 lb 1 oz NoB11971 RAv 1 lb 2 oz NoR2148. Correspondence: Fishing Hut, Eyebrook Reservoir, Caldecott, Rutland.

Great Ouse Water Authority. **Grafham** NT Buckden DP BP Ht144 Dp70 pH8·3 BAv 2 lb 6 oz NoB10636 RAv 1 lb 12 oz NoR21437. Correspondence: (Boats) Chief Engineer's Office, West Perry, Hunts. (Bank) Fishing Lodge, West Perry, Hunts.

Hanningfield Water Joint Management Committee. **Hanningfield Water** NT Chelmsford SP (maximum of 250 rods) BP

Ht181 Dp55 pH8·4 BAv 1 lb 11 oz NoB307 RAv 1 lb 11 oz NoR6226. Correspondence: The Secretary, Hanningfield Joint Water Committee, 13 Cambridge Road, Southend-on-Sea.

Tendring Hundred Waterworks. Construction of a reservoir has begun. Stocking policies not yet decided. Correspondence: Tendring Hundred Water Company, Manningtree, Essex.

Oxfordshire and District Water Board. **Farmoor** NT Oxford Cl Ht221 Dp35 pH7·8 NoB1260 NoR1257. Correspondence: Fred Taylor, 39a James Street, Oxford.

BLACK COUNTRY and NORTH-WEST MIDLANDS

Stockport and District Water Board. **Errwood** NT Buxton Ht917 Dp114. Fishing let to Errwood Fly Fishers' Club. Correspondence: W. F. Williams, 1 Westwood Drive, Brooklands, Sale, Cheshire.

North Derbyshire Water Board. **Linacre Reservoirs** NT Chesterfield, **Press Reservoirs** NT Chesterfield, **Crowhole** NT Chesterfield, **Stanley Moor** NT Buxton, **Lightwood** NT Buxton Cl in all cases. Correspondence: Board's Office, West Street, Chesterfield.

West Shropshire Water Board. Two unnamed reservoirs are let for private fishing only. Correspondence: West Shropshire Water Board, Shelton, Shrewsbury.

Staffordshire Potteries Water Board. **Tittesworth** NT Meerbrook Nr Leek DP SP BP Ht646 Dp98 pH6·8 to 7·4 BAv 1 lb 1 oz NoB2336 RAv 1 lb 3½ oz NoR621. Correspondence: (Advance Booking) Engineer and Manager's Office, Albion Street, Hanley, Stoke-on-Trent (Day Permits limited to 40). Same day bookings at Foreman's Office, Tittesworth Reservoir.

South Staffordshire Waterworks Company. **Blithfield** NT Abbots Bromley SP (guests permitted) Ht312 Dp47 pH7·1 BAv 1¼ lb NoB3589 RAv 1 lb 3 oz NoR1194. Correspondence: The South Staffs Waterworks Company, 50 Sheepcote Street, Birmingham, 15.

Birmingham Water Department. **Shustoke** NT Coleshill DP
Ht263 Dp22½ pH8·4 BAv 15 oz NoB3544. Correspondence:
Council House, PO Box 49, Edmund Street, Birmingham, 3.

WEST, CENTRAL and NORTH WALES

Central Flintshire Water Board. Correspondence: Board's
Office, Chester Road, Flint.

Wirral Water Board. **Alwen** NT Cerrig-y-Drudion DP SP
Ht1190 Dp90 pH5·3 BAv 10 oz. Correspondence: Wirral Water
Board, Cerrig-y-Drudion, North Wales.

Wrexham & East Denbighshire Water Company. **Pennycae
Upper** and **Lower** NT Pennycae DP Ht708 and 661 Dp30
pH7·4 BAv ¾ lb NoB188 total. Correspondence: Company's
Office, 21 Egerton Street, Wrexham, Denbighshire.

West Denbighshire and West Flintshire Water Board. **Dolwen**
and **Plas Uchaf** NT Llanefydd Nr Denbigh DP BP Ht525 and
475 Dp42 and 43. Correspondence: Board's Office, PO Box no
2, Plastirion, Russell Road, Rhyl, Flintshire. **Llyn Crafnant**
NT Trefriw Nr Llanrwst. Correspondence: The Cafe, Llyn
Crafnant, Nr Llanrwst.

Conway Valley Water Board. **Llyn Cowlyd** NT Dolgarrog DP
Ht1200. **Melynllyn** NT Llanbedr DP Ht2100 Dp102. **Llyn
Dulyn** NT Llanbedr DP Ht1750 Dp182. Some, at least of these
reservoirs are accessible only on foot. Correspondence: Conway
Water Board, 50 Mostyn Street, Llandudno, Caernarvonshire.

Eryri Water Board. **Cwmystradllyn** Dp Ht699 Dp27. Correspondence: Gwynfor Humphreys, Cwmystradllyn Water Works,
Garndolbenmaen, Caernarvonshire.

Anglesey County Council Water Department. **Cefni** NT Llangefni DP BP Ht98 Dp19·7 pH7·8 BAv 13 oz NoB1306 RAv
13 oz NoR46. Correspondence: W. J. Williams, Cefni AA,
Gronant, Caerwen, Anglesey. **Alaw** NT Llanddeusant DP BP
Ht130 Dp19 pH7·5 BAv 2 lb 3 oz NoB2117. Sea-Trout Av
2 lb 3 oz Number 230. Correspondence: County Water Engineer
and Manager, Frondirion, Llangefni, Anglesey.

Birmingham Water Department. **Elan Valley Fisheries** NT
Rhayader DP Ht822 at Caban Coch to 1210 at Claerwen Dp122
to 184 pH5·8 BAv 9½ oz NoB3507. Correspondence: Elan Office,
Elan Village, Rhayader, Radnorshire.

Clywedog Reservoir Joint Authority. **Llyn Clywedog** NT
Llanidloes DP BP Ht927 Dp216 BAv 1½ lb NoB2600 RAv 1¾ lb
NoR1600. Correspondence: Edgar Spooner, Montgomeryshire
Federation of Angling Associations, Memorial Gallery, New-
town, Mont.

Cardiganshire Water Board. **Teifi Pools.** Correspondence:
South West Wales River Authority, Llanelli. **Craig-y-Pistyll**
Cl. Correspondence: D. Fleming-Jones, Aberystwyth AA, 7
Bridge Street, Aberystwyth.

Merioneth Water Board. **Llyn Cynwch** NT Dolgellau Cl
Ht734 Dp60 pH6·0 to 6·5.

SOUTH WALES and MONMOUTHSHIRE

Tredegar UDC Water Department. **Shon Sheffrey** Cl. Correspondence: B. James, Tredegar Angling Club, Highlands,
Scwrfa Road, Tredegar. **Scotch Peter** and **St James' Reservoirs** Cl. Correspondence: G. Gurmin, Markham Angling
Club, 26 Railway Terrace, Hollybush Blackwood, Mon.

Ebbw Vale UDC. **Carno** NT Ebbw Vale Cl Ht1290 Dp90
pH5·5. **Llangynidr** NT Ebbw Vale Cl Ht1445 Dp45 pH5·5.
Correspondence: W. Muggeridge, 116 Bryn Glas, Gilwern,
Mon.

Taf Fechan Water Board. **Nant Hir** NT Hirwaun Cl Ht850
Dp57 pH4·5 to 5·2 (efforts being made to raise pH by bagged
limestone at intakes) BAv ½ lb RAv ½ lb. **Rhymney Br II** NT
Rhymney Cl Ht1167 Dp40 pH7·0 to 7·6 BAv ½ lb RAv ½ lb.
Clydach NT Ynysybwl Cl Ht932 Dp25 pH6 to 7·2 BAv ½ lb.
Bwllfant NT Aberdare Cl Ht711 Dp22 pH7·5 to 7·8 BAv
¾ lb. **W Neuadd** NT Pontsticill DP Ht1504 Dp72 pH6·8 to 7·5
RAv 1 lb. **Pontsticill** DP Ht1082 Dp107 pH6·8 to 7·5 BAv
1 lb RAv 1 lb. **Lluest Wen** NT Maerdy Ht1336 Dp64 pH6·9 to
7·6 BAv ¾ lb RAv ¾ lb. **Castle Nos** NT Maerdy Ht1100 Dp38
pH6·9 to 7·4. **Llyn Fawr** NT Rhigos Ht1208 Dp46 pH6·5 to

7·2 BAv ¾ lb. **Penderyn** NT Penderyn Ht700 Dp31 pH5·9 to 7·2 BAv ½ lb. Correspondence: Board's Office, Castle Street, Merthyr Tydfil.

West Glamorgan Water Board. **Usk** NT Trecastle Nr Brecon DP Ht1006 Dp94 pH7·6 BAv ¾ lb NoB2000. **Cray** NT Cray DP (3 only per day) Ht1001 Dp101 pH7·0. **Upper** and **Lower Lliw** NT Felindre, Nr Swansea DP Ht615 and 389 Dp67 and 43 pH6·5 and 7·0. **Ystradfellte** NT Ystradfellte DP (10 rods per day) Ht1204 Dp90 pH6·9. Correspondence: Reservoir Keepers or Board's Offices, 86 The Kingsway, Swansea.

Cardiff Corporation Water Department. **Llandegfedd** NT Pontypool and Usk DP BP Ht280 Dp120 pH7·8 BAv 1 lb 3 oz NoB6085. Rainbows first stocked 1969. **Beacons** NT Cefn Coed, Nr Merthyr DP Ht1340 Dp54 pH6·9 BAv 1¼ lb NoB1400 RAv 1¼ lb NoR150. **Cantref** NT Cefn Coed DP Ht1073 Dp73 pH6·9 BAv 1¼ lb NoB500 RAv 1¼ lb NoR100. **Llwyn On** NT Cefn Coed DP Ht854 Dp65 pH6·9 BAv 1½ lb NoB1800 RAv 1½ lb NoR200. **Llanishen** and **Lisvane** NT Llanishen Nr Cardiff Ht151 and 146 Dp23 and 21 pH7 B and RAv 1 lb NoB and R2490. All waters season permit; includes Llanishen and Lisvane. Correspondence: Cardiff Corporation Water Department, Municipal Offices, Greyfriars Road, Cardiff.

Llanelli & District Water Board. **Upper Lliedi** NT Felinfoel Cl DP Ht276 Dp53 pH7·8. Correspondence: Llanelli Angling Association, 2 Hedley Terrace, Llanelli. **Lower Lliedi** NT Felinfoel DP Ht208 Dp51 pH7·8. Correspondence: Board's Office, 13 Park Crescent, Llanelli.

Pembrokeshire Water Board. **Prescelly Rosebush** NT Maenclochog DP BP Ht750 Dp65 pH6·8 BAv 11 oz NoB225. Correspondence: Board's Office, 23 Hill Street, Haverfordwest.

Abertillery and District Water Board. The riparian rights of the reservoirs are retained by the ground landlords.

SOUTHERN ENGLAND AND THE CHANNEL ISLES

Mid-Kent Water Company. **Eccles** NT Aylesford SP only Dp50 pH8·0 BAv 1¼ lb NoB220. Correspondence: Company's Office, High Street, Snodland, Kent.

East Surrey Water Company. **Bough Beech** NT Edenbridge SP only.

North-West Sussex Water Board. **Weir Wood** NT Forest Row Nr East Grinstead DP BP Ht245 Dp35 pH7·4 B and RAv 14½ oz NoB2190 NoR2554. Correspondence: Board's Offices, Hurst Row, Horsham.

Hastings County Borough Water Department. **Darwell** NT Mountfield DP BP Ht132 Dp51 pH6·9 BAv 15½ oz NoB185 RAv 15 oz NoR1713. **Powdermill** NT Sedlescombe Cl DP BP Ht78 Dp35 pH7·6 BAv 9 oz NoB382 RAv 11 oz NoR514. Correspondence: W. H. Mee, Hastings Fly Fishers Club Ltd, Mountain Ash, Pett Road, Pett, Sussex.

States of Guernsey Waterworks Department. **St Saviours** NT St Peter's Port Cl Ht136 Dp71 pH7·2 BAv 12 oz NoB2100. Correspondence: Dr John C. Bulstrode, X-Ray Department, Princess Elizabeth Hospital, Guernsey.

Jersey New Waterworks Company, Ltd. **Val de la Mare** NT St Helier Cl DP BP Ht150 Dp75 pH7·0 BAv 14 oz (Estimated) RAv 1 lb (Estimated). Correspondence: H. H. Willis, Jersey Model Laundry, Vallée des Vaux, St Helier.

WEST MIDLANDS AND SOUTH-WEST ENGLAND

Swindon Borough Water Department, **Wroughton** NT Wroughton Nr Swindon DP BP Ht455 Dp20 pH7·1 RAv 1½ lb NoR34 (probably an incomplete return). Correspondence: Civic Offices, Swindon.

Bristol Waterworks Company. **Chew Valley** NT Chew Stoke DP BP SP Ht185 pH7·8 BAv 1 lb 10 oz NoB7248 RAv 1 lb 11 oz NoR4139. Correspondence: Fishery Department, Woodford Lodge, Chew Reservoir (night issuing service for bank tickets). **Blagdon** NT Blagdon DP BP Ht147 pH7–8 BAv 1 lb 12 oz NoB2723 RAv 1 lb 10 oz NoR2260. Correspondence: Anglers' Hut, Blagdon Lake. **Barrows No 2 and No 3** NT Bristol SP (includes Blagdon) Ht326 and 317 pH7·8 BAv 1 lb 10 oz NoB488 (total) RAv 1 lb 8 oz NoR525 (total). Correspondence: Woodford Lodge, Chew Reservoir. **Litton** Two small reservoirs fishable by company invitation.

Wessex Water Board. **Sutton Bingham** NT Yeovil DP BP
Ht182 Dp40 pH8·0 B and RAv 1 lb 2½ oz NoB2433 NoR700.
Correspondence: Fishing Hut, Sutton Bingham, Nr Yeovil.

West Somerset Water Board. **Clatworthy** NT Wiveliscombe
DP BP SP Ht640 Dp95 pH6·8 BAv ¾ lb RAv 1½ lb. **Durleigh**
NT Bridgwater DP BP SP Ht73 Dp27 BAv 1 lb RAv 1½ lb.
Otterhead Lakes NT Churchstanton SP Ht600 Dp12 pH7·4
BAv ¾ lb RAv 1 lb. **Hawkridge** NT Bridgwater SP (available
to season permit holders of other waters) Ht320 Dp65 pH7·2
BAv 1½ lb RAv 2 lb. Correspondence: Board's Office, 150
Priorswood, Taunton.

North Devon Water Board. **Wistlandpound** NT Barnstaple
DP Ht797 Dp77 pH7·3 BAv 5 oz NoB1000 RAv 5 oz NoR100.
Correspondence: Board's Office, Barnstaple. **Slade** (two reser-
voirs) NT Ilfracombe BP Ht432 and 367 Dp32 and 39 pH7·3
BAv 5 oz NoB600 RAv 5 oz NoR50. Correspondence: Ilfra-
combe UD Council Office.

South West Devon Water Board. **Kennick** NT Hennock SP
Ht820 Dp30 pH6·6 BAv 11 oz NoB793. **Tottiford** (two reser-
voirs) NT Hennock SP (jointly with Kennick) Ht780 Dp24
pH6·6 BAv 14 oz NoB445. Correspondence: Board's Office,
King's Ash Road, Paignton. **Fernworthy** NT Chagford DP
BP Ht1125 Dp63 pH6·2. Permits from Caretaker, Fernworthy
Reservoir at the reservoir bank only.

City of Plymouth Water Undertaking. **Burrator** NT Yelverton
DP BP Ht718 pH6·0 to 6·5. Correspondence: Municipal Offices,
Plymouth.

East Cornwall Water Board. **Siblyback** NT Liskeard DP BP
Ht725 Dp60 pH6·5 to 7·2. Correspondence: Reservoir Keeper's
House, Trewitham, Liskeard.

North & Mid Cornwall Water Board. **Porth** NT Newquay DP
SP BP Ht85 Dp25 pH7·4 BAv 1 lb NoB2500 RAv 1 lb NoR150.
Correspondence: Board's Offices, Victoria Square, Bodmin.

South Cornwall Water Board. **Argal** NT Falmouth DP BP
Ht230 Dp50 pH7·2 BAv 1¼ lb NoB1187. Rainbows stocked for
first time 1969. **College** NT Penrhyn DP BP Dp25 pH7·2
BAv 2 lb NoB196. Rainbows stocked for first time 1969. **Stith-**

ians NT Camborne DP BP Ht532 Dp60 pH7·2 BAv 2 lb NoB145 RAv 3½ lb NoR206. **Cargenwyn** NT Camborne SP (Limited) Ht520 Dp25–30 ft pH7·0 BAv 1 lb. Correspondence: Board's Office, 100 Pydar Street, Truro.

West Cornwall Water Board. **Drift** NT Penzance DP SP Ht275 Dp45 pH7·0 BAv 10 oz NoB1500. Rainbows stocked first time 1969. **Bussow** NT St Ives Cl Ht395 Dp16. Correspondence: The Agent, Chyandour Office, Chyandour, Penzance. (The riparian rights of the water were retained by Mr Charles Williams, the estate owner.)

Note: Empingham Reservoir when filled will extend to some 3,000 acres and become the second largest body of water in England and Wales. Its maximum depth will be 110 ft and its average 32 ft, 7 ft more than the Grafham average. It will be filled by pumping from the Rivers Welland and Nene, dissolved solids will be high, and the lake very fertile.

The lake will probably be opened for fishing in 1976, and will be managed by the Welland and Nene Rivers Authority. The raw water will be sold to water undertakings.

At last, it seems, a major reservoir is to be managed as a fishery by professionally trained fishery workers who will take up their duties long before the reservoir opens.

CHAPTER 20

A discourse on lakes

From a fishing point of view there are only two kinds of lake in which large trout may be expected to occur, namely: 'oligotrophic' lakes and 'eutrophic' lakes. A third type, 'dystrophic' lakes, in which the water is stained by peat and other organic matter, seldom contains any but small trout and is of little importance in our discussion.

The unfamiliar words are not of my choice, but they occur in many books about freshwater and were first used by Professor Theinemann. Their importance lies in their meanings: oligotrophic meaning 'little nourishing', eutrophic 'well nourishing', and dystrophic 'badly nourishing'.

It is important that the reader understand how and why these names are applied and I must therefore try to explain some of the behaviour of a body of water throughout the year.

Stratification

Water is at its heaviest when its temperature is 4°C. During the late autumn and winter, the surface-water of a lake cools to 4°C and sinks to the bottom and remains there, being added to by further cooling at the surface until the bulk of the water is at the same temperature. During spring the surface-waters are warmed by sunlight and are therefore less dense than the lower body of water. This upper layer is known as the 'epilimnion', the lower as the 'hypolimnion', and the narrow belt between the two, in which the temperature changes rapidly from that of the epilimnion to that of the hypolimnion is, not unnaturally, spoken of as the 'thermocline' (*vide* diagram 20.1b).

The epilimnion is in constant circulation owing to wind action and is thus well oxygenated. The depth to which the upper layer extends is dependent upon the mixing effect of winds sweeping across the surface and possibly also on the depth to which the warming rays of the sun penetrate.

During calm weather when the epilimnion is not in circulation, there will be, during the heat of the day, a tendency for the fish to lie in the thermocline because of its higher oxygen content. Those who 'troll' in deep lakes are well aware of the fact that it is most important to spin their spoon or minnow at the right depth, but few realize that they are in fact searching for the

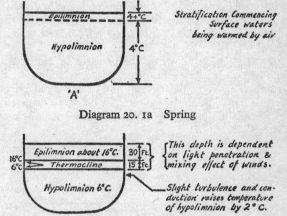

Diagram 20. 1a   Spring

Diagram 20.1b   Summer

thermocline. A minimum thermometer on a measured cord would help them to find the correct depth without guesswork.

The epilimnion will remain intact until its temperature is the same as the summer temperature of the hypolimnion, that is: 6°C. At this point the whole of the water will have the same density and will be readily mixed by the autumn winds as shown in diagram 20.2.

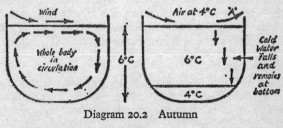

Diagram 20.2   Autumn

253

Further cooling below 6°C results in the winter stratification shown to be beginning in 'A' of the above diagram.

With the whole body of the water at 4°C, equal density throughout again permits of complete circulation as in diagram 20.3. Cooling below 4°C results in an insulating layer of water forming at the surface, since water near to freezing point is markedly lighter than water at 4°C. When ice forms the water is protected from wind, and further cooling of unfrozen water can occur only by conduction. Thus a few feet below the ice, water is well above freezing point and fish continue their normal lives.

In shallow lakes, however, particularly in North America where winters are long and severe, a layer of snow over the ice may entirely prevent plants removing carbon-dioxide from the water, and in addition the oxygen may become exhausted; serious mortality in the fish population then occurs, and is known as 'Winter Kill'.

The slightest increase of surface temperature above 4°C in spring restores the position shown in 'A' of diagram 20.1.

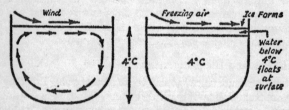

Cooling process shown at Diagram 20.2 'A'

Diagram 20.3   Winter

Summarizing, we may say that during the summer the water becomes stratified into two distinct layers which do not mix: an upper warm layer or epilimnion and a lower cold one or hypolimnion. The region of the epilimnion where a marked temperature change occurs is called the thermocline.

Oxygen

Oxygen is acquired by water in two ways: first and most importantly by the diffusion of air into the water at its surface, and secondly by solution of the oxygen produced by green water-plants. The carbon of the carbon-dioxide dissolved in the water is used by the plant to form carbohydrates, and simultaneously a quantity of oxygen is released and can often be seen as small bubbles upon the leaves of water plants. This process only occurs in daylight and only plants whose cells contain the green pigment chlorophyll can use carbon-dioxide in this way. It must not be thought that plants 'breathe' carbon-dioxide, for they breathe-in oxygen and exhale carbon-dioxide, just as do all other living things except the anaerobes. But during day-time they use more carbon-dioxide to form carbohydrate than they exhale carbon-dioxide in the process of breathing. Carbon assimilation and plant breathing are two completely different functions going on side by side.

After the autumn water-mix has taken place and stratification is broken down the quantity of oxygen at all depths is approximately the same. Later, as decomposition of dead animal and vegetable matter takes place, the quantity of oxygen in the lower waters is reduced and by summer time the oxygen of the hypolimnion may be entirely used up. Thus there is not only a great difference in temperature between the epilimnion and hypolimnion, but also a chemical difference such that fish may be found in the former but not in the latter.

This phenomenon requires further explanation.

Plant life and the nutrient cycle

Proteins are substances found in all living cells, and they are built up from over twenty different amino-acids. These acids are organic compounds, all of them containing carbon, hydrogen, oxygen, and nitrogen, while some also contain phosphorus and sulphur.

The hydrogen and oxygen are supplied to the cell in the form of water, the carbon is extracted photosynthetically from carbon-dioxide, but the other substances must be obtained from soil-water in the case of land plants or from the water itself in the case of the small drifting plants, of which algae form the major part found in lakes and ponds.

Nitrogen is the most important of the protein-forming elements and it is never completely absent from the waters of the earth's surface. Even in complete absence of organic matter some nitrogen will be found in the form of nitrates, for whenever electric storms take place atmospheric nitrogen is combined with oxygen to give ultimately a nitrate. It has been calculated that in England about 8 lb of atmospheric nitrogen are combined as nitrate in this way each year for each acre of land. In monsoon lands it reaches 80 lb of nitrogen per acre or the equivalent of 4 cwt of sulphate of ammonia. Nevertheless, in most waters the nitrate occurs principally as a result of feeder streams flowing through cultivated land from which soluble nitrates are constantly leached out in the drainage-water. Whenever animal or vegetable matter decomposes in the presence of oxygen, nitrate will be produced, thus all waters draining into a lake will carry some nitrate nitrogen.

In spring when surface waters warm up and stratification begins, the algae commence to multiply. If the quantity of nutrients is high the crop will be a big one; conversely, low nutrient supply will mean a small crop. The green algae use up the available nutrient until at last when one of the essential elements is entirely gone the 'crop' ceases to increase and starts to die off. It is not necessarily lack of nitrate which causes this decline. An investigation of Wisconsin lakes showed that a lack of carbon-dioxide which limited the production of carbohydrate was probably responsible, while at Windermere, our scientists found that lack of silica probably limits the growth of diatoms. It is often difficult to assess the cause, for often a species of algae has started to decline when the dissolved nutrient seemed entirely adequate. It is now believed that some species produce substances, antibiotics, which poison their competitors.

When these tiny plants die their soluble body nutrients pass back into the water. Some of them are completely decomposed by bacterial and fungal attack in the epilimnion, while the insoluble residues of others will slowly sink through the cold hypolimnion to the lake bottom. Here they are attacked by ammonifying bacteria and possibly later by nitrifying organisms, or they may be eaten by the bottom-dwelling animals. Whatever their fate the organic material forming their bodies is broken down to something simpler. It is because decomposition is carried out by living organisms that the oxygen of the hypolimnion is depleted while the carbon-dioxide content increases.

Meanwhile all is not static in the upper water: other algal organisms will have established themselves, reached a population peak and gone into a decline. There is a continuous rain of bodies from the upper water throughout the year. Sometimes the rate of deposition is so rapid that bodies are covered before they have decomposed, for in the low temperatures of the hypolimnion decomposition is always slow. If this should happen decomposition without oxygen, that is, anaerobic decomposition, must take place. This is extremely slow – in fact pollen grains over 1,000 years old have been recovered from the mud of Windermere, still

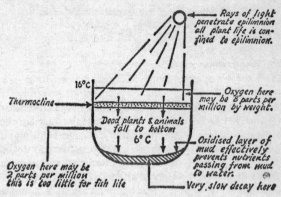

Diagram 20.4 'Oligotrophic' lake

identifiable. More dramatically, human bodies, centuries old, were brought up in excellent preservation from the mud of a small Norwegian lake. This preservation of proteins in the bottom mud means that the chemical nutrients they contain are lost to the water for all time.

When a lake is deep, the hypolimnion consists of a large volume of water whose oxygen will never be completely used up and the mud surface will always be in an oxidized state. This oxidized layer effectively insulates the water above from the products of anaerobic decomposition below. Such lakes will always be 'little nourishing' or 'oligotrophic', because they preserve their protein instead of breaking it down to simple plant foods for re-use.

But let us suppose that the lake is a shallow one perhaps only 50 ft in depth. Such a water would form an epilimnion extending to a depth of about 35 ft while the hypolimnion would be so small that its oxygen would soon be completely used up. The oxidized surface of the mud, a colloidal ferric complex, would then be broken down to the soluble ferrous state, and the nutrients locked up in the mud would pass through the mud surface into the water of the hypolimnion as illustrated in diagram 20.5.

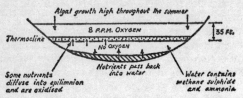

Diagram 20.5 'Eutrophic' lake

The absence of oxygen in the hypolimnion would mean that the products of decomposition would exist not as carbon-dioxide, nitrate and sulphate, but as methane (CH_4) ammonia (NH_3) and sulphide (H_2S). These noisome substances would not be oxidized until the autumnal mixing of the water, when these nutrients would be dispersed throughout the lake.

Although the epilimnion and hypolimnion do not mix during the summer, substances in solution in the lower layer will slowly diffuse into the upper layer. Thus during the summer, if the oxygen of the hypolimnion becomes exhausted the nutrient content of the epilimnion will be replaced to some extent, and algal production will continue at a higher rate than in an oligotrophic lake. Lakes whose hypolimnion oxygen becomes exhausted in this way are said to be 'eutrophic', because they 'nourish well' their upper productive waters.

In the case we have just considered a certain amount of nutrient does remain locked up throughout the summer and maximum productivity is never achieved. A water of about 30 ft depth, or less, presents a very different and markedly more productive type of eutrophy. As with other lakes there is a spring 'flush'. During March and April high winds keep the whole water circulating and the bottom temperature will be similar to that at the surface.

The rate of decay at the bottom will be much higher than in a deep stratified water, and as soon as calm weather settles in and the water becomes still, slight thermal stratification will occur and the bottom water will lose its oxygen. The nutrients of the mud will then pass into solution as in diagram 20.5, and the next breeze will start the water circulating, and disperse the nutrient throughout the water. This process may occur every few days and the algal production in the surface waters is correspondingly high.

Just to keep the story correct, I must mention that when a water contains much dissolved or suspended organic matter such as sewage or animal excreta the blue-green algae appear. Some of these organisms are able to use atmospheric nitrogen to make their body-protein and in this respect resemble some bacteria. When they die, their bodies decompose, and they therefore increase the nitrate of a water. Ordinary plants and algae can use only nitrate or in some cases ammoniacal nitrogen, the atmospheric nitrogen is no use at all to them. The blue-green algae are responsible for water bloom and also for odours and flavours in drinking water, and are therefore most unpopular with water-engineers.

The productivity of still water

The algae are the basic food of all waters. Except where they exist as 'slime'-colonies upon weed-stems or rocks they are visible only as 'colour' in the water, but they are nevertheless the food of the small water animals such as daphnia, rotifers, hydra and so on, collectively known as 'zooplankton', the plants being known as the 'phytoplankton'.

These tiny animals are in turn the food of larger species and small fish, and these in turn are eaten by large fish. It should be obvious that the larger the algal crop the greater will be the production of fish. Thus the shallow lakes and reservoirs have an advantage over deep lakes, although some exceptions to this rule do exist.

It is most regrettable that we cannot remove from the water the whole of its crop of plankton.

Professor Juday found that the standing crop of plankton in Lake Mendota, an eutrophic water in Wisconsin, was 214 lb of dry matter per acre. If we assume that the crop is replaced every ten days of the growing season, total production will be of the order of $1\frac{1}{2}$ tons of dry matter per acre per annum. Obviously such figures are approximations, but Worthington and Macan accept Juday's findings as being reasonable.

The analysis of this mixture of tiny plants and animals shows that 44·5 per cent is crude protein, 7·5 per cent is fat, and 48 per cent is carbohydrate. From a nutritional point of view we may compare plankton with soya beans, with 53 per cent crude protein, 17·5 per cent fat and 30 per cent carbohydrate. Medium fat beef dry analysis shows 79 per cent first-class protein and 21 per cent fat . . . but you get very little of it from an acre of land.

The high fat-content of the plankton deserves some mention. John Clegg in his book *Freshwater Life of the British Isles* tells us that during the 1939–45 war German scientists obtained twice as much oil per unit of plant-nutrient from cultures of the Alga *Chlamydomonas* as was obtained from the same nutrient used for culture of oil-seeds.

In addition to the algal crop there is of course a crop of attached, higher plants. Professor Juday found that these grew to a depth of 23 ft in Mendota and amounted to about 350 lb of dry matter per acre of the whole water. This crop appeared only once a year and it was therefore deemed of less importance than the algal crop.

In very shallow lakes the standing crop of rooted plants per acre might well be much higher, and in fact it may, by taking up nutrient and holding it through the summer, restrict algal development.

Dr Gross, writing in the July 1941 issue of *Nature*, tells of Allen's figures of 1915 which showed that the yield of protein from a Continental carp-pond was 20 lb per acre heavier than the production of beef from grassland. Again, in 1939 the Munich fish-ponds yielded 400–500 lb of carp per acre which compares very favourably with Wye College's 250 lb live-weight increase for bullocks on each acre of land. The dressed carcase-weight would be only 60 per cent of this amount.

Though no guide to fish production in temperate Britain, crops of carp and tilapia in Israel, tropical Asia and Africa have, in recent years, far exceeded Munich figures.

Macan and Worthington have given us a 'magical' factor '7' in the food cycle of water. Each unit of vegetable food yields one-seventh as much animal matter. If this animal matter is itself used as food, it in turn yields one-seventh of its weight as fish. If a fish lived only on algae, 49 lb of algae would produce 7 lb of fish, but if the fish lived on small water-animals which in turn had lived on algae, 49 lb of algae would yield only 1 lb of fish. The result of this is, that a water with a given algal production will produce at least two and a half times as great a weight of carp-flesh each year as it will trout-flesh, since carp utilize plants for at least a part of their food while trout are almost completely carnivorous. (See also page 313).

A typical unmanured eutrophic lake with a highly fertile bottom should produce *in theory* from 150 to 200 lb of carp per acre per year or about 75 lb of trout per acre. In practice such high returns will not be obtained and oligotrophic waters would have much lower yields. Stocking of water must obviously be related to productivity. Particularly must it be borne in mind that most of the productivity figures available to us relate to the conditions of Continental fish farms, where ponds average perhaps 6 ft in depth and where the ratio of margin length to area is high. It has long been established that fish 'graze' marginal waters more effectively than the middles of ponds and lakes. Small lakes are thus more productive per acre than big ones, other characteristics being equal.

Reservoirs by their very size cannot hope to produce acre for acre as great a weight of fish as a farmed pond.

Utilizing waters for fish production

If a water contained only phytoplankton and bottom plants the process of decomposition and regeneration of a 'crop' would be slow. The addition of small animals which eat the plants and excrete part of them as simpler organic substances would speed up the return of nutrients to the water. But the maximum rate of regeneration is achieved only when fish are added to speed the decomposition of the small animals.

The rapidity with which the excreted wastes of fish and the bodies of dead water-creatures are broken down into inorganic nitrate and phosphate is dependent upon the calcium content of the water. The bacteria which carry out the processes of ammonification and subsequent nitrification are most active at pH values above 6·5.* In addition Juday has shown that the carbon

* Neutral water is said to have a pH value of 7. Figures above 7 denote alkalinity, figures below 7 acidity. A fluid is said to be acid when the quantity of hydrogen ion (H+) is in excess of the hydroxyl ion (OH−).

pH means the concentration of hydrogen ion (in grammes per litre) expressed as the reciprocal of the logarithm. If a litre of water (1¾ pints approx) contained ·0000001 gm of hydrogen ion we could express this small amount as a logarithm i.e.: 10^{-7}gr/litre. Usually in logarithms we omit the dioxide content of a water is dependent upon the amount of calcium present, and that where the calcium is low there may be a limit to algal growth by reason of carbon-dioxide deficiency. In Europe 65 parts per million of calcium carbonate and bicarbonate have been found to be necessary for the heavy cropping of water, and where waters are acid, up to 3 tons of calcium carbonate per acre may be added depending on the degree of acidity. Mild acidity itself does not harm the fish; it merely limits the natural productivity of the water and lowers the growth rate.* Quite obviously, calcium-deficient waters cannot support a large population of those species which construct their shells of calcium carbonate, and such species are an extremely important item in fish diet.

Following correction of the acidity it has been found profitable to manure with superphosphate or basic slag (this last itself corrects acidity). Krügel and Heinrich claimed that each pound of superphosphate added to a water with an organic mud bottom gave an increased production of 2·13 lb of fish. A normal dressing of superphosphate is 1½ cwt per acre per annum applied as ¾ cwt in spring and the remainder in summer. When fertilizer is applied, a large algal population develops, and the resultant coloration of the water restricts the amount of light penetrating to the bottom and depresses the growth of attached bottom-plants. In deep water only the surface waters would receive sufficient light to produce algae, and the economical depth for

---

'10' (the base) and use only the index, in this case '−7'. The reciprocal of −7 is 7, thus we say a fluid containing ·0000001 gr/litre of hydrogen ion has a pH of 7 and is neutral. Since the figures are logarithmic reciprocals, a decrease of 1 unit means that the concentration of hydrogen ion has *in-increased* 10 times, pH 5 is ten times as acid as pH 6 and contains 100 times as much hydrogen ion as a fluid at pH 7. pH 9 is 10 times as alkaline as pH 8 and contains 1/100th the quantity of hydrogen ion that a fluid at pH 7 contains.

* Exceptions to the general rule, that acid waters do not rear good trout, are sometimes found. Lough Shure with water as acid as pH 4·8, little above the iso-electric point of many proteins, produces rainbow trout around the pound mark. The pH measurements were taken in May and August 1931. Presumably several measurements were taken at varying times of the day, though this point is not expressly referred to in Dr Winifred Frost's paper in *Salmon and Trout Magazine* of September 1940. It has been found in investigation of United States lakes that the pH value may vary by as much as 3 units in a twenty-four-hour period, owing to removal of dissolved CO_2 from the water by photosynthesis.

fish-ponds has been found to be 6 ft, i.e.: that depth of water in which the whole is actively productive. It is reasonable to suppose that the greatly increased growth-rate of trout in experimentally fertilized Quebec lakes would be repeated elsewhere.

Fish production in reservoirs

We have seen how the dissolved plant-nutrients fed into a lake by feeder-streams are built up into vegetable protein and eventually into fish-flesh. The logical result of this is that the outlet-water from a lake contains less nutrient than the inlet water, and the lake becomes a reservoir of plant-nutrients, its productivity increasing as the years pass.

If the lake is a water-supply reservoir this increase of productivity brings in its train a number of problems for the water engineer, for the algal crop to be removed by filtration will increase with the increasing fertility of the water. Loch Katrine, which supplies Glasgow with water, is an excellent illustration of this, and it now produces a heavy algal growth quite unknown in the 1870s.

There are numerous ways by which plant-nutrient in a water can be reduced or controlled. The easiest is perhaps that used in stratified reservoirs, from which nutrients are easily removed by using the enriched water of the hypolimnion as compensation water. In shallow waters this method is seldom a practical proposition, and the methods employed include removal of a crop of fish, removal of organic mud, removal of marginal vegetation and, alas, the use of systemic poisons such as copper sulphate.

The removal of a crop of fish is the method advocated in pamphlet no 11 of the Freshwater Biological Association of the British Empire (henceforward FBA). The writers suggest that removal of fish should absorb a very large part of the annual increase of nutrient. Macan and Worthington in their book subscribe to this same view, and state that theoretically it is possible to check completely the accumulation of nutrient.

Where this means of control is to be used it is essential that the fish in the water shall have a high economic value. It is not enough for them to be nutritious if the angler finds them unpalatable. We possess an important sea-fishing industry, and coarse fish are here regarded as unfit for table.* The fact that the attitude may be a result of prejudice in no way alters the case, and the angler returns his catch to the water at the end of the day. The Continental approach to fish-farming cannot succeed in England until we confine our fish production to those species which find a ready sale: the salmonidae and eels. For removal of a crop of fish from a reservoir by angling, common sense dictates that the species stocked shall be trout, for such fish will always be retained by the captor and used as food. It is true that a crop of coarse fish could be removed by netting and subsequently used to stock the waters of a nearby angling association, but such a method has nothing to recommend it: nothing is contributed to the national larder; the sporting amenities of the neighbourhood are merely maintained but are not increased, and netting itself is an expensive and often unsuccessful venture.

By keeping down rushes and choking-weed, silting is reduced, and water engineer and angler benefit alike. Labour costs have hastened the employment of hormone weed killers such as 2,4-D and 2,4,5-T to control 'herbaceous' weeds, and very recently we have been able to kill rushes and reeds with chemicals such as 'Dowpon'. In concentrations sufficient to kill vegetation these substances are harmless to fish and food creatures. Restricting the growth of emergent weeds does not, of course, remove nutrient, which being unused by attached plants may increase the algal crop.

Threatened with algal trouble on the filter beds, water engineers tend to think about applying copper sulphate to the reservoir and thereby reduce the total crop of algae. If reservoir anglers know the facts and hazards they can at least try to ensure that it is applied in an enlightened manner, unlikely to result in serious fish mortality.

In USA, when copper sulphate was first used it was applied at rates up to 10 lb per million USA gallons (US gallon = 8·3 lb of water) and produced concentrations up to 1·2 parts per million. Hale carried out experiments and found that as little

* There is a limited market for carp to Jewish members of the community, and eels too have always found a ready market. The Lough Neagh eel crop has in recent years been the bone of contention between owners and poachers and the cause of blood letting on more than one occasion. The eels taken by both factions find their way to London and the Continent.

as ·14 parts per million of copper sulphate was toxic to trout, while perch succumbed when the concentration was ·67 ppm. Only sunfish and black bass could survive at 1·2 ppm concentration, but their survival is no triumph if they subsequently starve.

Fortunately, for the angler, it was found that following the use of copper sulphate secondary growths of copper-resistant algae occurred. Some of these organisms were so tiny that they passed through the filter-beds, and the resultant spate of complaints from consumers that their tap-water was green caused engineers to modify their methods. Pamphlet no 11 of the FBA reports on the work of Domogalla who used only ·05 ppm of copper sulphate to control the algae of Lake Monona, Wisconsin.

Domogalla's method aimed, not at wiping out the algal growth, but at reducing the peak population to one which did not hinder filtration. That he succeeded in doing so is shown by population figures, but more important from the anglers' point of view is the fact that the protozoa and fish populations were undisturbed. No secondary growths of copper resistant organisms occurred.

Most water engineers are loath to interfere with the biological balance of a water; nevertheless anglers may be faced with such disturbances of the fishery. Application of copper sulphate is not a job for a labourer: Domogalla's methods require very careful use of powder spraying equipment.

The effect of lake type upon the feeding habits of fish

Investigations of Swedish lakes by Alm showed that the weight of fish produced each year was approximately proportional to the weight of the available bottom feed. Fish production, he found, varied from 1 to 100 lb per acre per annum while the standing crop of bottom-dwelling food animals varied from 1 to 215 lb per acre.

It has been found that waters with peat or inorganic rock bottoms tend to be deficient in bottom fauna, and the bottoms described as being of 'organic' mud are those most productive of food animals. An organic mud is one consisting of finely-divided mineral particles, i.e.: silt or clay, together with plant and animal residues.

Under the best conditions this mud will exist as an ooze over the mineral bottom. The colloidal particles of this ooze play an important part in the adsorption of the cations of calcium, potassium etc. and in the adsorption of the phosphate anion. Where superphosphate is applied, the organic mud is of great economic importance by its retention of the phosphate ion which otherwise would be removed in the outflow from the pond. But for most of us this mud is important because it is a perfect environment for snails, mussels, worms and fly nymphs and larvae. In addition its rich supply of nutrients will give rise to an abundance of rooted plants which supply additional food for snail, and whose leaves and stems become covered with algae and protozoa on which other water-animals feed.

In ponds used for commercial fish-culture luxuriant bottom-vegetation is discouraged, but in fishing waters such plants are desirable. As a fish grows it tends to select larger food-forms. This fact is particularly true of trout and other carnivores. In a fish-pond, trout are seldom more than $\frac{3}{4}$ lb in weight, and their diet of planktonic water-animals is adequate. But fish of, say, 2 lb or over could not grow on such small organisms, for they would expend more energy in catching their food than was yielded from its assimilation and combustion. Large trout tend to be bottom-feeders and only an organic mud bottom can satisfy their demands for food species of sufficient size: caddis larvae, snails and other molluscs, corixa and so on. Very large trout are of course found in oligotrophic waters which are deficient in bottom-feed, but these fish have attained their size by feeding upon small fish which in turn have fed upon the small planktonic animals.

The food chain in such lakes would be, algae, protozoa, small fish and trout; and the addition of an extra link again, bringing in the factor '7', further reduces the fish crop.

Scale-readings of trout taken in two Midland reservoirs show that the fastest growth occurs in fish weighing from 1 to $2\frac{1}{2}$ lb, that is to say, when the fish are big enough to take advantage of the supplies of stickleback. Over 3 lb in weight the fish lose their beauty of form, probably because a stickleback diet is not a large enough food-form. In Lake Pend Oreille, USA, many rainbow trout over 30 lb in weight have been taken. Many of these fish are but four summers old, and they are not ugly fish since they have access to a large enough food-species: a degenerate land-locked salmon about 6 in. long. If trout are to carry on growing while retaining their beauty, they must be able to select larger food-forms as they grow. It is possible that we could greatly improve the trout of the Midland reservoirs by using the true minnow instead of stickleback as a food species. Minnows can feed directly upon algae, whereas the stickleback is carnivorous. Thus the crop of food-minnows each year would be heavier than the stickleback crop, and the use of minnows would provide a diet of greater variation in size, for large minnows weigh perhaps eight times as much as large sticklebacks, while their fry are no larger. Their use entails none of the risks associated with large coarse species which compete with trout for available bottom-food animals.

Summing up, we may say that eutrophic lakes will usually provide an abundance of bottom-feed because the bottom itself is rendered fertile by the deposition of large quantities of organic material from the surface water. Further, the relatively large area of the bottom receiving light from the sun will produce a heavy crop of attached vegetation among which heavy fish may find the large food-forms they require. In eutrophic lakes, trout can attain a weight of 4 lb without resorting to cannibalism, and at that weight their diet will still include food-forms which can be imitated by a fly. The bottom-feeding habits of trout in eutrophic lakes will render them difficult to take on a dry-fly at the surface.

For the trout inhabiting oligotrophic lakes with restricted bottom-feeding facilities, surface flies are a more important item of food and in such waters the dry-fly may well give good results.

The Midland reservoirs

There is no doubt that the reservoirs of, and close by, the Midland Plain provide the cheapest good-class trout fishing in the whole of England. They are usually flooded farmland of high fertility. The soil is sweet, and thus the water is not acidified as it would be over marshland or bog. The dam is constructed across the headwaters of a river or tributary stream above all sources of pollution, and the incoming water is thus pure and well oxygenated. The Midland valleys are usually wide and shallow and form typical eutrophic lakes with fertile organic mud bottoms. Many of these waters are no more than 35 ft deep.

I am sometimes asked why it is that reservoirs constructed many years ago continue to produce large trout, while other lakes of a similar age will produce only poor stuff, and in many cases have become suitable only for coarse fish. The answer lies in a combination of factors.

By contrast with the ornamental lake a reservoir does not suffer from lack of cleansing. The weed is kept under control, and is seldom allowed to decompose in the water and take up valuable oxygen, while many lakes, uncleansed for years, develop thick beds of blanket-weed in their upper shallows.

In shallow lakes the value of weed lies in its power to remove excessive and harmful carbon-dioxide from the water during photosynthesis. The release of oxygen during the process is relatively unimportant, for this essential gas readily diffuses into the water at its surface.* Heavily weeded, shallow water may, at night-time, create actively poisonous conditions by its release of large quantities of carbon dioxide in normal respiratory processes, when no carbon dioxide is being turned into carbohydrate owing to absence of light. Certainly the decomposition of these blanketing weeds is a contributory factor to the deterioration of lakes. As the quality of the water drops over the years, so does the quantity of scavenging life in the water and with that the food supply of the fish. It follows then that when the rot sets in, it continues increasingly swiftly.

One of the unfortunate side effects of the accumulation of detritus in 'matured' lakes is the proneness of their fish stocks to Winter Kill when decomposition of the bio-mass drastically reduces the oxygen when the lake is ice- and snowbound.

Within a species, the oxygen requirement of an individual fish, under given conditions, is governed by body-weight, which is related to the cube of any dimension. In contrast, the ability to assimilate oxygen varies with the surface area of the gill filaments which is related to the square of any dimension. Put simply: as a fish grows the ratio of body weight to gill area increases, and in water low in oxygen big fish survive less ably than small ones.

With big fish (predators) gone, the myriad small fish survive the better, living on less and less food each year and the fishery becomes valueless.

* During hot weather on 28 August 1931, Birge and Juday found a layer of water at from 9 to 10 metres depth which was supersaturated with oxygen resulting from photosynthetic action of algae. Solar energy at these depths was found to be only $1\frac{1}{4}$ per cent of the surface energy. The oxygen content of this layer was markedly higher than that of water near the surface, and although no reference is made by the investigators to the presence of fish, there is little doubt that they would tend to be concentrated some 28 ft down because of the high oxygen concentration.

Although Winter Kill is usually thought of in connection with shallow lakes of the North American Continent, I believe it to occur fairly frequently in Britain too. Wherever the seasonal catch of a shallow loch or tarn set in hilly country ceases suddenly to include large fish, the previous winter having been severe, Winter Kill should be high on the list of suspects. Winter Kill decimated stocks in many lakes in the severe 1962–3 winter. Pix Lake, a famous big pike and carp water fished by the Boxmoor and District Angling Society, had its stock almost wiped out; and George Hollands, writing in *Angling* February 1969 records a similar disaster in 1962–3 winter on the Sussex Hammer Pond that he fishes.

The reservoir has one tremendous advantage over the lake in that its level drops from 7 ft to 15 ft each year in high summer. In years of excessive drought, 75 per cent or more of the bed is exposed to the cleansing influence of sunlight and air.

It was many years ago that I read M. Louis Roule's book *Fishes: Their Ways of Life*, but I recall that he mentioned the emptying, drying, harrowing and manuring of Continental carp ponds. Most books on fish-culture stress the importance of an occasional drying of the pond bed and its resultant improved fertility. Our reservoirs receive at least a part of this treatment each year, and when the water rises in October and November it does not cover a growth of rushes, for these are mown and removed while the water is low.

In one respect, however, most of our reservoirs are seriously lacking, and this is in regard to spawning facilities. This problem is dealt with in the following chapter.

CHAPTER 21

Thoughts on stocking

We have already seen that inland waters may be highly product-ive, and that the coarse species are unsatisfactory for reservoir stocking because they are a crop which the angler does not remove from the water. Nevertheless, whether or not they are introduced by man, they will inevitably appear after a few years, either entering the water from the feeder streams or as ova carried on the legs and feet of wading birds such as the heron.

In recent years pike and perch have appeared in Hollowell Reservoir, Northamptonshire. It is fair conjecture that entry, here, has been effected via the pipe-line through which water is pumped from one of the head streams of the River Nene – which, above Kingsthorpe Mill, was always well known for its pike and quality perch. Whenever water is pumped from a river into a reservoir, coarse fish will get through no matter how elaborate the fry and spawn traps may be.

In most eutrophic lakes, bream, rudd and carp find them-selves in an environment perfect in every respect, and being enormously prolific they will soon establish a heavy population. Brown trout, on the other hand, produce only about seven hundred eggs per pound of body weight and furthermore, because their eggs must be covered by well-oxygenated running water not normally found in most lakes, few of the eggs hatch out and natural regeneration is inadequate. For these reasons, trout in a lake populated with coarse species will be suppressed, unless good management and stocking maintain the supremacy of the trout. Perch are perhaps the greatest menace in trout lakes and at Grafham they are already a problem. I hear rumours that selective poisons are now being tested in America and that within a year or two we shall be able to hit a complete vermin population while leaving the trout – and the ratepayers – quite unharmed.

In all problems of management we are faced with a lack of precise information on matters of every kind. Earlier, I mentioned Edward Hewitt's plankton theory, a theory worthy of investigation for Hewitt has been actively concerned with fisheries and hatchery management for most of his active life. He quotes a case of an experiment in England by Stratton Gerrish. A lake which provided an abundance of plankton feed, but few larger food forms, contained artificially reared trout which seldom grew to be more than ¾ lb. A similar water stocked with naturally reared fish produced large trout which were plankton feeders throughout their lives. The substitution of fry stocking in the first lake resulted in the establishment of a plankton-feeding population whose members grew to large size. If Stratton Gerrish's findings are generally true they are of enormous importance. The officers of the Freshwater Biological Association have no information on the subject and it would appear that no 'controlled' experiments have been carried out over here. United States sources are similarly devoid of information on the feeding habits of hatchery-reared and wild fish. There was, however, a brief reference in the 1937 report of the US Bureau of Fisheries which may throw some light on the matter. Artificially reared rainbow and brook trout were released in streams and later caught by angling. Examination of the stomach contents showed that the rainbows had consumed large quantities of plankton in addition to insect food, while the brook trout contained only the larger food forms. On the face of it, the findings of Stratton Gerrish and the US workers conflict, but allowance must be made for the differences of habit of the species involved. On the available evidence I cannot accept it as proven that naturally reared fish are plankton feeders whereas hatchery-fed fish are not but I certainly feel that a full investigation would be worthwhile. In particular it might pay to investigate the feeding habits of rainbow trout and brown trout reared under identical conditions and placed in the same water. It has long been known that the active rainbow can satisfy his appetite and thrive on smaller food forms than the brown trout; if in addition he can use plankton to supplement his diet his value as a species for stocking is greatly enhanced. So far as Grafham is concerned I have proved that rainbows are plankton feeders. It must be borne in mind, however, that habitat and the available food supply will have an enormous bearing on the diet of fish: in Lough Derg naturally reared trout are plankton feeders while in Lake Windermere they are not.

On a northern reservoir where in 1968 we added five hundred 8 in rainbow trout to an indigenous brown trout population at the commencement of a diagnostic fishing programme, we found that whilst the average weight of the brown trout caught increased between June and September by only ¾ oz, the average weight of the rainbows increased by 4 oz.

It is clear that up to 10 or 12 oz, the rainbows can use the available foods better than the brown trout, but we do not yet know whether they survive the hard northern winter as well, and can grow on past 12 oz, the weight at which some unknown factor limits the further progress of the brown trout.

Side effects of hatchery life discussed

In October 1952 H. Spurway's article 'Can Wild Animals be Kept in Captivity' was published in *New Biology No 13*. If its implications may fairly be applied to fish, we must assume that the trout in all but a few remote and wild-stocked lochs are today different from those our ancestors knew. Life in the feeding ponds of a hatchery must have shown preference to fish genetically suited to domestication, while, by definition, fish better suited to wild existence must have been selected-out. It is doubtful whether hand-fed fish can ever take full advantage of the natural feed in a water when they look to and, literally, rush to man for the food they require during their early life.

Spurway's article expressed far better than I could the doubts in my mind when I described in my first edition a method of rendering a reservoir head stream suitable as a nursery for wild-rearing a stock of growers. A supply of natural food was the basis of the system but my layout, though practicable, was subject to hazards of storm, silting and difficult recovery of the grown fish. Overcoming these factors required storm-water channels, penstocks and sluices, and capital cost and supervision would have made the young fish far more expensive than those grown commercially.

Many of the 'advances' in the cost-conscious world have nothing to recommend them apart from an economic advantage which is too often short term. But there is no question at all that with the rearing of fry in compensation water we have taken a fundamentally sound step ahead.

'Trout for nowt'

Starting in 1948 the fishery staff of Bristol Water Works Company reared trout in the compensation-water channel below Blagdon Reservoir. The results were impressive. Spring-planted fry averaged in the autumn 5¼ in: 1 in longer and approximately double the weight of fry reared for the same period by usual hatchery methods. It was noticed, too, that growth at nine months was very even and that young fish appeared more resistant to disease than those in the hatchery. Better dispersal of the stock and a two million gallon per day volume of flow (about ten times the flow at Ubley Hatchery) must, of course, reduce the incidence of disease, but the quality of the natural food and the fishes' freedom from digestive trouble would have made its contribution.

I first saw the system applied at Durleigh Reservoir in 1955 where Mark Holford had for several years reared ten thousand fry in specially constructed but quite simple pools through which a controlled quantity of compensation water passed. As at Blagdon, the fish ate only the plankton contained in the compensation water and when planted out had never known the delights of horse liver and other offals. Though there is no evidence to connect the fact with their plankton diet, Durleigh Brownies are probably the hardest fighting brown trout I have ever caught.

That the system is not of recent origin is clear from one of Mark's letters. He writes: 'In 1928 at Talybont on Usk Reservoir I had my first experience of rearing trout in compensation water. We had a temporary intake with a 150 ft dam across the stream to enable the Newport Corporation to take up to 5,000,000 gallons per day, while the Reservoir was in course of construction.

'Under the supervision of Supt H. Graves a temporary tank was built where 250,000 gals of compensation water per day was flowing through. This was stocked with fry from Wentwood reservoir.'

But at Chew Valley Lake, the system has been adapted by Kennedy Brown to full-scale commercial production.

Since 1955 about forty-five thousand fry have been reared each year to between 4½ and 5½ inches length without any food other than that carried to them by the flow of 3·15 million gallons per day. Labour costs are restricted to approximately thirty minutes each day to clear the screens of debris and algae by means of an ordinary broom. Commercial value of the crop? £3,200 a year – a highly satisfying return for an initial capital outlay of about £2,000.

Each of the three tanks is 150 ft long and 9 ft 6 in wide with depth so graduated that the strength of the current alters considerably to suit the needs of fish at various stages of growth. The tanks can be drained to a fish trap at the lower end when the growers are required for planting out.

There is no reason why trout should not be grown in the compensation water from reservoirs in any part of the country. Once the tanks are built and the fry turned in, the only care needed is the daily clearing of the screens. The provision of taut strands of nylon monofil over the tanks will deter herons and kingfishers without need for watching. At long last we have a method of rearing fish which should make it possible to stock our waters adequately without having to spend large sums of money. Even a Chief Financial Officer must approve this system.

While discussing sources of natural food we should do well not to forget the cleansing waters from the rapid filters now in use in many large water undertakings. Briefly, these relatively new-type filters are designed quickly to remove bulky material including small water animals before the water passes on to the familiar but much slower sand-and-clinker filter beds. By this pre-treatment of the raw water, the slow filters are able to handle a very much larger volume before cleaning becomes necessary.

The water over the rapid filters soon becomes grey with the accumulation of water fleas etc, and after a period the filter is washed and the washing water (complete with natural feed) is passed to the compensation channel, whence it could pass to fishponds.

It is nothing new, of course, for trout fry to be reared on the filter beds themselves, though I doubt if the practice is officially approved.

With a supply of naturally reared plankton-feeding fry now available at several fisheries it is high time we checked their value to the angler after planting out and growing-on to takeable size. Marking the naturally reared fingerlings before stocking would enable the angler to identify them readily, and a contrasting marking system used on the normal hatchery-reared stock of the same age would enable comparisons of the two types to be made quickly.

The assessment of results is quite simple. The date of catching, weight and age are recorded for each fish and a table similar to the one below is prepared.

Table 1 – Hypothetical comparison of two stocks of marked brown trout

Total number of hatchery fish stocked: 400

Total number of naturally reared fish stocked: 400

Age of fish	Month taken	No of wild fish caught	Average weight	No of hatchery fish caught	Average weight
4	April	40	1 lb 1 oz	40	15 oz
4	May	30	1 lb 2 oz	25	1 lb
4	June	30	1 lb 4 oz	25	1 lb 1½ oz
4	July	15	1 lb 6 oz	20	1 lb 3 oz
4	August	15	1 lb 8 oz	15	1 lb 5 oz
4	September	30	1 lb 9 oz	20	1 lb 6 oz
Total		160		145	

Similar tables for older age groups would soon reveal the story. From such a table as that above it would be reasonable to conclude that the naturally reared fish were growing faster than hatchery reared fish, and in addition the numbers taken show that their recovery rate was higher. If this were also true in the other age groups it would mean either that the naturally reared fish were rising more readily to the fly or had a better survival rate. In either case they would be more useful fish. Probably the best method of comparing the value of two methods of stock rearing is to divide the cost of rearing the fish by the total weight of mature fish caught, and thus arrive at the stocking cost for 1 lb of each type of fish produced.

The necessity for marking all fish

Tables such as the one above could not be compiled without data. The fishery officer or association managing the water must be able to identify each fish caught at a glance.

Scale reading is an exact science and the method makes it possible to calculate the length and weight of a fish at any time in its life if we know its length and weight when caught, for the weight of a fish varies directly as the cube of the ratio of its lengths at two stages of growth: if we multiply the length by 2 we multiply the weight by 2 cubed, or 8.

Let us presume that we have caught a fish 12 in long and weighing 1 lb. Scale reading and micro-measurement show the fish to have been four years old and the distance from the centre of the scale to the second annual ring to be two-thirds of the distance from the centre to a newly forming fourth ring or line of erosion. The ratio of the lengths of the fish at two years and four years will therefore be as 2 is to 3, and our 12 in fish was therefore 8 in long when two years old. Further, the cube of the ratio, 2:3, ie 8:27, tells us that our fish at two years of age weighed $\frac{8}{27}$ of its weight when caught. $\frac{8}{27}$ of 16 oz gives us its weight as having been $4\frac{3}{4}$ oz. This method of calculation would be useful only when the conformation of the fish had not altered between the second and fourth year.

Useful though it is to know the past history of a fish, scale reading is of limited application in fishery management because it is a task for a trained worker. Its very exactness, resulting in limitation of the number of scales which can be read in a given time, is a serious drawback and for practical purposes we must have methods which can be used by the angler. In fertile reservoirs there has been the additional difficulty that many fish continue feeding hard and growing fast through the winter so that winter rings are often hard to discern and sometimes entirely absent.

We carried out our first stocking at Hollowell and Ravensthorpe Reservoirs with trout marked by removing the left pectoral fin, removing only the rayed portion so avoiding any bleeding that might accompany cutting into the stub of flesh at the fin-base. In the following season we found many small fish with fins so well regenerated that only by comparing lengths of left and right pectorals was there any evidence at all of earlier cutting. The method fell flat on its face because the mark we used was not quickly apparent to the lay angler on whom we relied to identify and record his catch.

Contrary to general belief, a fish does not use its fins for locomotion but as stabilizers: even the tail is unessential. I have before me at the moment a letter from Lloyd Meehean written in 1953 in which he mentions seeing a trout caught which had had *all* its fins removed a year earlier. The removal of one or more fins is a standard practice in the United States where hundreds of thousands of young salmon have been marked in recent years as part of the research on West Coast salmon stocks and their migrations. Immediately following fin-clipping there is a little inconvenience, but within a day or two the young fish learns to swim as well as before.

Unfortunately, in some ways, the average angler loves trout and loathes scientists: the word mutilation has after all most unpleasant associations. At Northampton, after the partial failure of the first experiment, we were prevented from improving upon the clipping method used the previous season as a result of a highly emotional attack at the AGM on the clipping procedure. The committee's policy was finally reversed by an appeal to members to reject a practice which resulted in being unable to set up a specimen trout because it had a fin missing!

Clearly we had boobed horribly in our public relations work!

No matter where we turned in 1953, information on fin-cutting techniques was scanty and often conflicting. One of the few common factors was the use of Urethane to anaesthetize fish so that they could be handled safely and cuts made accurately.

But in 1958, HMSO published T. A. Stuart's monograph 'Marking and Regeneration of Fins' which makes it quite clear that a completely satisfactory cutting method has now been devised. The paper illustrates the various types of cut and their effect after the passage of several years.

In principle, he relies not upon the absence of a fin or its seriously distorted growth, but upon a cut which will afterwards be discernible as a ridge on a fin of otherwise almost normal appearance and size: a ridge such as is commonly seen in trout which have suffered a natural accident. The charge of permanent disfigurement cannot fairly be applied to Stuart's methods, and I feel they are likely to prove acceptable to many anglers who opposed the earlier 'stub cutting' methods.

Once marking is adopted, effective fishery management becomes possible. Guesswork is no substitute for facts and facts we can certainly get by marking.

We most of us believe we know the answers to at least some of the following questions. But at the best our answers are inspired guesswork, at the worst they are hopelessly inaccurate.

1. Which survives the better, a fish stocked in spring or a fish stocked in autumn?

2. Which is cheapest to stock, fry, yearlings or two-year-olds ?

3. How many fish are there in the water in each age group ?

4. Do young fish rise more freely than old fish and do fast growers rise better than slow growers ?

5. Is it weight or age which controls the trout's inclination to feed on the bottom ?

6. Of two stocks of fish from different hatcheries, which has the better survival rate ?

7. Of two stocks of fish, which grows the faster ?

8. Of two stocks of rainbow trout has one a more marked tendency to migrate than the other, and does one tend to spawn earlier than the other ?

9. Between what ages do the fish grow fastest ?

10. What is the extent of natural regeneration of the stock ?

After a few seasons' marking we would know all of these things.

At first sight it may not be easy to envisage how the answers to questions 3, 4 and 5 could be obtained. The method used is not 100 per cent accurate but it is considered sufficiently accurate by those engaged in deep-sea fishery research to warrant its use, and within the confines of a lake results should be more accurate than at sea.

A stretch of water is netted shortly before opening day, and the fish so caught are tagged and returned. In the case of a water stocked with marked fish, the number in each age group would be noted and the tag would be an additional marking; the fish would then be released in various parts of the water.

During the ensuing season some of the tagged fish will be caught, and the relationship of the number of tagged fish caught to the number tagged will be the same as the relationship of the total number caught to the total number in the water. The following table shows how the population is worked out.

Table 2 – Hypothetical Population Check

Age	Number tagged	Number of tagged fish caught	Total caught	Stock at beginning of season
4	50	15	300	50/15 × 300 = 1,000
5	45	13	200	45/13 × 200 = 690
6	30	11	100	30/11 × 100 = 273
7	15	3	40	15/3 × 40 = 200
8	7	1	15	7/1 × 15 = 105
9	2	—	—	—

Examination of such a table gives us a great a deal of information. Firstly, by subtracting the total caught from the stock at the beginning of the season we can find the number of fish in each age group remaining in the water. Secondly, we notice that the percentage of fish caught falls off sharply after the sixth year. In fact, although we tagged two fish which were nine years old, we have not caught any from this group, although judging from the number of eight-year-olds there should be a large population of nine-year-old fish. We could assume from our table that fish showed a tendency to become bottom feeders from the seventh year onwards and were no longer desirable in a water fished only by the fly. Such fish would be actively harmful for many of them would be capable of killing trout up to 1 lb in weight. Our figures would, in fact, justify the removal of all fish over six years of age by any means available. Probably the easiest method would be to net them out when they ran up the brooks to spawn, but it would also be possible to spin for them during July and August. If this latter method were adopted it would be necessary to lay down a minimum width for spoon baits, or adopt a standard size and pattern: the use of 'Devons' would lead to the killing of too great a number of the smaller fly-rising fish.

We all like to feel that there is a chance of taking a 10-pounder on the fly. D. M. Pilkington had a fish of 10 lb 10 oz at Shustoke Reservoir in 1947, and C. Inwood (who gave me my first lesson with a fly rod) took one of 10 lb 4 oz at Eyebrook in 1955. Eyebrook (the Corby Reservoir) has incidentally produced a fish over 11 lb on spinner, and an impressive number of fly-caught brownies over 7 lb making it probably our best producer of really big trout.

Grafham had the potential to produce a 20 lb rainbow trout and I rashly predicted that we should see a 15-pounder in 1968 as a result of heavy feeding by three-year-olds on shoals of small perch. But it has not happened. Very big trout are hooked from time to time on fly or lure fished deep, but I doubt very much if conventional flies and lures are capable of attracting double-figure rainbows intent on red-meat by the $\frac{1}{4}$ lb mouthful.

The chances of taking double-figure trout on the fly are, in fact, so small as to render it stupid to allow fish over 6 lb to remain in waters up to a hundred acres, with a top limit of 8 lb in bigger lakes.

Fish as food converters

The aim of good management is to take the largest possible weight of trout from the water in such a manner that the population from year to year remains constant. As a rough guide, if the average weight of each fish caught remains at a satisfactory constant over a number of years the stocking policy is correct. If, however, the average weight increases the water is understocked. The converse also tends to be true, but it must be remembered that a revised stocking policy to remedy understocking will itself result in a decrease of average weight which may continue over a period of seven or eight years. Panic alterations of a policy should be avoided at all costs: overstocking of trout in lakes where natural regeneration is low is very easy to correct, either by netting or increasing fishing pressure.

Biological factors and matters of heredity govern the growth of fish by influencing the use the fish makes of its food, and it is not possible to get the same increase of body weight per pound of food fed at all stages of growth. In general, young fish tend to be better food converters than old fish, and a given water containing young trout in their most vigorous stage of growth would produce a greater weight of flesh each year than the same water containing older fish. Let us presume our water produces 100 lb of fish food each season. Forty fish weighing 1 lb each could eat $2\frac{1}{2}$ lb of food and perhaps gain 9 oz each of body weight; thus the water would have produced $22\frac{1}{2}$ lb of fish during the year. On the other hand, ten large fish, each weighing 4 lb, could each consume 10 lb of food and perhaps gain only 1 lb each, giving a total production of only 10 lb of fish. Although the conversion ratios are not based on any experiment they are likely to prove true, for large fish require large food forms and the diet provided by the water, and which was so well suited to the smaller fish, would be unlikely to meet the needs of large fish; in fact the large fish might be unable to catch and eat the 10 lb available to each of them.

Dr Meehean has stated that the culture of trout is comparable to the culture of any other livestock: I do not think many of us would quarrel with that statement, and yet we do not apply its implications.

Marking of fish and/or scale reading will show that in any given water there is a period in the life of the fish when growth proceeds very fast as measured by the total gain in body weight. In the two Midland reservoirs which I fished hard from 1947 to 1953 scale readings showed that the period of fastest growth occurred between the fourth and sixth years; thereafter the fish grew more slowly, probably because they could not find a sufficiency of the large food forms required.

Under such conditions, perfect management would aim at removing all trout at the end of their sixth year, and all younger fish would be replaced to continue their fast growth. This method would result in a very heavy crop of fish each year, but it is obviously impracticable because anglers demand the right to catch fish bigger than 3 lb if the water will grow them to greater weight. As the corollary to rational cropping, the fish would be stocked as wild-fed pounders able to grow fast on the natural food supply of the water.

While agreeing that the ideal is unattainable because we cannot drain the water each year, we should not lose sight of the underlying aim: to ensure that the food supply is used by fish which can convert it into flesh economically. For many years Blagdon Reservoir produced only $3\frac{1}{2}$ to 7 lb of fish per acre, a ridiculously low figure for so fertile a water. On a similar water the highest production we had experienced when I wrote in 1952 had been a most unusual 16 lb per acre. At Blagdon the average weight of fish taken during the period of low productivity was around 3 lb. In the other reservoir it was about $2\frac{1}{4}$ lb. When the average weights are so high as these, it is inevitable that the angler will experience many blank days because the number of fish in the water is unnecessarily small. Many of the fish caught are, by reason of their great age, ugly and unpalatable. We most of us would prefer to catch more fish of a smaller size: young fish which were beautiful to the eye and a pleasure to eat. These smaller fish also fight, weight for weight, far better than large fish.

In formulating a stocking policy we must estimate the productive capacity of the water and the rate of growth of the fish we are going to put in. It has been found that the annual weight increase of fish in a given body of water remains remarkably constant among individuals of the same age and scale readings of the existing stock will therefore provide some facts to work on.

Table 3 – Probable fish population resulting from autumn stocking of 4,000 brown trout aged 1 summer, and fished at 50 per cent recovery rate

Col 1 March	Col 2 Population	Col 3 Av. weight based on scale readings	Col 4 Gain during previous year	Col 5 Total gain	Col 6 Number Taken	Col 7 Total weight removed
yearlings	*Under sized fish* 3,500	1 oz*				*Loss due to predators* 125 lb
2 summers	3,000	5 oz*	4 oz	750 lb		100 lb
3 ”	2,700	10 oz*	5 oz	840 lb		725 lb
4 ”	*Takeable fish* 2,500	1 lb	6 oz	940 lb	725	790 lb
5 ”	1,700	1 lb 8 oz	8 oz	850 lb	525	830 lb
6 ”	1,150	2 lb 8 oz	1 lb	1,150 lb	330	830 lb
7 ”	900	3 lb 4 oz	12 oz	675 lb	260	400 lb
8 ”	340	4 lb	12 oz	260 lb	100	180 lb
9 ”	125	4 lb 8 oz†	8 oz	65 lb	40	140 lb
10 ”	70	5 lb 8 oz†	av. 1 lb	70 lb	25	
		Old fish etc.†				
Totals	15,985			5,600 lb	2,005	4,120 lb

* Figures queried were either known to be variable or had not been sufficiently checked by scale reading.
† Old fish are sometimes found to be healthy and virile while others can barely put up a struggle.

Stocking and results

Table 3 opposite was related to the conditions of a water which, until 1954, I fished frequently. For many years the stocking programme had been inadequate. Losses from natural causes were unknown, but heron and grebe were numerous and otters occasionally visited the water. Spawning losses were difficult to estimate but carcases were often found. No matter how the fish were taken from the water all were counted as part of the crop. I presumed a recovery rate of 50 per cent and a theoretical productivity of 75 lb per acre based on the known high nutrient of this eutrophic water on good agricultural land. I assumed that the heaviest natural losses would occur early and late in life, that the weight for age would remain little changed and that equal percentages of each age group would be caught. Obviously, some of my assumptions were invalid, particularly the last, and where common sense dictated, I adjusted the figures. I deplored guesswork but I had so few facts. The annual rate of stocking most likely to be correct as judged by the theoretical annual crop was four thousand fish per year.

Table 4, extracted from Table 3, shows the estimated composition of the spawning loss. No attempt was made to reconcile the 1,755 lb total with the 1,480 lb difference between columns 5 and 7: the difference was considered too small to be significant.

Table 4 – Spawning mortality of age groups 7 and over

Age	Number of dead fish	Weight of carcases
7 summers	300	975 lb
8 ,,	115	460 lb
9 ,,	15	70 lb
10+ ,,	45	250 lb
		Total 1,755 lb

The number of dead spawning fish was obtained by reconciling the March population and the number of that age group caught, with the March population of the next older age group thus:

March population of 7-year-olds	=	900

Number of 7-year-old fish taken	=	260
Number of spawning casualties	=	300
Number of 8-year-old survivors	=	340
		Total 900

My general approach to the stocking problem at Ravensthorpe and Hollowell was probably sound but I had made seriously wrong assumptions (which argues strongly for marking policies!). We also suffered restrictions in the matter of money available for stocking, and as a result of the partial failure of the first year's fin-cutting. To be wrong in one thing is to be suspected of fallibility in all things.

So far as water productivity was concerned I had assumed the acreage to be 113 – that at high water – yet over the years the average area is probably nearer to 80 acres owing to lowering of the level. But the greatest single error was the adoption of the computed crop figure of 75 lb per acre deduced from Schaper-claus's tables for the productivity of German waters stocked with carp. These were intended to apply to sunlit shallow fish ponds; not to reservoirs where perhaps $\frac{1}{2}$ or $\frac{2}{3}$ of the area would consist of water over 12 ft in depth and therefore less productive.

Further error probably lay in underestimation of the nutrient loss in water run off to filter beds and down compensation channels. Nitrogen loss due to water-birds foraging on weed, and to the removal of weed and sedges after cutting is another probable source of error.

Tables 5 and 6 show what actually happened when we stocked Ravensthorpe and Hollowell Reservoirs. There were errors in our programme and setbacks galore, but we also enjoyed strikingly improved sport.

The immediate conclusions to be drawn are (1) rainbow trout are quite unsuitable in Ravensthorpe. (2) Since the first large numbers were caught in 1956 (2 years after stocking with two-summers fish) our earlier assumption that brown trout do not become takeable until their fourth summer is correct. (3) Heavy stocking and heavy fishing from boats and banks resulted in an average yield of 17·4 lb per acre between 1956 and 1958; much higher than has been known for many years, and probably the highest yield over this period of any large matured reservoir in the country. This reservoir was first opened to fishing in 1893 so that present high productivity is in no way attributable to its recent construction and high residual manurial content.

The figures for Hollowell were initially better than for Ravensthorpe because there was a stocking of 8 in fish in 1951, and in any case there was known to be some natural regeneration in this water.

Both tables show that the yearly average weights remained closely constant (over five years Hollowell showed a variation of only 1·5 oz) and the condition of fish was excellent, so we were stocking within the feeding capacity of the water. What I would like to know is, how much we could have increased the stocking rate before average weights and condition fell off. I suspect a 50 per cent to 70 per cent increase would have been quite safe provided fishing pressure was maintained or increased.

Now, if we assume that when stocking with 8 in fish, the results are apparent two years later (see Table 5: 1954 Stocking, and 1956 catch) the 6,450 brown trout stocked at Ravensthorpe in 1954, 1955 and 1956 yielded 2,954 fish in 1956, 1957 and 1958, ie approximately 46 per cent, so, clearly, we should not have achieved 50 per cent when stocking yearlings, say, 5 in long.

Further evidence on recovery rates for brown trout is provided by the statistics on Grafham at the beginning of Chapter 16. If you turn back you will see that up to autumn 1966, 65,000 brown trout were stocked. Up to the end of 1968 season we caught 23,293 browns, being about 35 per cent recovery. (Because the average weight in 1968 was 2 lb 6 oz I have assumed few of the 1968-stocked fish were caught.) We shall catch 1965- and 1966-stocked browns until 1971 or 1972 and the final recovery is likely to prove somewhere between 40 and 43 per cent.

For the future with 7 in to 8 in brown trout stockings I would assume 50 per cent recovery on lakes up to one hundred acres with intensive boat fishing and 40 per cent with light boat effort. On large lakes, 42 per cent and 35 per cent respectively. Rainbow trout, from the Grafham figures, taking all stockings and catches to the end of 1968, seem already to have achieved a recovery rate

Table 5

Ravensthorpe Reservoir: Stocking and Cropping, 1952 to 1958

Production figures are based upon an average of 80 acres of water through the season, and ignore the weight of each year's stock

Year	Late Autumn Stock			Catch				Crop in lb/acre
	No	Size	Species	No	Average weight	Fish/rod/day	Total crop	
1952	2,500	5″	Rainbow					
1953	2,500	5″	,,	164	2 lb 3 oz br. 15½ oz r'bow	·206	265 lb	3·3
1954	1,000 1,500	5″ 9″	Brown trout ,,	82	1 lb 3 oz br. 2 lb 2 oz r'bow	·134	139 lb	1·7
1955	450 1,500	5″ 9″	,, ,, ,,	289	1 lb 3 oz br. 2 lb 2 oz r'bow	·46	368 lb	4·6
						Boat Bank		
1956	2,000	8″	,, ,,	1,045	1 lb 8 oz br.	1·09 ·532	1,589 lb	19·8
1957	2,000	8″	,, ,,	915	1 lb 5 oz	1·16 ·366	1,201 lb	15
1958	2,000	8″	,, ,,	994	1 lb 6 oz	1·02 ·374	1,384 lb	17·3

Average: 17·4 lb/acre

Table 6

Hollowell Reservoir: Stocking and Cropping, 1952 to 1958

Production figures are based upon an average of 80 acres of water through the season, and ignore the weight of each year's stock

Year	Late Autumn Stock			Catch			Fish/rod/day		Total crop	Crop in lb/acre
	No	Size	Species	No	Average weight		Boat	Bank		
1952	3,000	5"	Brown trout							
1953	2,000	5"	" " "	275	2 lb 8 oz			·28	695 lb	8·6
	800	8"	" " "							
	500	9"	" " "							
1954	1,000	8"	" "	713	1 lb 11 oz			·59	1,211 lb	15·1
1955	1,200	8"	" "	389	1 lb 12 oz			·42	684 lb	8·5
	450	5"	" "							
1956	2,000	9"	" "	614	1 lb 13 oz		·95	·49	1,139 lb	14·2
1957	2,000	8"	" "	943	1 lb 11½ oz		·94	·65	1,631 lb	20·4
1958	1,500	8"	" "	695	1 lb 13 oz		·67	·3	1,270 lb	15·9

Average: 16·8 lb/acre

just over 50 per cent with one and perhaps two more seasons in which we may catch 1966- and 1968-stocked fish. Maybe 60 per cent recovery will be achieved. Rainbows, where they thrive, should always give better recovery rates than browns because they are at hazard to predators, disease, and climatic (Winter Kill) risks for a much shorter period between infancy and takeable size.

The table on Hollowell is less straightforward of interpretation than Ravensthorpe or Grafham figures because of the build-up of the perch and pike population from 1955 onwards, but it appears fair to look upon the 3,354 trout caught from 1954 to 1958 as resulting from the planting of 10,950 trout from 1952 to 1956, a recovery rate of 31 per cent.

A particularly interesting catch is that of 1954 at Hollowell. It is almost certain (despite lack of those vital fin markings!) that it resulted in greater part from the heavy stocking with 5 in fish two years previously . . . in other words, yearling 5 in fish in a fertile reservoir appear to grow in their second summer to be much longer than the 8 in or 9 in achieved by brown trout in a hatchery.

While yields of 75 lb and more are, as we have said, theoretically possible, the heaviest crop of trout actually taken from any unfertilized lake in Britain appears to be the 60 lb per acre per annum from Bury Lake, Chesham. In this water the maximum depth was only 4 ft, and conditions were as near perfect as possible. Natural spawning was discouraged and the whole stocking programme was rigidly controlled. The lake was managed as a rainbow water, although a few brown trout were also stocked each year.

The past tense is correct.

Dr Peter Gorer received the following letter and passed it on to to me; I am indebted to Major Hallows for permission to reproduce it here.

Berkhamstead, Herts
5 June 1953

Dear Dr Gorer,

The club has long ceased to exist. All over this part of the world springs have ceased to flow owing to a fall in the water table. This is due to the growing drain by artesian wells in London Buildings on the great subterranean lake which draws most of its water from the Chilterns. Except in very wet spells the Chesham Lake is now an expanse of mud and the headwaters of the river a mere trickle A tragedy!

To see it now you'd never believe that on one day in 1929 I had five fish weighing 15¾ lb.

Would you please let Ivens know? I receive many inquiries.

Your sincerely,
R. W. Hallows

In large reservoirs it is impossible to control a fish population closely, and equally impossible to fish the water with rod and line as intensively as a small lake where every fish must be covered many times each season.

In 1952 I postulated a production of 35 lb per acre of trout as achievable on lakes up to twenty-five acres, 28 lb per acre up to a hundred acres and 12 to 15 lb per acre on 'inland seas'. Grafham's 34 lb per acre was possible because it is a very new water in its first flush of production and because there are twenty-five boats to crop the offshore feeding grounds. In the long-term, my figures will probably prove close to the mark except that 'inland seas' will lie between 15 and 20 lb per acre with today's greater emphasis on boat fishing. Sufficient fishing pressure to ensure high recovery rate and relatively low natural mortality is as essential to heavy cropping as good stocking.

The cropping rates I have mentioned apply to hard waters (those with over 65 ppm calcium carbonate or equivalent bicarbonate) over organic mud. Very hard waters might crop a little more heavily, soft water much less. Any uncertainty as to the degree of hardness can be settled by washing your hands with soap in water taken well away from a weed bed.

In private lakes the use of superphosphate fertilizer would enormously increase the productivity of the water. Krügel and Heinrich found that each pound of 'supers' gave an increased yield of 2·13 lb of carp, so it would be fair to assume that in a lake having an organic mud bottom and a supply of calcareous water each pound of superphosphate should increase yield by ¾ lb of trout.

As I have said elsewhere we may yet see pond fertilization applied to our reservoir fisheries as their recreational value increases through the years.

CHAPTER 22

The how, when and what of stocking

'The worst enemy of a little trout is a big trout.'

If there is one time when big trout are less interested in food than any other, it is over the spawning period. During the spring and early summer they are most active in their feeding and would probably then indulge in cannibalism whenever opportunity occurred. Herons and grebe are also to be seen fishing hard in the spring, particularly when they have growing broods to feed.

Both fish and bird predators find spring-stocked trout easy meat. When placed in the water the youngsters often remain in a shoal, undispersed, for as long as three weeks. This may in part be due to the habit of life in the hatchery where there was no need to search for food, but I do not believe this to be the sole influencing factor: I have long believed that all trout show shoaling tendencies in still water. Early in the 1952 season we located a shoal of 6 in fish cruising fast near the corner of the dam. Since we had stocked with 8 in fish in 1951 we were inclined to believe that these were the young of a coarse species which had found its way into the water. Fortunately, I rose and hooked one on a tiny dry fly, and although it kicked itself free, its behaviour readily identified it as a small trout. These fish must have been bred naturally and hatched out in the spring of 1951. But although these wild fish were moving as a shoal, it was a very small shoal moving over a wide area and therefore unlikely to be subjected to continuous attack.

Just how serious can be the losses by predation is well illustrated by what occurred at a Midland reservoir several years ago. In early spring, 1,500 yearlings were placed in the water near the corner of the dam. At the time of delivery, the water-keeper, who was not expecting the fish, was engaged upon his duties around the catchment area and was therefore unable to prevent the whole lot being placed in the one spot. Within two hours, he later told me, seven grebe had arrived upon the scene, and these continued harassing the guileless young trout until the shoal broke up days later. A 50 per cent loss of the new fish in the first seven days after stocking was extremely likely in this particular instance.

A little research on the relative values of autumn and spring stocking has been done in the United States. Autumn stocking in rivers has been shown to give very poor results, particularly in mountain streams; but in lakes excellent results have been achieved, recovery rates being at least as good as those with spring stocking. Because of the dangers of loss due to predation it is imperative that yearlings enter the water in the autumn. Spring stocking with yearlings is a waste of money, and should give way to stocking fish at least 8 in in length; in the long run, however, autumn stocking of yearlings will prove the cheaper proposition.

The fish should be introduced, twenty-five or thirty at a time, at points all around the lake. Nearby cover in the form of weed beds, tree stumps and so on is a great advantage to the young fish. Never should they be dumped in one spot.

A short while ago I came across a case where it was decided to omit the year's stocking, because fewer fish than usual had been caught. In some seasons, takes will fall below normal and the two possible causes require quite different treatment. To cease stocking means that the fishing in three years' time and onwards will be adversely affected, and yet unless a marking policy has been in force for some time this may be the only safe thing to do. A marking policy enables one to assess the cause of the small catch. A dull-and-wet or a very hot summer is usually to blame, in which case the percentage of the total catch for each age group will be found to agree closely with the percentage of previous years. This would mean that the fish population had not suffered any disaster and was in excess of its usual end-of-season strength. Remedy? In season: increase fishing pressure and bag limits. Out of season: net a stretch of the water. Having removed a normal season's crop of fish, stock as usual. If on the other hand it were found that the number of fish caught was well below normal because the lowest age group had not contributed its usual quota to the total, then this may be taken as clear evidence that the stocking of the group was followed by severe mortality, and in this case the normal stocking programme should be continued since the water is already understocked.

A rough and ready guide to the survival of any group of stocked fish is provided by separating the fish caught each season into their weight groups roughly corresponding to age groups thus:

$$
\begin{array}{ll}
1 \text{ to } 1\tfrac{3}{4} \text{ lb} \dots\dots\dots & 490 \\
1\tfrac{3}{4} \text{ to } 2\tfrac{1}{2} \text{ lb} \dots\dots\dots & 580 \\
2\tfrac{1}{2} \text{ to } 3\tfrac{1}{2} \text{ lb} \dots\dots\dots & 460 \\
3\tfrac{1}{2} \text{ to } 4\tfrac{1}{2} \text{ lb} \dots\dots\dots & 210 \\
4\tfrac{1}{2} \text{ to } 6 \text{ lb} \dots\dots\dots & 40
\end{array}
$$

Regular stockings will, over a period of years, show fairly even percentages of fish in any age group and variations from the norm should be investigated. Pollution of reservoirs is unlikely to occur, but if such mishap does take place then it will do so during the summer months when the dead fish will be found and will tell their own story. If subsequently the season's catch is below average, it may be assumed that many fish have been killed and the stocking policy should be continued. I would not, however, advise an increased number of stocked fish for they would hinder the re-establishment of a normal population.

Put and take

Stocking programmes so far considered relate to turning small fish into the water to grow on for a season or two before they attain takeable size. Probably this approach is feasible in these days of intensive fishing pressure only for large and highly productive lakes. For smaller lakes and those set in hill country over peat or rock bottoms, it is sometimes necessary to use the available food supply as a maintenance diet for takeable-sized fish stocked at intervals through the fishing season. Particularly is this so when the water is hard fished. Even Grafham was put-and-take stocked with rainbow trout in 1969 to avoid the opening slaughter of 1968 mentioned earlier. (Probably the May 1968 excesses would not have occurred had the water been stocked in Autumn 1967 enabling the young rainbows to disperse and adapt to their environment before opening day.)

It is sad to think that we are having to resort to the same stocking policies as the chalk streams on our reservoirs. I now know just how Plunkett Greene felt about the artificial stocking of the River Bourne in 1905. Incidentally, when you read his chapter, 'The Tragedy of the Bourne', you are reminded very much of our own UDN crisis by his descriptions of ailing trout.

Vermin species

Darwin in 1856 stated that the manner of increase of any species was a geometric progression, but that the total population was limited by the available supply of food and the action of parasites and predators; thus we may say that a given environment will be found to support a vermin population which remains remarkably constant from year to year whenever the control methods are not aimed at complete elimination. The rabbit and rat provide classic examples of man's failure to control by 'persecution'.

Shooting, trapping, ferreting and snaring up to 1955 merely resulted in temporary reduction of the rabbit population. Whatever good was achieved was entirely offset by the fact that the survivors with less competition multiplied at a higher than normal rate and brought the population back to its previous 'high' in a very few months. Campaigns against the rat have followed much the same course and with similar results.

In America and Canada the bounty paid on certain predators such as the coyote has had little effect on the populations. Year after year the bounty money paid out has been a fairly constant sum, due to the fact that the number of animals killed is approximately the same each year. Today the conservation officers and pest control officers understand why their past efforts have met with failure and they are directing their attacks on undesirable species in new ways.

The method used by the forestry officer against rabbits is the complete extermination of all the rabbits within an area enclosed by a rabbit-proof fence. In 1952, a forestry officer told me that it had cost £55 to kill the last rabbit in a clear felled area which had been due for replanting. But since it was still free from rabbits and none of the thousands of young trees had been damaged he deemed the money well spent. That £55 would be nearer £150 at today's values.

The other method of control is that of changing the environment to render it unsuitable for the vermin species under attack. The rat is now being controlled by just such means. Farmers and warehousemen are rat-proofing their food stores; householders clear up food scraps; holes and cracks in walls are sealed up, and life is made difficult for the animal. Undernourished and lacking protection, the rat has to extend his feeding range and is thereby subjected to attacks by his natural enemies. His lowered plane of nutrition results in a lowered rate of reproduction: the rat menace is now under control. The same methods are also being brought to bear against the rabbit.

Changes in the environment of the rabbit have led almost to the complete extermination of that pest in many areas. The increased use of crawler tractors and combine harvesters in the mid-twentieth century has favoured big fields and has led to the removal of the hedges and banks in which the rabbit made his burrows. Some farms were virtually clear of rabbits even before the myxomatosis wipe-out began. Disease is, of course, an environmental control, even though man may be, as with myxomatosis, an agency for its distribution.

Perhaps, reader, you wonder what all this has to do with fishing.

Most of our fisheries have a vermin problem. In the Test it is grayling*; at Windermere it is perch; in the Yorkshire streams it is chub; at Ravensthorpe it is rudd, and so we could carry on indefinitely. In most waters the coarse fishes thrive because in addition to their prolificacy they are better able to withstand the low oxygen content of the water in the summer months, and are less susceptible to the toxic substances in the effluents which find their way into the water. Very shallow lakes, whether the water be healthful or not, usually provide a better habitat for the relatively valueless coarse species than they do for trout. Let us face the truth, the trout goes under because the environment has changed against him. If a water is being polluted, control of the vermin is pointless for trout will not thrive in polluted waters even if they are the sole occupants. In a case like this the first step is to clean up the water and think about the vermin afterwards.

Until very recently, attacks on the vermin species of fish have followed the same course as past attacks on the rabbit and rat. The waters have been netted; a lot of useless fish have been removed,

* As one who has thoroughly enjoyed grayling fishing on the Ure and on the Test and several of its tributary streams, I find it impossible to regard the grayling as vermin. Grayling in many cases provide far better sport to the fly than the stew-fed browns and rainbows one finds almost everywhere and they put up a splendid fight once they are recovered from their spring spawning.

and a few have been left behind to restore the population rapidly. Man has done nothing except prevent the vermin species competing within its own ranks.

Ravensthorpe Reservoir has held vast shoals of rudd for sixty years. Before the war, thousands of fish were removed each year by netting, and yet the population from year to year was roughly constant, fluctuating only according to the natural population cycle of the species. Exactly this same sort of thing is happening at Shustoke: netting will never be the answer, and indeed it cannot be because it fails to take into account the fact that the vermin population is controlled by the environment and not by removal of a percentage of the members.

Any method of control which falls short of an extermination policy is fore-doomed. Let me tell you what happened when the lake mentioned above was partly drained during a drought. When there remained but a small area of water this was thoroughly netted and the very few rudd present were removed. Subsequently the lake was refilled. The following year we caught adult rudd! I can only presume that they had undergone a period of dormancy in the mud. But whatever the reason for our failure, it would appear to be necessary to drain, dry out and plough the lake bottom if the opportunity to do so should present itself again.

A reservoir cannot be emptied merely because the coarse fish are a nuisance, and most water authorities do their best for the angler by bringing out the nets and effecting a temporary reduction in the ranks of the coarse fish. Several years ago I attempted to obtain the services of a gang of netsmen to clear some of the fish from a reservoir. I found that the task could not be undertaken during the coarse fishing closed season. Requests for aid elsewhere met with the same astonishing reply. In an off-the-record conversation with the extremely able secretary of a very famous fishing organization I found that the netting authorities frowned upon the disturbance of the coarse fish during their spawning season. I can appreciate their point: they want to take the fish out and use them to stock other waters without serious mortality to the gravid fish. But from the point of view of the trout fisherman the idea is not a good one because he has to put up with the shoals of fish in the shallows during the early season and then when their spawning is over the shoals break up and heavy hauls of fish are difficult to take. Many reservoirs are over 30 ft deep and netting can only be fully successful when the shoals are spawning in the shallows. In any case what is the point of removing the parent fish after they have successfully spawned and sown the seeds of a new crop?

My dissatisfaction led me to consider other methods. 'Electric Fishing', then in its infancy, offered no solution: the expanse and depth of the water were and still are insuperable problems. I then recalled an article on selective poisons which appeared in *Fishing Gazette*.

The substance referred to was Rotenone, the active principle of the Derris used by every gardener for controlling greenfly. A letter to the Ministry of Agriculture and Fisheries elicited the information that it was a most effective poison, but that I would be liable to a fine of up to £50, or up to three months' hard labour, if I used it. This was under the relevant section 9(b) of the Salmon and Freshwater Fisheries Act of 1923.

Rotenone had been extensively used in the United States, but even there, there was less than wholehearted enthusiasm. US Fishery Leaflet No 350 opened as follows: 'The laws of all States prohibit the use of Derris or other poisons to fish, in public waters.' Having thus covered himself, the writer then went on to tell us all how to get the best results from it.

The application of only 1·4 lb of Derris (5 per cent Rotenone) per acre foot of water, as advised in the leaflet, results in a lethal Rotenone concentration of 0·03 ppm.* The poison causes constriction of the capillaries of the gill filaments and consequent asphyxiation of the fish. Before the substance can be used the quantity of water in the lake must of course be calculated. Because of the rapidity with which a vermin species will re-populate a lake, it is probably wise in the long run to poison out the whole water, trout included, and start all over again. In large lakes, however, a 100 per cent kill is unlikely and selective poisoning would then appear to be the best compromise. The method relies upon the fact that when the temperature of the surface waters rises above 65°F the trout will seek deeper water which, being cooler, will be better oxygenated. The coarse species on the other hand will often remain in very shallow water, and spray-

* The American pamphlet probably contains a misprint. In one paragraph it advises ·5 ppm of Rotenone. It is probable that it should read ·5 ppm of Derris.

ing of the shallows in the noon heat will result in the poisoning of the vermin while the trout remain unharmed. The trout will not normally re-enter the marginal shallows until evening time and by then the concentration of Rotenone will have been reduced by dilution with unsprayed water. This method should be very effective in dealing with shoals of fry.

It has been found that fish affected by Rotenone rapidly recover when placed in a tank of uncontaminated water. It would thus be possible to render first aid to the occasional trout. The carcasses of the coarse fish may safely be fed to stock, and in any case should be removed from the water. Being non-poisonous to farm stock, pets and human beings, Rotenone is safe for use on a reservoir and has a great advantage over copper sulphate in that the small water animals and plants appear to remain unaffected by it. Rotenone offers new hope to those who fish vermin-infested trout lakes: but its use in rivers could be disastrous. Rotenone cannot give good results unless its application is carefully supervised and the habits of the vermin species thoroughly understood. Its action is retarded below 60°F.

The 1923 Act was altogether too sweeping in its condemnation of fish poisons. Around 1953 or 1954, I attended a Rotenone-poisoning operation in Southern England where part of the good work was carried out by local magistrates and supervised by a senior member of the Thames Conservancy, and another gentleman, who was perhaps our foremost commercial fish-farmer!

The account would have been published several years ago – and at least one very senior gentleman in the Ministry looked forward with genuine enthusiasm to seeing the matter ventilated – but I had given an undertaking to the association concerned to leave the final decision on publication to them. They were forced to withhold their permission because they could not afford to fight a test case . . . it seemed that in 1959, thirty-six years after the passing of the Act, its Law had still not been tested in a case involving the use of poisons for good purposes!

Thank heavens, the position has now been clarified. When in March 1969, I wrote to the Minister to seek information on the present position, I was very pleased to learn that whilst the 1965 Act retains very valuable safeguards against abuse, fish poisons are now accepted as fishery aids.

Probably I can do no better than quote the relevant parts of the letter:

It is confirmed that section 9 of the Salmon and Freshwater Fisheries Act 1923 has been repealed and replaced by the Salmon and Freshwater Fisheries Act, 1965. This Act raises the penalties and strengthens the provisions against the use of explosives, poisons or electrical devices, etc., with intent to take or destroy fish but contains provisions controlling the use of any device or noxious substance in any waters for a scientific purpose, or for the purpose of protecting, improving or replacing stocks of fish. All such users require the permission in writing of the appropriate authority, and in addition, permission for the use of poison or other noxious substances requires the approval of the Minister of Agriculture, Fisheries and Food.

For your guidance, the first part of the 1965 Act reads as follows:

... No person shall use in or near any waters (including waters adjoining the coast of England and Wales and within the exclusive fisheries limits of the British Islands) any ex-explosive substance, any poison or other noxious substance, or any electrical device, with intent thereby to take or destroy fish:

Provided that this subsection shall not apply to the use by a person of any substance or device –

(a) for a scientific purpose, or for the purpose of protecting, improving, or replacing stocks of fish; and

(b) with the permission in writing of the appropriate authority; ...'

The Act then defines the 'appropriate authority' as being the River Authority, the Thames Conservancy or the Lee Conservancy, but states that in respect of the use of any noxious substance such permission may not be given without the approval of the Minister.

Probably broad-spectrum poisons for fish lack the precision that we are accustomed to in germ or insect control, but there is hope that this may change. 'Toxaphene', an American pesticide, has proved useful for killing fish less than 3 in in length in hardwater lakes and left longer fish unharmed. Indications are that it takes considerable time to degrade (become harmless), and it is clearly too dangerous to use with our present state of knowledge, but it points to a line of future research.

Basic facts about animal breeding and our fish

If today your butcher supplied as the Sunday joint a piece of mutton from the type of sheep grown in Britain two hundred and fifty years ago, you would not be grateful to him, and would very soon shop elsewhere. A joint from Bakewell's 'Leicester' sheep, or from Ellam's improved 'Down' sheep of the 1780s would be a very different proposition, for the lean meat would contain much more intermuscular and intramuscular fat and the resultant roast would be deliciously tender.

Our poultry, cattle, rabbits, pigs, horses and sheep have all been improved by selective breeding, and until recently the method used consisted of the breeder mating two animals of the type he deemed most nearly perfect. From the progeny he again selected the animals which best suited his purpose and used them either for brother and sister mating, or crossing back to sire or dam, or other inbreeding method, until eventually he had a strain of sheep or cattle which would produce young which were all of the type he desired. If the original parents had been of differing breeds, the new true-breeding progeny would be a new breed. If, however, they were of the same breed and the farmer had merely set out to improve his stock, we should say he had produced a new strain or race.

Bakewell in the eighteenth century was considerably ahead of many of today's farmers who will buy and use a young stud animal merely because it has a pleasing body conformation. Bakewell found that it frequently happened that an animal of inferior appearance sired better progeny than another animal of apparently better quality, and before he died he made a practice of hiring out his rams to serve the ewes of a neighbour's flock. If the ram produced good lambs of the type Bakewell wanted, he brought the ram into one of his own flocks, and conversely a ram which sired poor quality lambs would remain for hire. Bakewell assessed the value of a breeding animal by the quality of the stock it sired, not by its own appearance. His method, now known as progeny testing, has come back into use in this country following the success which the Danes have achieved with it.

But although breeders are now becoming interested in progeny testing, the stud animal is still the result of in-breeding because it is desirable that he produce stock of consistently high quality. It must be faced that in any system of the mating of close relatives there must be as many cases of the bad qualities of the parents being combined as there will be of only the good qualities combining, and there must also be a number of offspring in which good and bad qualities will be mixed. I do not wish to embark upon a discourse on 'genetics', the science of inheritance, for that is outside the scope of this book and is a job for the man who has made a life study of the subject, but it is important that you, reader, should appreciate how inheritance works, for the basic facts of breeding a milking cow apply equally well to breeding a trout.

The unit of inheritance is an infinitesimally small amount of chemical substance called a gene. Genes exist in chains called chromosomes and a number of chromosomes are found in the nucleus of every cell of every living thing. Except in certain cases the chromosomes exist in pairs and the genes being always in the same order lie side by side. That is to say, a gene controlling hair colour will be paired with a gene which also controls hair colour, though not necessarily a gene giving the same hair colour. Of each pair of chromosomes one is inherited from the male parent and the other from the female, and the appearance and behaviour of an individual depend on the way the inherited genes interact, but we must also remember that environment too plays an important part.

Let us suppose that A represents a gene for fast growth and A_1 a gene for slow growth (or, if you prefer it, absence of a gene for fast growth). A fish descended from true-breeding fast-growing parents would be fast growing and would have the constitution AA. Another fish descended from true-breeding slow growers would have the constitution A_1A_1 and would itself be slow growing.

In the production of ova and milt, there is a halving of the chromosomes in the cells which results in each egg or sperm containing only one set of genes. Such a cell is called a reproductive cell, and in the case of a female fish of constitution AA all eggs would carry the factor A for fast growth, while the male fish having the constitution A_1A_1 would produce sperms each carrying the factor A_1 for slow growth. The diagram below shows the mating of these two fish. The progeny of this mating will all carry the factors of both slow and fast growth, and if neither factor is more powerful than the other, the progeny will have a growth rate intermediate between that of the two parent fish.

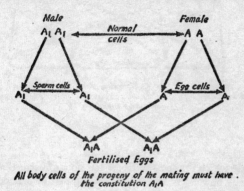

All body cells of the progeny of the mating must have the constitution A_1A

Diagram 22.1

But now let us suppose that A is 'dominant' to A_1, that is to say the power of the fast-growth factor overcomes the influence of the factor for slow growth. Our fish with constitution A_1A would then be fast growing, but as shown below could not breed true. In Diagram 22.1, only one type of gene combination was possible because each parent produced only one kind of germ cell. Parents with A_1A constitution, however, will produce equal numbers of A germ cells and A_1 germ cells, and because the union of sperm and egg is quite haphazard the ordinary laws of chance result in three types of progeny being produced in a predictable ratio.

Thus from our fast-growing parents we have produced 25 per cent of slow-growing fish and 75 per cent of fast growers but of these fast growers only 25 per cent will breed their like. The only way in which the breeder could pick out the true-breeding fast-growing fish would be to mate several male fast growers to a slow-growing female whose eggs have been separated into as many batches as there are males. Any batch of progeny which contains slow-growing fish must have come from eggs fertilized

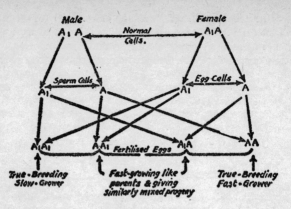

Diagram 22.2

by a male which carried the factor for slow growth. Such a test would only be valid if the factor for fast growth were completely dominant.

If before using a pair of fish for breeding it were necessary to test the quality of their offspring, it would mean waiting an extra twelve months before either of them was used to breed fish for stocking, but until we do accept this delay we are unlikely to find the best combinations of parents.

A hen fish produces about 1,500 eggs when she weighs 2 lb and it would be possible to split the eggs into ten batches, fertilize them with milt from ten different males and observe the rate of growth and other characteristics of the progeny. All progeny would need to be kept separate, but under identical environmental and feeding conditions. With ten hen fish and ten males, a hundred combinations are possible, and in the following season one could mate the fish giving the best-quality progeny. But, I would add, the assessment of the quality of the progeny must have regard to the ability of the growing troutlings to survive as 'wild' fish after stocking. Only by rearing the many batches of youngsters under wild feeding conditions such as those in the Compensation Water System should we learn their true value and be able to distinguish the best mating for our purpose.

If, reader, you are an animal breeder you will know that I have over-simplified the matter of inheritance. The characteristic of fast growth might easily be controlled by a dozen or more genes, and in mating the number of combinations possible would make it extremely difficult to recognize differences between one fish and another. Nevertheless, the principles underlying breeding problems remain the same and systematic work will have to be undertaken before progress is made. I have mentioned fast growth as being a desirable quality in a fish, but it is not the only or even the most desirable quality as will become apparent when I refer to the breeding work carried out with fish in the United States.

As we have implied in referring to wild or hand feeding of fry, environment has an enormous influence on the visible (phenotypic) effects of a fish's genetic make-up. If a fish with a constitution for fast growth is given or can obtain only a small amount of food each day, it may well be considerably smaller at the end of the growing season than a fish with a constitution for slow growth which has been given as much food as it will take. In other words, to get the best results from our breeding work we must feed our fish up to their genetic capacity. But although the fast-growing fish on a starvation diet may have appeared insignificant by the side of his less well-bred physical better, in breeding work he would be a much more valuable fish, his genetic constitution being uninfluenced by bad feeding.

The food which a fish eats can be divided into two parts, the maintenance ration which enables it to live in a state of rest, merely holding its place in the stream and keeping its organs functioning, and a production diet which is expended as energy for movement and metabolized as flesh and fat. The longer any animal takes to reach a certain size, the greater becomes the proportion of its total food which is used for maintenance. Conversely the greater the percentage of food used in making flesh, the more cheaply can the animal be raised to the predetermined weight or size.

The measure of the economic value of a fish which is raised in a hatchery is the cost to raise 1 lb of flesh as compared with the price for which that flesh can be sold. Because fast-growing fish will always use a greater percentage of their food for flesh forming, they must always be cheaper to produce than slow-growing fish, just as a fast-growing beast is a more economical producer of beef than a 'poor-doer'. Even when reared on 'free' food in compensation water there remains the advantage of planting out fish which are bigger for their age and which will reach takeable weight perhaps a season sooner. Apart from that, against the value of the yearlings must be set the interest on capital outlay and the depreciation of the plant. Why rear only, say, 200 lb of young stock when the plant is capable of yielding 300 lb ?

There are possible objections to this reasoning and the first is that a fish is a cold-blooded animal and does not waste flesh in the form of surface heat in winter time as does a store beast on an inadequate winter diet. The second is, that one may deliberately hold an animal on a low plane of nutrition and then fatten it when the high-quality foodstuffs required are cheaper. But neither objection is valid, for no matter what the system of management the fast grower must always produce its flesh with a greater economy of food than the slow grower.

I have posed this matter of food and growth for a very simple reason: so far as I am able to discover no work to improve our trout has ever been carried out. The advertisers in our angling magazines draw attention to the fact that their stock is bred from wild fish as though this in itself were some wonderful achievement. What the advertisements mean is that the stock is of mixed origin and variable in type, and possibly that the hatchery does not go to the expense of rearing the parent fish to maturity. I can think of but one type of water which might require to be stocked with the progeny of wild-bred fish and that is the moorland stream, and here again there is no proof of necessity. If hardiness were important it is more than likely that the hatchery rearing would do much to destroy the very qualities which made it necessary to use wild parent fish, just as the offering of foodstuffs to Dartmoor ponies and hill sheep would tend to encourage them to rely upon man rather than upon their own ability to find their food under all conditions. It is strange too that the fish breeders should place emphasis on heredity in this one respect and ignore it in all others.

Moorland streams usually contain enough fish without any stocking at all, and there is no doubt that 50 per cent of the wild-bred stocks are placed in waters which provide them with better feeding conditions than they knew in the hatchery, while another 20 per cent will be no worse off. To put fish bred from wild parents into highly productive waters is as wasteful as using a first-class lowland pasture to rear and fatten slow-maturing hill sheep.

Experiments with trout in the United States

It was in 1919 that Embody and Heyford commenced their series of experiments on the inheritance of the capacity for fast growth. By 1926, their work at Hackettstown Hatchery, New Jersey, had proved that it was possible to raise strains of fish which grew much faster than wild-bred fish. By mass selection of their breeding stock over three generations they raised the average length of brook trout at 1 July from 2 in to 4 in. The improvement meant that the new strain was able to increase its weight to eight times as much in the same growing period. (You may check this by applying the rule regarding the cubing of the ratio of the lengths.)

In 1928 another series of experiments was commenced at Pittsford, Vermont, under Davis and Lord, who replaced mass selection of breeding stock by individual matings, and by this means were able to observe what characteristics were inheritable and the extent to which given fish transmitted their own characteristics to their progeny. In other words Davis and Lord were progeny-testing their fish.

In 1930, the selection of the forty-five pairs of breeding stock of the second generation was carried out on a basis of rapid growth, vigour, fecundity, body symmetry and coloration. In practice it is impossible to improve more than one characteristic at a time and the breeder would therefore select his fastest-growing fish which were satisfactory in all the other respects; he certainly would not use any fish which lacked vigour or prolificacy or was abnormally shaped, no matter how fast it grew. Insistence on these other desirable characteristics ensured that the improved strain of fish was viable and capable of breeding to perpetuate its type. The progeny of these matings were tagged and it was thus possible to trace the ancestry of every fish raised.

One of the points noticed at the mating of the second-generation fish was that they each tended to come into spawning condition at the same time as their parents had done, and that the duration of their spawning period was similar to that of their parents. By 1933 all doubt had been dispelled: consistently, fish had become 'ripe' at the same time of year as their parents, and furthermore, once having spawned at a certain date they continued in later years to spawn at approximately the same date. In two cases, the coming into spawning condition of the progeny had coincided to a day with that of the parent fish.

In point of fact there were two types of improvement going on at Pittsford, for fish which were not good enough for individual matings were used for the production of fish used in stocking, and between 1928 and 1933, the beginning of September weight of these fish was increased from an average of 2·1 gm to 6·09 gm, while the progeny of the individual matings were reaching 12·7 gm. But whereas Embody and Heyford's fish had been extremely variable in growth rate, Lord and Davis found that the progeny of an individual mating all closely resembled one another; that is to say, the strain was beginning to breed true to type, and this end had been hastened by choosing the breeding stock for a new generation from fish of a good, even-sized group rather than from outstanding specimens of several variable groups. This is now common practice in pig breeding in this country, for the most useful sow or boar is one which produces litters of even and fast growth rather than one or two giants among a group of runts.

Quite apart from the steady improvement in growth rate, other improvements had been noted. The fast-growing fish were more prolific, and the number of ova per pound of body weight of brook trout had been increased by about 20 per cent, and at the same time there had been the steady increase in the resistance to furunculosis of fast-growers, which had originally been noticed by Embody and Heyford. In fact a furunculosis-resistant strain was being deliberately developed.

A check of the Pittsford results was made at Leetown Hatchery in 1933. At 29·5 weeks of age, wild fish averaged 4·6 gm; fish from parents of one generation of domestication averaged 4·9 gm, and the fish hatched from Pittsford eggs averaged 11·5 gm. These results are impressive in themselves, but become more so when we refer to the health of the stocks.

When the Leetown check commenced there were 1,200 fish in each group. An outbreak of furunculosis occurred and was allowed to proceed without attempt at control. Of the wild fish, no fewer than 718 died; of the fish from parents of one generation of domestication 546 died, but of the fish hatched from Pittsford eggs only 169 died.

The combination of fast growth, increased prolificacy and heightened resistance prompts one to feel that it is not so much that a new characteristic was bred into the fish as that several undesirable characteristics were selected out.

It was always noticed that when eggs from a number of different sources were used in one hatchery, quite serious mortality occurred in all groups except that of local origin, and Dr Davis suggested in 1930 that the trout culturist should raise his own selected strain of fish from the stock native to the hatchery district. It is doubtful whether the advice still holds good, for the use of eggs of an improved strain may save several years' work, and the fact that some fish survive in their new environment means that they have acclimatized themselves. The eggs from which the Ennis Hatchery, Montana, raised its fast-growing rainbow trout were 'special' eggs imported from Birdview Hatchery, Washington, and the results there have been excellent.

All of the later breeding experiments were accompanied by others designed to determine the value of a hatchery-raised fish to the river fisherman. Results showed that the well-nourished trout released as a legal-sized fish was at no disadvantage by comparison with the wild trout in a stream. He rose freely, fought well and satisfied his appetite, though apparently he did not often use plankton foods. Under difficult conditions for fishing he appeared to be quite as shy as a wild fish. Experiments in 1933 and 1934 confirmed the tendency of rainbow trout to move downstream, and in the latter year it was noticed that the hatchery fish were exceedingly difficult to catch. In more recent stocking experiments it has often been found that wild trout are more easily caught than newly introduced stock. This is believed to be due to the fact that the less well nourished wild fish are more easily tempted to seize a lure.

The flesh colour of trouts has been the subject of a great deal of argument. W. C. Kendall as long ago as 1918 stated that the factor for red coloration was something borne in the fish. If a fish had a genetic capacity to produce red flesh and was well nourished, his flesh would be red; on a low plane of nutrition his flesh would be pale, but no amount or quality of food would change to redness the flesh of a trout which had not the necessary genetic constitution. In recent years Holloway and Chamberlain found that hatchery fish soon recovered their redness when released in a stream or when held in a dirt-bottomed rearing pond. Their finding seemed to support the oft-expressed conviction that some item of natural diet is responsible for redness, but of course it did not mean that Kendall was wrong, for there are many streams containing very pale-fleshed trout.

Probably the argument is now settled for there are in use today feeding pellets which include artificial carotene capable of producing red-fleshed trout for table direct from the hatchery. I heard some years ago, too, that feeding pellets which included meal made from the waste products of the shrimp- and prawn-canning industry had a similar effect. Everything points to the probability that those who through the years insisted that pink flesh was the result of a diet which included freshwater shrimps and other crustaceans were correct.

May I quote from Alex Behrendt's letter of 10 March 1969:

> In close and lengthy cooperation with Cooper Nutrition Products, I developed a pellet, 'Beta Trout Food', which is now used by most British trout farms, some using it nearly exclusively. I was the first to introduce into this country from the Continent the artificial carotene, Canthaxanthin, which Cooper Nutrition used in some of their pellets. Trout became pink-fleshed in about six to eight weeks after being fed with these pellets. The taste of their flesh improves considerably, but most important, in my opinion (although not all trout breeders agree with me) is that a trout needs carotene from an early age if it is to grow into a good big fish. In its natural state it gets carotene in its food.

The practical importance of the American experimental work

The more quickly a trout can be brought to saleable size the lower per pound of fish produced are the costs of production. In Britain at this moment the vast majority of 8 to 9 in brownies used in stocking are two-year-olds; fish which at 3 to 5 in length were held through one winter, eating $2\frac{1}{2}$ per cent of their body weight in food each day without making any growth. Fish which are stocked in their second spring will, of course, have been held through two winters. Where an adequate supply of spring water is available, water temperatures through the winter may be high enough for growth to continue.

All foods fed to growing trout are very high in protein, much higher than the food fed to farm livestock, though today trout health is no longer dependent upon the feeding of a high percentage of fresh meat for normal development. Again, let me quote from Alex Behrendt's letter:

As you know, the old conversion figures for average quality meat or sea-fish were between six and eight, mostly quoted as seven. Then in the 1950s trout pellets were used increasingly. The very best trout pellets on the British market have a conversion rate of two. It sounds unbelievable, but two pounds of pellets can produce one pound of trout flesh. This applies on many trout farms, and certainly applies at Two Lakes.

But however good may be the conversion factor of today's foodstuffs, improvement of trout stocks will further decrease the cost of producing a pound of fish flesh.

Selective breeding for high growth factor should make it easy to produce 8 in fish by the first summer, and the quantity of food used to produce 1 lb of trout suitable for stocking would be reduced by reason of the fact that fast-growing fish are better food converters than slow growers, and the fact that the fish were not fed over the winter period.

Let us compare the position in Britain twenty-odd years ago with the position at that time in the USA.

Dr M. F. Brown, here, in 1946, found that it took 6 lb of meat to produce 1 lb of trout. At Ennis, Montana, the US Fish & Wildlife Hatchery raised 32,574 lb of trout by feeding to them 85,360 lb of horse flesh, 1,742 lb of horse liver, 19,069 lb of beef tripe, and 838 lb of brewer's yeast. This represents 1 lb of trout from every 3·77 lb of food. These figures were given to me by Dr Meehean and Mr Hagan of the Fish & Wildlife Service.

In Britain we were using $1\frac{1}{2}$ times as much food for the same result. The difference, almost certainly, was the better genetic capacity of Ennis fish to turn their food into flesh.

The poultry world has changed out of recognition in the last twenty-odd years, and both the egg and the broiler industry use strains of chicks genetically far different for ovulation and growth characteristics from those reared in 1945. (Broiler houses and Stilboestrol implantation are contributory factors only.)

Chicks are produced from what are known as 'nicking strains'. Closely inbred lines, 'true' for certain characteristics are crossed to provide super-chicks with a double parental dose of those characteristics plus the further factor generally known as hybrid-vigour.

It can be done with trout at any time that an efficient hatchery sets out to achieve it. Ten years should see the hard work virtually completed.

I have been told that it would be pointless to increase output because the existing demand does not justify it. What rubbish this is! The existing demand is low because prices are too high. Very few associations can afford to stock their waters adequately at the moment, but if the price were reduced to £40 to £50 per thousand for 8 in fish many associations would increase their stocking commitments, and many others would swing from coarse fish to trout. We should not forget that Continental rainbow trout are sold as food in Britain for as little as 20p per lb wholesale and that 25p to 30p per lb for home-produced stock fish should therefore be an adequate price. It is true that at least some of the imported rainbows are produced in sewage ponds, but they are no less valuable for all that, and if they can be produced cheaply by such means it is up to us to learn how to do it.

The rainbow trout

I have examined a number of documents originating in both this country and the USA in order to get a clear picture of the classification of the rainbow. The only account which was fully satisfying was that written by Dr E. B. Worthington published in the *Salmon and Trout Magazine* (Nos 100 and 101).

The Americans seem to have done with their rainbow classification exactly the same thing that we did with our brown trout, that is to say they have given races the status of species. In addition, several scientists have revised the classification so that several names exist for the one race of fish.

Much of the classification relied upon differences in the scale counts of the lateral line, but later it was shown that this method was invalid because the variation appeared when fish of the same stock were reared in waters of differing temperature. It was reported in *Fishing Gazette* that American workers had found it possible to increase the number of vertebrae by subjecting the ova to shock treatment by quick freezing. Such shocks occur naturally from time to time, and result in specimens which are slightly different from the original stock; nevertheless they are of the same species since these differences are environmental rather than genetical.

The most useful classification of the rainbow trout is that which ignores the appearance of the types and relies upon their differences of habit. The method was adopted by Worthington and has the advantage that it is of practical importance.

The name *Salmo gairdnerii* is given to the migratory rainbow trout known as the steelhead and which corresponds to our sea trout. (The word steelhead has also been used in the USA to describe the migratory type of dolly varden trout, *Salvelinus Malma*.) *Salmo irideus* is the rainbow trout of the Pacific coastal rivers. It is partly migratory and a spring spawner and is the predominant type used in stocking work in Britain. *Salmo shasta* is the fast-growing, non-migratory(?) November-spawning fish which originated in the McCloud River near Mt Shasta, California. Although not given by Worthington as a separate type, the Kamloops trout, a rainbow, native to Lake Kamloops, has such amazingly fast growth that it deserves mention. In Lake Pend Oreille, Washington, these fish have reached 40 lb in weight by the end of their fourth summer. The water teems with a degenerate race of landlocked salmon and this fact no doubt has greatly contributed to the rapidity of growth. Haig-Brown refers to the Kamloops rainbow in his book *A River Never Sleeps* and states that these fish spawn at the end of their fourth year. Other races of rainbow trout spawn at three or even two years of age and the Kamloops trout thus appear to enjoy a longer period of uninterrupted weight increase and incidentally avoid for an extra twelve months the complications of spawning to which I refer below.

The Ennis Hatchery used rainbow trout for its selective-breeding work, and in 1952 80 per cent of their yearling output consisted of 9 in fish while the remaining 20 per cent of yearlings weighed over 1 lb. The hatchery enjoys an exceptionally useful supply of water which remains at or near 54°F all the year round; growth is thus continuous through the twelve months. Nonetheless eggs from wild-bred parents will not give such good results. Today, such results are almost commonplace and where selected strains of rainbows are employed most fish reach 1 lb at twelve months.

The strain of fast-growing fish was developed at Ennis to enable the hatchery to stock the streams of the area with 3 in to 7 in fish in early summer. Stocking in autumn gave poor recovery rates but the summer-stocked fish grew away well, and were able to acclimatize themselves to withstand the winter conditions of the water. Any tendancy for the trout to spawn in spring had to be selected out and all the brood fish are now winter spawners. The fry are frequently graded during rearing to ensure that large specimens selected for breeding are not merely the result of social hierarchy resulting from a slightly stronger fish getting more food than his fellows and being thus able to increase his lead over the others. The Ennis fish are made to compete against others of their own size.

The rainbow trout remains a mystery fish. At Blagdon and Chew Valley Reservoirs, and at Grafham, they do well and very large numbers are taken, in fact they feature in the returns to about the same extent as or better than brown trout. At Ravensthorpe, on the other hand, of the five thousand fish stocked in 1952 and 1953 only eighty-six had been recovered by the end of the 1954 season, although the water is very similar in character to Blagdon and Chew. Water had not passed over the bye-wash since the rainbows had been turned in, and the oldest rainbows in 1954 were only three-summers fish so few could have died in spawning. Fish which migrated to the filter-beds through the draw-off were returned to the reservoir.

But the returns do not tell the whole story for thirty-eight fish were caught by one angler, making it abundantly clear that the low return resulted partly from the inadequacy of the techniques employed by other anglers.

As we now know, Dick Shrive had discovered that rainbow trout could be taken by fishing very deep and had developed suitable techniques ten years before the rest of us. He attributed some of his success to autopsies which showed a quantity of Quillwort, *Isoetes lacustris*, in the stomach contents in April and May, and much of the time he fished where this weed was plentiful. This same plant has been noted in the diet of brown trout in Welsh lakes.

From June to September the stomach contents of Ravensthorpe rainbows were always fry and Mr Shrive tells me that his best catches at Eyebrook and Ravensthorpe were made when the water was too warm for good brown trout fishing.

The most interesting point in his letter was his reference to the capture of a rainbow trout at Ravensthorpe in April 1958 – four and a half years after the last rainbow stocks were turned in. Clearly there are some fish which find the water a suitable environment, and were we to use them as brood stock we should most probably be able to develop a strain of real sporting value to that lake.

In 1955 Mr Alexander Macintyre wrote of his experiences on a fifteen-acre loch in the north country. Of a stocking about thirty years ago none were caught at all – the inlet is a field drain, the outlet is valve-controlled. At one of the reservoirs at Wylam, on the other hand, he tells me they put in some seven hundred rainbows and two or three years later (1954) they caught four hundred averaging $1\frac{1}{2}$ lb, the heaviest being $2\frac{3}{4}$ lb.

There seems no guiding principle: only an experimental stocking will show whether rainbow trout will do well in a water or are useless.

Another serious drawback on most waters is the rainbow trout's tendency to spawn in spring. In one of the published articles on rainbows that came my way, an English trout farmer stated that he had found it convenient to use spring-spawning fish as brood stock, so that he could hatch his rainbows after the brown trout hatch. Again, another breeder admitted to me in conversation that he used spring-spawning fish in order to make up the number of rainbow eggs. Clearly, both these workers have perpetuated the nuisance we seek to avoid; spring spawners should not be used as brood stock if the progeny are to be placed in a water containing brown trout: on their own, it would be possible to open and close the season later.

Undoubtedly the best method would be to stock them on their own and manage the water as a rainbow fishery. An association having two lakes could stock spring spawning rainbows in the one and brown trout in the other, and thereby enjoy a nine-month trout season. If, on the other hand, an autumn-spawning strain of rainbows were available, a brown trout water would provide better sport in summer time if the stock included 20 or 25 per cent of rainbows, allowance being made for their faster growth by reducing the total number of fish stocked by 25 per cent. Although I have no concrete example of its efficacy, it may well be that biological control of a vermin population could be achieved by stocking rainbow trout in place of brown trout. I have little doubt that the larger appetite and greater vigour of rainbows would enable them to compete against a coarse species and reduce the fry population far better than can the brown trout.

Perhaps, reader, you have gathered an impression that only the rainbow stocks of this country need to be improved; this is far from being the case: the brown trout is also a very variable quantity. I have occasionally noticed a condition of egg binding in females, and earlier in this book I mentioned the tendency of many of the fish to spawn after the season had opened. We must face the fact that our stocks of fish are well below standard, either as a result of chance methods of breeding or because the type used has been selected for the convenience of the hatchery manager rather than for its suitability as a sporting fish. So far as lake management is concerned, spawning streams would be a great help by encouraging natural shedding of ova in the early winter so that fish were again in good condition by opening day.

From time to time the policy of in-breeding becomes the subject of most unfair criticism. It is quite true, of course, that the mating of close relatives does produce physical and mental freaks, but it does so only because the parent stock had these weaknesses to a lesser degree. The trouble appears to occur when breeders try to improve the beauty of an animal rather than its utility. Beauty lies in the eye of the beholder, and judging by the appearance of some of our modern show gun dogs there can be many conceptions of beauty and few have much bearing on field work. If arbitrarily members of a breed society decide to develop an animal with a longer head and narrower skull, automatically they will have to mate specimens which are not typical, and in the quest for the 'new-look' fine-boned animals with poor stamina are quite likely to be used and the result of their mating may well be undesirable specimens. In-breeding can only be successful when the parent stock is sound.

The future development of our fisheries

It is all too easy to blame those who have bred our existing stocks for their present lack of quality. But before we do so let us examine the difficulties under which the fish-farmer works in Britain.

The cost of labour and high-protein foods makes it difficult to feed commercial stocks let alone experimental groups. The British trout-farmer paddles his own canoe: he has to pay for his own experience, there is no adequate organization to carry out research on his behalf and solve his many problems for him. Although there is a Brown Trout Research Station at Pitlochry, its work has been largely of academic rather than practical importance; Stuart's work on fin-marking being a notable exception. In many ways the research has been parallel to that of Freshwater Biological Association at Windermere, or that in the USA twenty-odd years ago. It would appear that the scientists are happy to work with our existing unimproved stocks of fish. Surely, work to improve the quality of the fish should be proceeding side by side with work to increase the fertility and resultant productivity of the water!

By contrast the Fish and Wildlife Service and the State Governments in the USA are operating many experimental hatcheries staffed with research workers and the information so gained is passed on to the industry.

As long ago as 1949, research staff engaged upon the problems of freshwater fishery management totalled 324 and the expenditure on research work was $1,473,448.

There are plenty of unworldly boffins working on a shoe-string research budget who are convinced that the quality of their laboratory's output is not related to the money spent. And maybe they are right so far as 'original' research is concerned. But once we advance to the stage of checking laboratory experience on a field scale, money is a controlling factor, and the availability of sufficient money is the reason for America's rapid development of new ideas.

At one time it was easy for the small business to work out its own salvation. Particularly was this true when materials and labour were cheap, for one could then afford to use both on enterprises from which there was no direct profit. Experimental work today is a matter of costs, and hit or miss methods are too expensive. This in turn means that the research work has to be undertaken by a trained – and sometimes highly paid – scientist, and only the highly capitalized companies can afford to run their own research departments. Some industries have pooled their resources to set up a joint research centre to solve problems for the industry as a whole, and in other cases, the responsibility for the research is undertaken by a government department. An example of this last type of research and advisory organization is the National Agricultural Advisory Service which exists to serve every farmer in the country . . . except the fish farmer.

It is true that the FBA can help with water problems, but primarily the organization exists for pure research, not for applied fishery research and experimental work in hatchery techniques. The Ministry of Agriculture and Fisheries has taken little interest in freshwater matters and when recent legislation threatened to undermine the ability of riparian owners to protect the water from pollution, it was not the Ministry but the fishermen who through ACA, their pollution-fighting organization, strove successfully to ensure that the Common Law right of the riparian owner was retained in the Bill to act as a check upon the actions of the new River Boards (now River Authorities) whose members are predominantly dwellers in industrial towns.

What a farce the much-lauded legislation turned out to be! Despite the opening of the Water Pollution Research Laboratory at Stevenage river authorities have been slow to adopt an effluent standard, and the right to clean up the estuary seldom seems to be exerted when the estuary needs cleaning. The nationalized industries seem in many cases to continue to pollute with impunity, and there was the astonishing spectacle of the late 'Bessie' Braddock speaking up in the Commons for fishermen (including the riparian owners) on a salmon river, the Welsh Dee, when the authority failed to act in a pollution in which its chairman's company was later proved in an ACA action to have been implicated.

More recently, the Federation of British Industries, in a pamphlet on pollution and the common law, suggested that actions for damages and injunctions are contrary to the national interest . . . 'If the effluent is good enough for a river board,' they argued, 'it ought to be good enough for everyone.'

How cynical can we get ?

Most major pollutions emanate from the industrial towns and cities. Urban representation on river authorities is usually paramount and disinclined to burden the rates (and voters) unless the river is a proven danger to public health.

When Pride of Derby Angling Association sought an injunction to stop the pollution of the Derwent, the defendants were British Celanese Ltd, the Derby Corporation and the British Electricity Authority.

Pride of Derby were backed by ACA ... Pride of Derby won!

To join ACA is the clear duty of every angler ... it is the only deterrent weapon we have that is feared by the polluter.

Reluctantly, I have come to the conclusion that our inland fisheries have suffered neglect by reason of the fact that they fall under the jurisdiction of the Fisheries Department of the Ministry of Agriculture, Fisheries & Food. This department, with its laboratory and library in Lowestoft, had always shown itself interested chiefly in our sea-fishing industry. There is little doubt that inland fisheries would be much better off were they legislated for and administered by the agricultural section of the Ministry, when fishery work would become another department of NAAS and the agricultural-research centres.

In Chapter 18, I stressed above all, the need for formal training in fish farming. Particularly do I feel it necessary to get away from this wretched ingrowing tendency of our older universities to train specialists who, having graduated, train more specialists who, having graduated, ... etc. You know the story as well as I do.

Many, if not most, of our present academically qualified fishery people are on the river authorities, and this sort of job seems to be the best available to them, at the moment. What we need is the best of these men working on commercial fisheries, doing not talking. Well-paid jobs ought to be there to attract them just as they are in industry. How valuable, too, these trained scientists will be as colleagues and advisers to the water engineers, enabling them to concentrate on water-supply matters instead of sport and recreation side issues.

Every angler should be aware of the fact that in America inland waters are used jointly for food production and sport, and under the Farm Fish Ponds Scheme some 270,000 ponds had been made in the ten years up to 1952. In many cases the farmer has been given a subsidy on the constructional work, and his stock fish are always supplied free of charge. Land so used is producing more flesh per acre than it would by grazing – even were the pastures as good as ours.

Our inland fisheries are a disgrace to any progressive society. It is not enough for ACA and similar organizations to fight the polluter: we need a positive approach to the whole matter of the usage of our waters. What is the gain if we stop them being used as open sewers, and do not then ensure that they are made to be productive of useful game fish to provide food and sport.

Our angling associations must share the blame. All too seldom do they attempt to interest their members in conservation: a great majority of the societies exist merely as a means of raising money to rent a fishery and there is no attempt to manage the water and make it productive. In the industrial North the pollution of the rivers and diminution of the size of the average fish has made contest fishing the only sport possible in many areas; the anglers are satisfied to catch tiddlers provided they catch enough of them. Surely as a gifted nation we can achieve something better than this as an angling recreation!

So far as game fishes are concerned, improvement of stock will have to be on a nationwide basis. Good brood stock may exist anywhere and it is very probable that there are better naturally bred fish in some of our waters than exist in the hatcheries. When really fine specimens are caught in a water containing marked fish, they should not be killed, but should be transferred to a holding pond for possible use as breeders. It would be simple enough to fit a 'well' to every boat capable of holding fish alive and unharmed until their return to the jetty in the evening.

CHAPTER 23

Books about fish and fishing

Below is a short list of the books which I have found most helpful in forming my angling technique and in writing this book:

Game species and fishing techniques

(1) *A Trout and Salmon Fisherman for Seventy-Five Years*, by E. R. Hewitt. Scribner: New York.

(2) *Salmon Fishing: A New Philosophy*, by R. Waddington. Peter Davies.

(3) *The Life of the Sea Trout*, by G. H. Nall. Seeley, Service.

(4) *The Practical Angler*, by W. C. Stewart. Black.

(5) *The Way of a Trout with a Fly*, by G. E. M. Skues. Black.

(6) *Wye Salmon and Other Fish*, by J. A. Hutton. Sherratt.

(7) *This Fishing*, by Captain L. A. Parker. Bennett Brothers of Salisbury.

(8) *The Angler's Cast*, by Captain T. L. Edwards and E. Horsfall Turner. Herbert Jenkins.

Tackle

(9) *La Canne à Mouche à Truite, Objet d'Art*, by Joannès Robin. Bosc Frères: Lyon.

(10) *Professional Fly Tying and Tackle Making*, by G. L. Herter. Herter, Waseca, Minnesota.

(11) *Professional Split Bamboo Rod Building Manual*, by G. L. Herter. Herter, Waseca, Minnesota.

(12) *Rod Building for Amateurs*, by Richard Walker. Belfield & Bushell.

(13) *Anglers' Knots in Gut and Nylon*, by Stanley Barnes. Cornish Brothers.

Robin's is undoubtedly the best book ever written on fly rods. I do not think that there is an English translation available, but the book is quite easy to read in the original.

Robin's method of assessing the value of a rod is based upon analysis of its curve under a given load. He states, and I agree with his statement, that a multiplicity of rod actions is unnecessary: there must be one action more efficient than all others and that same action could be had in different lengths and weights. A method which would enable a maker to price his rods according to their performance rather than their appearance should not lightly be set aside. Of the rods he examined, a 'Halford Knockabout' by Messrs Hardy Bros showed as good a performance as any.

Mr Herter's two books are probably the most complete on these subjects available. The writer is a manufacturer of some importance in America.

Rod Building for Amateurs is a shorter book than either of Mr Herter's but is nevertheless very complete. Mr Walker is an engineer, a wonderful craftsman and above all a superlatively good fisherman well able to check the value of his ideas before putting them on paper.

Freshwater biology

(14) 'Blue Green Algae', by G. E. Fogg. *New Biology No 5*, Penguin.
(15) 'Control of Algae', by F. E. Hale. *U S Waterworks & Sewerage Magazine*, 1939.
(16) 'Copper Sulphate', by Paul Weir. *U S Waterworks & Sewerage Magazine*, June 1945.
(17) 'Effect of Copper Sulphate on Organisms', by Paul Weir. *U S Waterworks & Sewerage Magazine*, May 1939.
(18) *Freshwater Biology and Water Supply in Britain*, by W. H. Pearsall, A. C. Gardiner and F. Greenshield. The Freshwater Biological Association, Windermere.
(19) *Freshwater Life of the British Isles*, by John Clegg. Warne.
(20) 'Freshwater Snails', by T. T. Macan, *Country Sportsman*, February 1949.
(21) *Life in Inland Waters*, by Kathleen Carpenter. Sidgwick & Jackson.
(22) *An Angler's Entomology*, by J. R. Harris. Collins.
(23) *Life in Lakes and Rivers*, by T. T. Macan and E. B. Worthington. Collins.
(24) 'Industrial Wastes and Fish Life', by M. Ellis. *U S Waterworks & Sewerage Magazine*, May 1945.
(25) *Progress in Biological Enquiries*, published yearly from 1928 to 1939. U S Fish and Wildlife Service, Washington.
(26) 'The English Lakes and Their Development', by W. H. Pearsall. *New Biology No 6*, Penguin.
(27) 'Can Wild Animals be Kept in Captivity', by H. Spurway. *New Biology No 13*, Penguin.

(28) 'The Freshwater Shrimp', by T. T. Macan. *Country Sportsman*, March 1950.

(29) 'The Reaction and Resistance of Fishes in their Natural Environment to Acidity, Alkalinity and Neutrality', by M. W. Wells. *US Biological Bulletin*, October, 1915.

(30) *Water Supply Today*, by John Bowman. Oxford University Press.

Pure research in connection with freshwater biology is as far advanced in England as it is anywhere in the world, but it is true to say that it is easier to obtain information from United States sources than from our own. As yet we have not compiled complete bibliographies in the way that the American Information Service has, and much of the valuable work carried out and published by our scientists remains hidden away in little-known journals which are filed by the researcher but which are completely unknown to the man who could make practical use of the information.

No 18 on the above list is a brief but complete account of water, algae, plankton crops, algicides, stratification and water sampling.

No 23, *Life in Lakes and Rivers*, is a book which should be in every fisherman's possession. It is well written, beautifully illustrated and has the great advantage that the authors explain their terms as they go along. No 22, *An Angler's Entomology*, is published in the same series and is equally fascinating – and I write this although I do not believe in 'entomological angling'.

The Reports of Progress in Biological Enquiries contain not only accounts of the work on Wisconsin lakes by Professors Birge and Juday but also accounts of the experiments on Trout Breeding, Disease Resistance and so on which were carried out at Pittsford, Vermont; Hackettstown, New Jersey; Leetown and elsewhere.

Water Supply Today is written from the water engineer's viewpoint; a viewpoint which should be appreciated by those who fish in reservoirs.

Fish and fish culture

(31) *Text Book of Pond Culture*, by Wilhelm Schaeperclaus PhD. Published in German by Paul Parey, Berlin. English translation by Frederick Hund for Stanford University under the sponsor-

ship of the California State Division of Fish and Game. Now published as *U S Fishery Leaflet No 311.*

(32) 'Artificial Propagation of Brook Trout and Rainbow Trout with Notes on three other Species', by G. C. Leach. *U S Fisheries Document No 955.*

(33) 'Care and Diseases of Trout', by H. S. Davis. *U S Research Report No 12,* 1947.

(34) 'Commercial Trout Culture', *Fisheries Notice No 29,* Ministry of Agriculture and Fisheries, 1950.

(35) 'Disease Control in Hatchery Fish', by F. F. Fish. *U S Fishery Leaflet No 68.*

(36) *Fishes, Their Way of Life,* by Louis Roule. Routledge.

(37) 'Peculiarities of Rainbow Trout', by S. A. Young. *Salmon and Trout Magazine No 100,* September 1939.

(38) 'Rainbows in Acid Water', by Winifred Frost. *Salmon and Trout Magazine No 100,* September 1939.

(39) 'Sewage Disposal in Germany', by Dr Ing. Karl Imhoff. *U S Waterworks and Sewerage Magazine,* March 1939.

(40) 'Some Publications on Diseases and Parasites of Fishes', *U S Fishery Leaflet No 58,* 1947.

(41) 'Some Publications on Fish Culture and Related Subjects', *U S Fishery Leaflet No 6,* 1950.

(42) *Survey of Fish Culture in the United States,* by A. V. Tunison, C. Mullin and O. L. Meehean. 1949.

(43) 'The Culture of Fish in Ponds', by C. B. Hall. *Ministry of Agriculture & Fisheries Bulletin No 12,* 1930.

(44) 'The Effect of Slightly Alkaline Tap Water upon Spawn and Eggs of Trout and Perch', by E. S. Hopkins. *Journal of American Water Works Association,* 1928.

(45) *The Food of Coarse Fish,* by P. H. T. Hartley. Freshwater Biological Association, Windermere.

(46) 'The Nutrition of Fish in Hatcheries; a Literature Survey', by N. Karrick. *U S Fisheries Leaflet No 325,* 1948.

(47) The Pemberton-Warren (Western Australia) Trout Acclimatization Society's Annual Reports Nos 17 (1948), 18 (1949), 19 (1950) and 20 (1951).

(48) 'The Production of Freshwater Fish for Food', by T. T. Macan, C. H. Mortimer and E. B. Worthington. *Scientific Publication No 6* of the Freshwater Biological Association at Windermere.

(49) The Second and Third Annual Reports of the Supervisory Committee for Brown Trout Research. HMSO Edinburgh, 1951 and 1952.

(50) *The Story of the Fish,* by Brian Curtis. Jonathan Cape.

(51) 'The Trouts of North America', by S. F. Hildebrand. *U S Fishery Leaflet No 355,* 1949.

(52) *Trout Feeds and Feeding,* by A. V. Tunison. U S Fish and Wildlife Service, 1945.

Schaeperclaus is often regarded as the father of modern fishery management. The thoroughness, the completeness of this work defy adequate appreciation. I can only say whatever you wish to know is probably there.

In his book, *The Story of the Fish*, Mr Curtis made it his object to collect from little-known scientific papers facts of interest to fishermen. He has succeeded in presenting interesting matter in an easily read form.

The reports of the Pemberton-Warren Association are an example of thoroughness worthy of copy by all angling associations. The members are made familiar with the technical side of fishery management. The way in which this association has overcome its difficulties is an exciting romance in itself.

Mr Tunison's paper on Trout Feeding (No 52) gives very full information on every aspect of the subject, from the mechanical preparation of the foodstuffs to the relationship between the quantities fed and the length of the fish and the water temperature.

Fishery management

(53) 'Recreational, Use of Waterworks', by Walter Winterbottom, OBE and Leonard G. Brown BSC, MICE, MIWE. *The Journal of The British Waterworks Association*, July 1967.

(54) *Use of Reservoirs and Gathering Grounds for Recreation*. Ministry of Land and Natural Resources Circular 3/66. HMSO.

(55) 'Available Publications on Fisheries'. *US Fishery Leaflet No 9*, 1951.

(56) *Construction of Farm Fish Ponds*, by J. M. Lawrence, Alabama Polytechnic Institute.

(57) 'Construction of Farm Ponds'. *US Fishery Leaflet No 17*, 1951.

(58) 'Farm Fish Ponds and Their Management', by O. L. Meehean. *US Fishery Leaflet No 27*, 1945.

(59) 'Farm Ponds', by M. T. Gowder & D. P. Schwab. Publication No 333 of the Agricultural Extension Service, University of Tennessee.

(60) 'Fertilization of Ponds', by Krügel & Heinrich. *International Illustrated Fertilizer Review*, June 1939.

(61) 'Fertilizers in Fishponds: A Review and Bibliography', by C. H. Mortimer and C. F. Hickling. Published as *Fishery Publication No 5* by HMSO.

(62) 'Fish Stocking', by Meehean, James & Douglass. *US Conservation Bulletin No 35*, 1944.

(63) *Management of Farm Fish Ponds,* by H. S. Swingle and E. V. Smith. Alabama Polytechnic Institute.

(64) *Fishery Science. Its Methods and Applications,* by G. A. Rounsefell and W. H. Everhart. Chapman & Hall.

(65) 'Rainbows, a Report on Attempts to Acclimatize Rainbow Trout in Britain', by E. B. Worthington. *Salmon & Trout Magazine,* September 1939 and January 1940.

(66) 'Summary of Trout Stocking Experiments', by A. D. Holloway, *US Fishery Leaflet No 137,* 1945.

(67) 'Marking and Regeneration of Fins', by T. A. Stuart. Published as *Freshwater and Salmon Fisheries Publication No 22,* HMSO, Edinburgh.

(68) 'The Control of Aquatic Plants in Ponds and Lakes', by E. W. Surber. *US Fishery Leaflet No 217,* 1948.

(69) 'The Use of Rotenone as a Fish Poison'. *US Fishery Leaflet No 350.*

(70) 'Vital Statistics of Fish Populations', by G. L. Kesteven. *New Biology No 4,* Penguin.

(71) *Weed Control in Small Ponds,* by H. W. Jackson. Virginia Polytechnic Institute.

(72) 'Aquatic Plant Control with 2, 4-D', by S. W. Surber. *US Fishery Leaflet No 344,* 1949.

The first two papers in this section are the foundation stone on which British anglers may lay claim to a right to fish in water-supply reservoirs.

Of the papers on pond construction No 56 is the most complete from the technical point of view. No 63 on pond management is excellently illustrated and clearly demonstrates how fine is the dividing line between success and failure when stocking with a food species.

No 64 is a comprehensive text-book on both sea and inland fisheries. Dr G. A. Rounsefell is Technical Editor of the Branch of Fish Biology, US Fish and Wildlife Service, Dr W. H. Everhart is Head of the Fishery Management Division of the Maine (USA) Department of Fisheries and Game.

Dr Worthington's report and conclusions are extremely important; no stocking committee can afford to be ignorant of them.

Miscellaneous books

(73) *A Dictionary of Biology,* by M. Abercrombie, C. J. Hickman, and M. L. Johnson. Penguin.

(74) *Animal Breeding*, by A. L. Hagedoorn. Crosby Lockwood.
(75) *Genetics*, by Hans Kalmus. Penguin.

No 73 is a most helpful book and one which I use frequently. It will enable the average angler to learn the terminology of the scientist. The ordinary English dictionary seldom gives satisfying meanings of scientific terms and a specialized dictionary of this type is essential.

No 75 gives a clear explanation of inheritance, while No 74 is a book with which every breeder of animals (and the word includes 'fish') should be familiar. There cannot be improvement in our fish stocks until breeders follow genetically sound principles.

How to obtain scientific and other publications

Most books are quite easily obtained through the National Library Service, but scientific papers have a very limited distribution and in some cases there may be but two or three copies in the whole country. The local librarian cannot be expected to obtain such publications even if they are available for loan. It is often necessary for the would-be borrower to tell the librarian where copies of the publication are kept.

Because I had much difficulty in obtaining many of the papers and articles used in compiling this book, I have made the following notes which may be of assistance to others:

Nos 10 and 11 were imported direct from Herters'.

Nos 15, 16, 17, 24, 29, 39 and 44 may be obtained from the Library of the Science Museum through the Library Service.

Nos 25, 32, 33, 35, 40, 41, 42, 46, 51, 52, 55, 57, 58, 62, 66, 68, 69 and 72 may be obtained direct from the office of the United States Federal Fish & Wildlife Service, at the Department of the Interior, Washington DC free of charge. Some of the reports of 'Progress in Biological Enquiries' are no longer obtainable. Many of these United States publications are held by the Librarian of the Fisheries Laboratory, Ministry of Agriculture & Fisheries, Lowestoft, and this library holds copies of all the reports, 'Progress in Biological Enquiries' referred to in this book.

Nos 56, 59, 63 and 71 may be obtained free of charge from the librarians of the publishing colleges. I would like to mention that I have never been refused literature by any of the American authorities to whom I have written.

Nos 37, 38 and 65 are obtainable from the Salmon & Trout Association, at Fishmongers' Hall; alternatively they may be borrowed from the Librarian of the Fisheries' Laboratory, Lowestoft, through the Library Service.

No 60 is available in the Library of Rothamsted Agricultural Research Station.

It is unfortunate that some libraries, such as that of the Freshwater Biological Association, do not permit books to leave the premises. Relatively few people are able to afford to journey perhaps several hundred miles to refer to a book and it is a pity that it is not possible to have books transferred to the reference room of the local library where they could be consulted under proper supervision.

Index

Anglers' Library

CANAL FISHING   35p
Kenneth Seaman

The author deals with this increasingly popular
sport in a helpful, lucid manner. Traditional
methods and tackles are critically examined
together with advice on bait selection and preparation. There are chapters on angling for
all the well-known species as well as the more
unusual chubb, dace and rudd. Match fishing
techniques are fully discussed, a fresh approach to ground baiting suggested and the
problems of canal maintenance highlighted.

'Practical, down-to-earth approach'
                                    – SCOTSMAN
'An admirable series' – DAILY TELEGRAPH

These and other PAN Books are obtainable
from all booksellers and newsagents. If you
have any difficulty please send purchase price
plus 7p postage to PO Box 11, Falmouth,
Cornwall.
While every effort is made to keep prices low, it
is sometimes necessary to increase prices at
short notice. PAN Books reserve the right to
show new retail prices on covers which may
differ from those advertised in the text or
elsewhere.